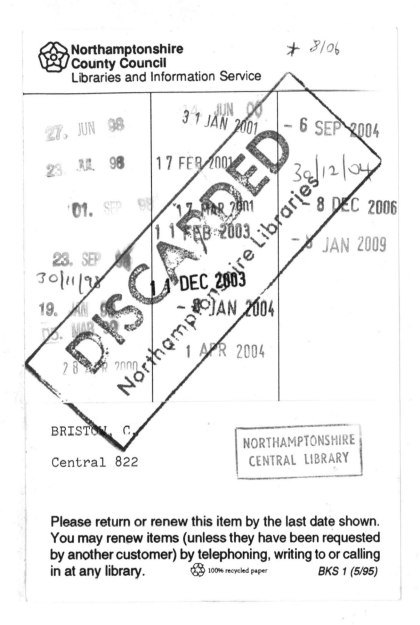

CENTRAL 822

CENTRAL 822

CAROL BRISTOW

BANTAM PRESS

LONDON · NEW YORK · TORONTO · SYDNEY · AUCKLAND

TRANSWORLD PUBLISHERS LTD
61–63 Uxbridge Road, London W5 5SA

TRANSWORLD PUBLISHERS (AUSTRALIA) PTY LTD
15–25 Helles Avenue, Moorebank, NSW 2170

TRANSWORLD PUBLISHERS (NZ) LTD
3 William Pickering Drive, Albany, Auckland

Published 1998 by Bantam Press
a division of Transworld Publishers Ltd
Copyright © Carol Bristow 1998

A catalogue record for this book is available from the British Library.

ISBN 0593 042085

Typeset in 11/13¼pt Linotype Sabon by
Kestrel Data, Exeter, Devon.

Printed in Great Britain by
Mackays of Chatham plc, Chatham, Kent.

For Janie

When to the sessions of sweet silent thought
I summon up remembrance of things past
Shakespeare's Sonnet No. 30

ACKNOWLEDGEMENTS

I am indebted to the many individuals who supplied the information, patience, advice and encouragement which enabled me to write this book.

In particular I would like to thank ex-Detective Chief Superintendents Henry Mooney, Roger Lewis, Peter Cornish and Guy Mills along with ex-colleagues and friends from the Metropolitan Police, too numerous to mention, and officers from the Hertfordshire Constabulary.

Special thanks also go to the late Michael Kalisher QC, who gave invaluable advice but who sadly died during the writing of this book.

I would also like to express personal thanks to Camilla Sampson, Ross Francis and Geraldine Warne-West who gave precious help and to the countless others who are not mentioned here by name.

This book would not have been possible without the encouragement and friendship of Julian Alexander, the commitment and patience of Wendy Holden, my co-writer, who worked slavishly with words, rescuing me time and again from the despair of mental paralysis, and the skill of Broo Doherty, who made useful suggestions as to the book's structure.

Last but never least, I must thank the hundreds of courageous women who inspired me to tell their remarkable stories. But for them, this book would not have been possible. To preserve their anonymity, I have changed their names and some of the identities of their assailants. Janie Shepherd and Jill Saward are the only women correctly named.

CENTRAL 822

1

'I HAVE A HIGH-POWERED RIFLE LEVELLED AT YOUR HEAD,' THE
Middle Eastern voice hissed down the telephone. 'If the police
have become involved, I will have no hesitation in killing you.'

My heart pounded. Posing as a secretary who was meant to
deliver a ransom demand to a foreign terrorist who was threatening to blow up part of London's Mayfair, I was standing in a
telephone box outside Earl's Court underground station in the
summer of 1971 and wondering what on earth I had got myself
into.

There have been several times in my police career when I
have felt really frightened. The fear starts low in my stomach
like butterflies but gradually rises to my chest, getting higher
and stronger as I start to lose my bottle. By the time I heard the
terrorist's threat, it had knotted in my larynx.

I stood stock-still, scared to move a muscle, listening to the
caller's calm breathing in the earpiece, afraid he could hear my
terror.

He paused, before adding abruptly: 'Go to Redcliffe Gardens
and throw the money into the back of the skip which has been
left at the junction with Redcliffe Square. You can't miss it.
It's half on the pavement and half on the road and people are
having to walk round it. If the man in the white shirt follows
you, I will shoot you dead. Do you understand?'

I understood only too well. My knees were trembling, I felt sick and my fear was beginning to suffocate me. I replaced the handset and spoke as slowly and calmly as I could into the tiny microphone taped across my throat under the neck of my jumper.

'Redcliffe Gardens. I've been ordered to put the money into a skip at the junction with Redcliffe Square. I am going there now.' The man in the white shirt stood watching me out of the corner of his eye.

The day had started unremarkably. Recently posted to Harrow Road Police Station in Paddington, west London, for the second time in my career, I was expecting nothing more than a bit of run-of-the-mill detective work.

On that fateful afternoon in June, I was working the late shift, 2 p.m. to 10 p.m., when I turned up for work fifteen minutes early. 'Where the hell have you been?' my governor asked, grabbing me as I walked into the CID office. As I began to mumble that I was actually early for my shift, he bundled me into the back of a car and told me we were heading for Oxford Street to see a man called Leslie Perrin, who had his offices there.

I had no idea who Mr Perrin was, but it turned out he was quite famous, working as the showbusiness impresario and publicity agent for the Beatles, the Rolling Stones, Frank Sinatra, Lulu, Slade and a few others. The Max Clifford of his day.

Mr Perrin had summoned the police after receiving a series of telephone calls from a man who said he was calling from America. The foreign-sounding voice claimed that unless Mr Perrin coughed up £10,000 (a small fortune in those days and the equivalent of £100,000 today), the Beatles' Apple company recording studios in Savile Row, Mayfair, would be blown up. He was told there were two bombs inside the building which could be operated by a remote-controlled radio device.

The caller told Mr Perrin that his secretary should be ready to take the ransom money to a destination which he would be given later. On no account was he to involve the police, he was told, although of course he did. Savile Row was discreetly

14

evacuated and I was drafted in to play the part of his secretary, something I hadn't fully appreciated until I pulled up in the car outside his office.

'Don't worry,' my boss said as he filled me in on the gist of the blackmail plot. 'It won't be real money you're carrying cos it won't get that far. We've arranged a huge police operation and officers from Scotland Yard's Surveillance Team will be following you everywhere you go. We'll arrest the buggers long before they get anywhere near you or the money.' I tried to look convinced.

Just after we arrived in his office and were met by two intelligence officers, Mr Perrin received another call. The blackmailer instructed him to put the money in a large brown envelope and give it to his secretary, who should make her way to a telephone box in Queensgate in Kensington, where she would receive instructions telling her what to do next. By this time I knew there was no going back.

'Take your blouse off,' one of the intelligence officers barked.

'What?' I said, forgetting the usual 'sir'.

'Your blouse,' he said. 'Take it off. We have to fit you with a throat mike. It has to be slipped up inside your bra.'

'Oh, right, sir,' I answered hesitantly.

Standing in front of a mirror in the ladies' lavatory threading a piece of wire up the centre of my cleavage, I felt more like Mata Hari than a woman detective sergeant in the Metropolitan Police. The intelligence officers fitted the end of the lead with a tiny circular microphone, which was held across my windpipe with sticky tape. The wire from it ran down my arm and into a hand-held button switch which, when pressed, allowed me to communicate with the officers by talking quietly. I was given a green polo-neck jumper to wear which would cover up the mike, and – what with my own nervousness and the boiling hot day – I was soon sweating like a pig and in danger of passing out.

Stepping cautiously out of Mr Perrin's office with the brown envelope containing nothing but pieces of paper, cut to size and wrapped in a few genuine notes, I hailed a black cab, which was driven by one of the undercover officers. As I left the building, I could hear my boss mutter: 'Intelligence Branch say it looks as if fanatical Arab terrorists are involved.' My mouth felt suddenly dry.

By the time I got to Queensgate and said goodbye to the cab driver, it was mid-afternoon. There were two telephone boxes, not one as expected, and both were full. I waited for what seemed like an age until a woman replaced the receiver and stepped out of the right-hand box. As she did so, the telephone rang almost immediately, so I rushed forward and, pushing her to one side, snapped: 'Thanks, but I think that's for me.'

A voice with a thick Arab accent gave me further instructions. 'Go to Kensington High Street Station. The phone boxes there have numbers on the door. Go into number seven and wait for my call.' I caught a taxi to Kensington High Street, and this time the cab driver was genuine. He tried to chatter on about various current affairs issues which enraged him, but I wasn't listening. 'Now that Education Secretary Margaret Thatcher says she's going to stop free school milk,' he told me. 'I mean, what's the world coming to? Free milk was the only thing that kept me growing as a kid.' I nodded distractedly and watched as the station appeared in the distance.

As I entered Kensington High Street Station that scorching summer afternoon, the fear in my gut had just started moving up.

Phone box number 7 was occupied so I loitered outside until it was free. Once inside, I peered out self-consciously at all the people milling purposefully around the station. None of them had a clue who I was or what I was doing. I wondered how they would have reacted if they had known.

As I watched, I saw a short Arab man, wearing dark glasses and carrying a white stick, being led towards the phone boxes by a tall European-looking woman. It was the pretty mauve tint of his lenses that drew my eyes to his face. Seconds later the telephone rang and the voice said: 'Go to Earl's Court underground station. There are four telephone boxes opposite the main entrance. Enter the first and wait for my call.'

Leaving the phone box, I spoke quietly into my throat mike

to tell the others where I was heading. Looking at the myriad faces of the people all around me, I hoped that several of them were on my side protecting me, as I had been promised. I would have been reassured had I been able to recognize one or two of them, but I didn't see a single sod that I knew and the fear in my stomach was pulsating just below the bottom of my ribcage. I had never felt more lonely in my life.

I joined a long queue of people waiting to buy a ticket when suddenly, out of nowhere it seemed, a detective called Phil, with whom I used to work, approached me. 'Have you got the time, please?' he asked politely, his face expressionless, a *London Evening News* tucked under the arm of his white shirt.

I looked at my wristwatch. 'Earl's Court underground station,' I said. 'The phone boxes opposite the main entrance.'

'Thank you,' he responded before disappearing into the crowd. He must have missed my last message, I thought, as I nervously adjusted my throat mike.

My ticket in one hand, the envelope in the other, I went down to the platform and caught a District Line train. By this time I was wound up like a corkscrew, so in my anxious state I accidentally caught the wrong train. I didn't realize my mistake until the next stop, Notting Hill Gate, when I jumped off, ran round to the other platform and caught the right one. Throughout all this confusion, I kept up a running commentary through my throat mike. I could see Phil following me out of the corner of my eye and I guessed he must have been wondering what the hell I was playing at.

At Earl's Court it was almost rush hour and the station and surrounding streets were packed. Four people were waiting to use the telephone boxes and I had to hang about for some time before I could get into the first one. I stood for several minutes in this stifling hot box, but the telephone didn't ring. I tried to ignore the queue of people standing outside, who were getting so impatient that they began making rude and agitated gestures with their hands. By now my body temperature was up to simmering point and, if it hadn't been for the sight of Phil standing on the corner of the street, leaning nonchalantly against a wall reading his newspaper, I think I might have lost it.

The telephone finally rang and I grabbed the handset, almost dropping it in my haste. 'We know you are a police officer,' the foreign voice snarled. 'We have seen the man in the white shirt following you.'

'You're m-m-mistaken,' I stammered, 'I'm not with any man in a white shirt, I don't know what you're talking about. I'm just a secretary.' I looked down at the brown envelope, clutched in my sweaty hand. As I did so, the door to the kiosk was suddenly wrenched open by a young man who looked as though he was about to explode. This is it, I thought, he's after the money and he's going to kill me. I dropped the telephone handset in my panic, sending it crashing into the metal window frame.

'How much longer are you going to be in there?' the impatient young man screamed. 'Can't you see the queue out here? For Christ's sake, show a bit of decency and hurry up.' In a trice he had stepped back, the door had slammed shut and I was alone, trembling from head to foot.

I retrieved the dangling handset and, trying to control my chattering teeth, I said: 'Sorry about that, but I guess you heard the young man who—'

The voice interrupted me and spat: 'I saw it all. I have a high-powered rifle levelled at your head.' My heart missed a beat. 'If the police have become involved, I will have no hesitation in killing you. Now listen carefully to what I have to tell you.'

I tried to focus on what he was saying as he told me to put the money into the skip at Redcliffe Gardens and repeated his warning that I would be killed if the man in the white shirt followed me. Whispering now into the neck of my jumper to alert my colleagues, I added, as calmly as I could: 'Phil is not to follow. Repeat Phil not to follow or I will be shot.' I let the door swing shut behind me and, resisting the urge to shout out to Phil to keep away, I started slowly walking towards Redcliffe Gardens.

I didn't notice him at first, as I was far too busy looking for the skip. When I eventually spotted it I was so relieved that all I wanted to do was run towards it, throw the envelope in and get the hell out of there. But I maintained my pace, keeping my eyes strictly in front of me to avoid any distractions. As I drew level with the skip, I dropped in the envelope. It was virtually empty save for some light domestic rubbish which meant my envelope would not look too out of place. Wiping my sweaty palms together, I turned slowly and started heading back towards the station, the words of the gunman repeating themselves in my head.

When I caught sight of Phil standing across the road under a white plaster portico, my heart stopped and my step faltered visibly. I wanted to run at him, screaming: 'Didn't you hear what I said? Get out of here, go away!' but the knot of fear was lodged between my tonsils and I couldn't utter a word. I had never felt so frightened in my life. I tried to make eye contact with him, to urge him to turn away as I passed, but he ignored me and I had to walk on towards Earl's Court Station. In my mind's eye, I visualized myself through the telescopic sights of a rifle. I could see the finger on the trigger and feel the tension in the hands of the gunman as he held the rifle in position and kept me within range. As a bead of sweat trickled down my cheek, I imagined a similar bead rolling down his face and his dark eyes concentrating on his prey.

I ran on to the platform. It was only when the train doors slid shut behind me that I finally felt able to exhale. Flushed with anxiety and heat, I collapsed into the one vacant seat in the carriage, wiping my damp face and hands with a handkerchief, trying to avoid the prying eyes of commuters around me, as they must have wondered what on earth I was doing wearing winter clothes in the height of summer.

As I endeavoured to get a grip on things, I focused on the massive police operation that was carrying on in my absence in Redcliffe Gardens and the intense activity of the surveillance lads. Armed officers would have been drafted in, additional uniforms would be on standby, ready to clear the area in case of any trouble, and senior detectives would be liaising with the Anti-Terrorist Branch. They'll have that skip 'plotted up' from every angle, I thought, and when the bugger makes his move, they'll have him. Not once did I register my good fortune at being alive. In my shaken state, my brain had been incapable of stretching itself that far.

I got off the train at Oxford Street and made my way back to Mr Perrin's office where I knew I would be able to monitor any developments. Once in the sanctuary of his publicity agency, I realized that my mike had cut out at Kensington High Street Station and consequently Phil and his fellow-officers had been at a loss as to where I was going. That is when they had decided to send Phil up to me directly, to ask me the time. From that moment, he had stuck to me like glue and it was left to him to keep the others updated with directions, having established the route I was taking.

The Apple building had been searched from top to bottom with police using sniffer dogs but they found no explosives. Phil joined us at Mr Perrin's office later and told me that the 'blind' Arab I had seen at Kensington High Street Station had also been spotted at Earl's Court. It seemed as if he was our man, and a good disguise it had been too. An Arab in Kensington in the 1970s on a summer afternoon – nothing unusual there. Presumably he had waited for me to enter the telephone box each time and had then rung me directly from the one next door or nearby. That way he was always able to keep me in sight.

As I had predicted, armed undercover detectives had surrounded Redcliffe Gardens and the skip, but no one ever came to collect the envelope, almost certainly because the sight of Phil following me had blown the operation and made them lose their bottle.

So that was it, job over. I was instructed to go back to Harrow Road and carry on with my normal duties. It would have felt like a terrible anticlimax after my surreal dice with death, but Mr Perrin had other ideas. He was over the moon that the Apple building hadn't been blown to pieces, and produced several bottles of celebratory champagne. I had never tasted champagne before and it didn't take me long to decide I liked it very much. Phil and I stayed until after 7 p.m. and I for one thoroughly enjoyed being treated like royalty.

Over a glass or two, Phil ribbed me about what my family would say when they heard I had been the subject of a terrorist assassination threat. 'You must be flippin' joking if you think I'm even going to mention it,' I told him. 'My mother would have kittens and, since she never wanted me to join the force in the first place, she'd probably never speak to me again.'

When I finally left the building, Mr Perrin kissed me on both cheeks and thanked me warmly. In passing, he mentioned that I shouldn't be surprised if there was 'the odd photographer' waiting for me at the door. What he didn't tell me is that he had rung up the whole of Fleet Street to tell them what had happened. It was just too good an opportunity for him to miss. As I stepped out into the street, a blaze of flashbulbs exploded in my face. I pushed my way unsteadily through the mêlée, trying to ignore their clicking cameras, but it appeared the damage had been done. I was well and truly captured for posterity.

The following morning, my dad was sitting in his local barber's shop in Alperton, waiting for a haircut. 'Sod that for a game of soldiers,' said the bloke sitting next to him, reading a newspaper. 'There's a story here about a woman detective who nearly got shot by some terrorist yesterday. What's the bloody world coming to?'

My father shook his head. 'I know. It's a worry. My daughter's in the police force, she'd sort them out.' With that he leant across to see what the man was reading and nearly fell off his chair. There, on the front page of the *Daily Mail*, was a full-length photograph of me leaving Mr Perrin's office with the caption *Carol Bristow: 'Very brave'*. The headline read: POLICE GIRL TOLD: YOU'RE IN RIFLE SIGHTS.

'Don't ever do that to me again,' my dad said when I saw him at home later that evening. 'I nearly had a bloody heart attack when I saw it was you.' Then he put his arms around me and hugged me, just like he had always done.

When I arrived for work the next day, I was told that the Chief Superintendent wanted to see me. I might have been forgiven for thinking that he wanted to congratulate me. But no. His face was as black as thunder.

'I've just had the Commissioner's office on the phone,' he said. 'Seems the powers that be didn't know about your little escapade yesterday because nobody bothered to ring and tell them. Someone up there is pretty miffed about you making the front pages, particularly when the Commissioner made a speech yesterday and got relegated to the back. What have you got to say for yourself, young Bristow?'

'I don't think I have anything to say, sir,' I replied, honestly.

'Just passing the message on, you understand,' the Chief Super said wearily. As he looked at my bewildered face, he softened. 'Well done, anyway. Keep it up.'

Somewhat flummoxed, I returned to my desk in the CID office. Sitting in the middle of it was a huge bouquet of flowers. The card read: *Thank you for being such a star. Much love, Les Perrin. XXX.* God, I love this job, I thought.

Later that same day, I was called to the front desk to receive a large box delivered to reception by a cab driver. 'I've got strict instructions to make sure this gets to someone called Carol who works in the CID,' he said, waiting for me to sign for the crate. Ripping open the packaging, I lovingly examined the dozen bottles of pink champagne sent courtesy of Mr Perrin, and was delighted that he at least thought I had done a good job.

My boss took one look at the crate and winked. 'You know you'll have to return this lot, don't you?' he said. 'Police officers aren't allowed to accept gifts.'

'I know, sir,' I said, grinning. 'But is there anything that says I can't return the bottles empty?'

There are not many people who can say they have Adolf Hitler to thank for their birth, but in my case it is true. If one of his bombs hadn't blown in the front of our house in October 1942, then my dad – who was away fighting the war – would never have been given special leave to come home and inspect the damage at first hand. My parents had tied up all the money they had in the world in that mid-terrace three-bedroom house when they bought it new, surrounded by fields and part of the prestigious Stonebridge Park development near Wembley, north-west London.

I was born on 7 July 1943, nine months after my father came home. I was born. It was three years later that I spotted a man I had never seen before walk up the North Circular Road towards me and my mother. As soon as she saw him, my mother abandoned me in my pushchair and ran into his arms. When later he handed me a little leather bag from India with a picture of the Taj Mahal on it, I was overjoyed. This handsome man said he was my father, and he was everything a little girl's father should have been and more.

I had never seen my mother so happy as when my brother Peter was born, almost nine months to the day after my father's return. Her husband was safely home from the war and her life seemed complete. She had suffered real hardship as a child and she was the type of woman who always feared its return. Her own father had been killed in the First World War and she and her older brother John had been brought up in considerable poverty by my grandmother.

My mother was very frugal and saved every spare penny for 'a rainy day'. I know that she did her best for me and loved me as well as she could, but from an early age I was painfully aware that I was not her favourite child. At the age of eight I asked her outright whom she loved the most. 'Your father, your brother and then you,' came the reply, and I felt as if someone had punched me in the stomach. Knowing I was third in the batting order coloured everything. I became a fearful child and would worry for hours that she was going to leave me or perhaps even give me away. I was literally afraid to go to sleep, because I imagined that when I woke up she would have seized the chance and walked out.

Her rejection of me and my perception of it made me totally insecure; I couldn't fathom what I had done wrong. As an adult, it has occurred to me that maybe she didn't like me because I was a girl. Before I was born she had already lost a baby son in childbirth, having carried him to full term. I think she came to resent me for not being a replacement for him. Perhaps it is no wonder that I was a real disappointment to her for no other reason than that I was female.

Fortunately for me, I had my dad. From the moment I set eyes on him I adored him, and I always knew that he loved me because he never stopped telling me. He would sit me on his knee and make it abundantly clear that no one cared for his 'little girl' more than he did. I never wanted for any love and affection from him. It never occurred to me that Peter felt the same way about Dad and me as I did about Mum and him.

Shortly after war broke out, my father joined the RAF as an engineer and was posted to India in 1943. It must have been an incredible experience for a former tram driver who had barely left London before, but he rarely talked about it. After the war, he worked as a driver on the trolleybuses, and washed windows part-time to make a bit of extra cash. I remember him religiously handing his unopened pay packet to my mother each Friday. She had tins and little envelopes marked GAS, ELECTRIC and HOLIDAYS, and worked everything out to the last penny before returning any spare money to my father so he could buy his beloved tobacco.

My dad always struck me as very happy and contented with his lot. His clothes may have been old and worn and his pockets empty, but he was always spick and span, with scrubbed fingernails and shoes so highly polished I could see my face in them. When his best friend George was promoted to an inspector on the buses, I remember asking him: 'Why aren't you an inspector like George, Dad?'

He replied: 'For eight hours of the day you sleep, for eight hours you play and for eight hours you work. You have to be jolly lucky to get a job that you like for those eight hours, and I like being a bus driver.'

I guess he was telling me not to give up doing something I liked just for the sake of ambition. 'Count your blessings and be thankful for what you've got.' It was a message I have carried with me like a talisman.

Pete and I were very much the goody-goody kids in the neighbourhood. God only knows how we kept our noses clean but we did, at a time when many of Pete's friends got nicked for thieving and quite a few of mine got pregnant. Our parents were decent people who set uncompromising standards. We were never slapped or beaten; my father was a talker, who preferred to reason things through rather than chastise. My mother was a weeper and she would cry at the drop of a hat if things weren't going her way; this was punishment enough for me because I hated seeing her tears. To this day, I loathe witnessing others cry because it makes me feel so helpless. I am also rarely able to cry myself.

Whatever problems my mum and I might have had, she was undoubtedly a gifted mother and wife in other ways. She made beautiful clothes for us and appeared to compensate for any lack of affection through housekeeping skills that would have put Mrs Beeton to shame. We could tell what day of the week it was by the food that she served. It never changed. A roast on Sundays, cold meat with bubble and squeak on Mondays, shepherd's pie on Tuesdays, a fry-up on Wednesdays, steak and kidney pudding on Thursdays, liver and bacon on Fridays and fish and chips from the shop on Saturdays.

My father had a strong sense of right and wrong and was a great defender of the underdog. He wasn't one to make a big fuss, but we all knew he took the side of those who were less able to stand up for themselves. He became great friends with a group of West Indians who moved in down the street at a time when a lot of bad things were being said in Britain about the influx of foreigners. My dad would roll up his sleeves and help them tinker around under the bonnets of their old bangers as if they were long-lost friends. He appeared to want to let us know that you should never judge a book by its cover, or make assumptions about people based on others' interpretations. I inherited my strong sense of justice from him. He was the type of man who wanted to be everybody's friend, and was a great hugger in a very non-tactile age. Without him my mother wouldn't have had any friends, and she loved him all the more for it.

My brother and I were as different as chalk and cheese. He was a shy boy, taking after our mother, and was so withdrawn that people sometimes mistook his timidity for arrogance. A born saver, he also took after my mother when it came to being careful with money. When I was about eleven, we added up how much we had in our red moneyboxes. I had eight old pennies and blew the lot down the sweet shop. Peter had one shilling and sixpence and opened a Post Office savings account;

he was seven years old. Little wonder that by the time he was forty he was a man of considerable wealth.

By contrast I was a spendthrift without a cause. Even though I always had some sort of job to give me pocket money – from a paper round to selling bundles of wood for kindling – I could never keep hold of my cash. My father used to say: 'Carol, as long as there is a hole in your arse, you'll never have a penny in the bank.' And of course he was absolutely right. I had champagne tastes but beer money, and if I had it I spent it.

I did moderately well at secondary school and was a good sportswoman, becoming Middlesex Schools javelin champion. During my last year, I decided I wanted to be a teacher and slipped the suggestion into conversation at home. After my parents had picked themselves up off the floor, they asked me where I thought the money for further education was going to come from. Anyway, my mother continued, I would probably be married by the time I was nineteen, so what was the point?

Pete, on the other hand, passed his Eleven Plus and went on to grammar school. He could, my mother said, go on to college because he was bright and would have to keep a family one day. I thought it was sod's law when he dropped out of school, became a teddy boy and grew a long curly quiff which hung down so low over his forehead that it was a miracle he could see where he was going. Luckily for him, he got a job with an engineering firm who insisted that he take a day-release course to study his new trade, which set him firmly on the road to success.

After working part-time as a barmaid in my local pub, I left school at sixteen and got a job as a typist in a City bank, the first of eight jobs I was to have before I was twenty-one. I loathed office work; it was too claustrophobic and I knew that I had to get off that particular treadmill while I still had a chance. I took myself off to night school to try and get enough GCEs for teacher-training college, hoping that, if I passed, I could rely on a government grant to see me through.

With a great deal of effort I passed English Language and Art, but since there wasn't a single sod in the world who congratulated me or gave me any encouragement I quit the course without taking the rest of my exams. My mother insisted I was daft for having ideas above my station. Feeling utterly despondent and wallowing in self-pity, I took the view that she must be right and found myself a new job as a copy typist with the Geographer's Map Company in the Gray's Inn Road.

It was a case of out of the frying pan and into the fire. All I wanted to do was be outside those four walls and free. I dreamt variously of emigrating to South Africa, Australia and Canada. I gave serious thought to joining the Army, Air Force or Navy just to get away, and I fantasized about how different life could be. But, lacking confidence and feeling pretty mixed up inside, I did nothing about it.

After a brief spell at Mabey & Johnson, an engineering firm in Victoria, I applied to Butlin's as a domestic cleaner – anything to get away for the summer and breathe some fresh air. To my very great surprise, they wrote back and said that with my sporting background I would be better placed as a Red Coat (which seemed as glamorous as being an air hostess at the time), so I packed my suitcase and went off to Bognor Regis in Sussex for the summer season, my mother's tearful protestations ringing in my ears.

It was exhausting but exhilarating work. I was up at dawn and went to bed at midnight. Wearing my famous red blazer, I helped organize the sporting activities for the holidaymakers and in the evenings had to dance with the single, unwanted 'wallflowers' in the ballroom where, yes, I had a ball. I shared a chalet with another Red Coat called Hazel, and by five-past midnight I could think of nothing else but crawling into bed and sleeping. Hazel, I quickly learnt, had other ideas. I slept on the top bunk while she had the bottom, and I could have been forgiven for thinking that I was living in a knocking shop. Hazel's succession of suitors, which changed when their holidays were over and the new influx arrived, was a sight to behold. Night after night they climbed into her bunk and night after night I turned a deaf ear to the giggling and the naughtiness that went on in the bunk below.

I didn't approve one bit and I certainly took no part in it. I was quite the little goody-two-shoes who, having lost my virginity on an uninspiring night a few years earlier, failed to understand what all the fuss was about. His name was Robert, an Air Force cadet and Mummy's own, who had asked me to marry him. We met when I was working as a barmaid. By the time I had reached the age of consent I was painfully aware that all my girlfriends had 'done it' and thought Robert was the most obvious candidate with whom to try out sex. I knew if I waited for him to make the first move I would remain a virgin, so on a particular day, when things seemed right, I suggested that he go and buy some condoms.

After he walked me home from the pub later that night, I invited him in and we had sex there and then on my parents' living-room floor while my mum was asleep upstairs and my dad was on night shift. The experience did nothing for me at all, although Robert seemed to enjoy it hugely. He was even pottier about me after that, but as far as I was concerned I had tried it once and it wasn't something I was going to waste my time on again. When he asked me to marry him, I refused, although I tried very hard to love young Robert. Sadly, I never quite managed it with him. I had hoped sex might make the difference, but it didn't, and for many years I felt bewildered by the whole episode. In the fullness of time Robert disappeared, and who could blame him?

A few months later I signed up with a girlfriend at the Victor Sylvester Dance Studios above the Odeon cinema in Wembley High Road. I loved dancing and decided to learn how to do it properly. A really nice boy called Maurice became my dancing partner. He had bright ginger hair and I thought he was smashing. We became boyfriend and girlfriend, although I made it clear that sex was out of the question. Perhaps because of that, a year later he suddenly asked me to marry him. I was more than a little flattered, because I could see I meant the world to him, but I didn't love him and I had to turn him down. Fortunately, he went off and found himself another dancing partner.

When the Butlin's summer season ended, I came back to London to work as a full-time 'live-in' barmaid at the Cloudesly Arms in Islington, which was part-owned by the landlord for whom I had previously worked. It was such a relief to be away from an office, and although the money wasn't very good I enjoyed it as a stopgap until a 'proper' job came along.

At the pub I met Gerald, a twenty-five-year-old man whom I went out with for a couple of months and who suddenly surprised me by suggesting that we get engaged. We hadn't slept together, we hardly knew each other and his proposal frightened the life out of me. It was the third marriage proposal I had received in as many years. I turned him down, broke off the relationship almost immediately and decided to get away from pub work altogether.

My next job was assistant to the personnel officer at Ascot Gas Water Heaters on the North Circular Road at Neasden. By this time I had a motorized scooter and was driving to work each day in a white leather helmet with a peak which I thought looked the business. The money was good and the work quite enjoyable, so I stayed for a year, much to my parents' relief.

Then I found some real excitement – Associated Rediffusion Television were advertising for typists at their studios in Wembley Park. I felt quite the star when I started working in their property department, typing out inventories of the props owned or hired by the television company for the sets of some of the most popular programmes. The best part was sharing the canteen with the television celebrities. I remember sitting next to Hughie Green, the star of a quiz show called *Double Your Money*, and feeling lost for words. After my experience as a Red Coat, I had briefly fantasized about a career in entertainment but, imagining my mother's reaction, put it straight out of my mind.

A month passed before my pride allowed me to admit that, despite a good wage, the Rediffusion job was lousy. For eight hours a day I was confined to a scruffy little office which I likened to a prison cell. At the grand old age of twenty, I threw a wobbler and finally decided that I'd had enough. I knew I would shortly go bananas if I didn't get out, so I quit, vowing never ever to go back to office work again.

By this time I had swapped my scooter for an old Ford van, which had cost me all of £15. It couldn't be driven anywhere unless the windows were open because the exhaust fumes came up through a gaping great hole in the floor, but it gave me sufficient driving experience to consider applying for a job on the road. So, much to my mother's disgust, I secured a job as a driver with Dagenham Motors, a huge garage in Alperton selling Ford motors and spares which they supplied throughout London.

I was the only woman driver among ten men and I loved the freedom, but even this was short-lived. After driving round the North Circular for the umpteenth time, the idea of emigrating or joining the services came floating back into my head. What was I going to do with my life? I wondered aloud, but then came my salvation.

It was late 1963 and I was sitting in a traffic jam outside the old Wembley Police Station when I spotted a large poster pinned to the noticeboard outside. It read: WHY NOT JOIN THE METROPOLITAN POLICE? I'd toyed with this idea three years earlier, but dismissed it almost as soon as I'd thought it. They'd never want me, I told myself, I'm not qualified.

The prospect of being out on the streets, meeting and helping people, held enormous appeal, but it was the autumn of 1964 before I finally plucked up the courage to send off the application form I had painstakingly filled out in my very best handwriting. Driving around London over the following weeks, I fantasized about what it might be like to walk the streets in a blue serge uniform. I rushed home every night to see what the postman had delivered, but nothing ever fell on to my doormat. Obviously no one was considering my application seriously. They've lost it, I thought, or binned it.

In the summer of 1965, long after I had given up all hope, a letter arrived inviting me to attend an interview. I couldn't remember feeling this excited. Here was something that I knew I could do – but more importantly it was something I really *wanted* to do.

I was at home with my parents one day, preparing myself for the interview, when a woman police officer called at the door, introduced herself as Sergeant Helen Lunn and explained that she had come to vet me and my family as she needed to judge the sincerity of my application. I took one look at this vision in blue and my heart soared. That could be me one day, I dared to think.

The night before the interview, I was so excited I could hardly sleep. I arrived at Great Scotland Yard behind Cannon Row sporting a smart new haircut and wearing my favourite chunky white cardigan over my best skirt and blouse. I sat in a long corridor with a bunch of other applicants, nervously waiting my turn. I went to the ladies' lavatory and found the loo paper had a stamp on it, bearing the words GOVERNMENT PROPERTY. It tickled my sense of humour and I tore off a strip and gave it to the girl sitting next to me outside. 'Keep hold of this,' I told her. 'It's the only thing the government is ever likely to give you for free.' She looked at me as if I were barking mad.

The interview was a disaster. Three men and a senior woman officer sat stiffly opposite me in an airless room and asked me all sorts of questions I hadn't even considered. One of them, not surprisingly, was: 'Why do you want to join the police force?' Of all the clever things I could have said about wanting to help people and admiring the work the police did in serving the community, I actually answered: 'I don't want to work in an office any more. It's boring.' I knew it was the wrong answer, they told me as much there and then, and as I left the room I could have burst into tears, convinced that my stupid reply had cost me my big chance.

But, for reasons I've never been entirely sure about, I got through the interview. All I had to do now was pass the medical and I was in. I was sent along the corridor for the terrifying process of having to strip in front of a doctor and having my parts inspected to make sure they were in full working order. These kinds of examinations have always embarrassed the hell out of me. A male doctor and the senior woman officer who had been on my interview board were waiting for me as I stepped nervously into the examination room in a dressing gown.

'Take your dressing gown off, dear,' said the woman officer briskly.

'What? Right off?' I asked, reddening and clamping it as tightly as I could to my chest.

'Yes, yes. Right off. Come along.' I let the thin towelling robe fall to the floor. 'And your knickers, dear,' the voice said. 'Now turn around.'

Barely able to look at them for embarrassment, I did as I was told.

'Now bend over and touch your toes.' I did it for a split second, but it was just long enough for me to see both of them, bent over their desk, apparently staring at my bottom.

With my back still turned to them, I heard the voice say: 'Now left foot up, sole to us. Good, now the right. Fine, you can go.' The whole exercise was over in less than two minutes. Having apparently demonstrated that I didn't have haemorrhoids or flat feet, I was accepted as a trainee constable into the Metropolitan Police. I dressed as quickly as I could and raced home to tell my parents.

My mother, who had been nagging at me to get a husband and a job I liked enough to stay in for more than a few months, was unimpressed. Even though I now appeared to have achieved the latter, as far as she was concerned I had really burnt my boats on the marriage front. 'This will ruin your chances of finding a good man now,' she cried.

My father, on the other hand, smiled kindly and told me he was proud of me. He knew I had been unhappy for some time and hoped this would bring me the peace of mind I sought. He told me that a woman he used to work with on the buses called Jackie White had joined the police force and was now a uniformed inspector at Paddington. He painted a pretty frightening picture of this loud-voiced peroxide blonde before saying that underneath it all she had a heart of gold.

Pete wouldn't offer any opinion on the subject whatsoever. His only experience of the police had been when he was arrested for a minor driving infringement as a young teddy boy. The officers had clearly given him a very hard time and he hated them for it. But nothing anyone could say was going to change my mind. I truly believed I had found my vocation and I couldn't wait to get started.

By 15 November 1965 I had packed my few belongings and moved into Peto House, an all-girl section house off the Marylebone Road, ready for my three months' police training at Peel House in Victoria. I was twenty-two years old and for the first time in my life I felt like a grown-up.

2

CATCHING SIGHT OF MYSELF IN THE MIRROR, I GASPED.
Wearing my police uniform for the first time, I felt intoxicated.
With its shiny silver buttons and inky material, it made me look
like someone important, someone with confidence. This wasn't
the Carol Bristow I used to know. All this prestige and in-
fluence was new to me. It was more than a little frightening, I
thought, as I smoothed down the dark blue tunic. But it was
also wonderfully exhilarating and I couldn't imagine ever going
back to civilian life.

From the minute training started, I was hooked. There wasn't
a second that I disliked, even when it came to learning legal
definitions parrot-fashion, digesting law books or learning how
and when to make an arrest. We were split into groups and
acted out real-life scenarios with shoplifters and burglars. We
had to interview fellow-students as 'suspects' and learn how not
to jump to the wrong conclusion. My mind had never been so
challenged, my intellect so stimulated. I could only wonder why
on earth I hadn't joined up before.

With my new-found confidence and happiness, I blossomed. I
did very well in all my classes, getting top marks across the
board. I was made class captain, which was a great honour and
made me feel like a winner. I felt as if I need not be afraid of
anything any more.

Not only did the job seem like it was made for me from the outset, but I loved the camaraderie and the belief that I was helping people, another trait I inherited from my dad. The first time I went out on the beat with a trained woman constable, I was walking on air. If a member of the public smiled at me or glanced in my direction, I blushed with pride. Ask me the time, someone, please ask me the time, I prayed. But to this day no one ever has.

I also fell straight into all the socializing, the drinking and the parties that went with student life. I suddenly found myself surrounded by like-minded people, who wanted to break away from traditional, boring lifestyles and get their teeth into something meaningful while enjoying themselves at the same time. Their company surprised and delighted me. I was treated with respect and my opinion actually appeared to be worth something.

We worked hard but, believe me, we played hard too. At the Christmas party that year we put on a concert in which a male recruit and I dressed up and mimed our way through a rendition of *Help* by the Beatles, which had been the hit film of the year, before drinking ourselves into a stupor. I had never felt so at ease with my surroundings, and my fondness for alcohol was becoming legendary. 'Carol can drink any man under the table,' my female friends used to brag, and stupidly – with the added encouragement they gave me – I learnt that I could.

When my three months' training was up, I was posted to West End Central Police Station in Soho, as a junior 'plonk' (WPC), a young wet-behind-the-ears probationer. I was very lucky to be sent to West End Central. It was a prime training nick, one of the busiest in London, and I knew I had landed on my feet. At training school, word had gone round that if you could manage the work in Soho or Mayfair you could work anywhere. We all dreaded being sent to Uxbridge, Epsom or South Mimms, stations right on the periphery of the Met area which were considered to be as far away from the action as Timbuktu.

So West End Central it was, together with a tiny room of my own at Putney section house, a four-storey residential hall for police officers behind Putney Police Station. The upper two floors were occupied by women and the bottom two by men. Woe betide any officer found on a floor occupied by the opposite sex, for that could mean disciplinary action or even sacking. The fact that such clandestine meetings between the sexes went on all the time was largely ignored by the residents, who conspired to keep everything well under wraps and away from the beady eye of the section-house sergeant who was supposed to be in charge.

I never took part in the sexual shenanigans between floors. Not only was I not in the least bit interested, I was far too scared of getting caught to risk it. My mind was on higher things. I believed that, as I had found my rightful place in society after years of searching, I was going to do my very best to stay there.

I was given a small single room to accommodate me and all my worldly goods. By today's standards, there wasn't enough room to swing a truncheon, but it seemed strangely spacious to me then. The toilets and washrooms were along the corridor, while the ironing and laundry rooms were elsewhere in the same building. There was a canteen on the ground floor and, for better or worse, this was home. I felt like the cat that had got the cream.

But within minutes of arriving at the nick on my first day and being introduced to the Chief Superintendent, the smile was wiped clean off my face. Over six feet tall, with whiskers on his upper cheekbones and a strong Irish accent, he bawled at everyone he met.

'I have looked into your background, Bristow, and I'm not impressed. You are twenty-two and you have already had eight jobs which makes you thoroughly unreliable. If I'd been on your interview board you'd never have got this far. Why they've given you to me, God only knows. But now I've got you I am putting you straight on to monthly reports, and the second anyone tells me that you are not up to scratch you will be out on your ear. Got it?'

'Yes, sir,' I mumbled, terrified.

'I didn't hear that,' he barked.

'Yes, sir!' I virtually shouted, standing to attention and thrusting my chest out. He grunted and stalked off. I didn't move a muscle until he was completely out of sight, and then I exhaled. Great, I thought, everyone else is to be reported on once every six months, but I'll be scrutinized monthly. What a terrible way to start my new career. My fellow-plonks regarded me pityingly.

Women police constables have been called 'plonks' by the fellas for as long as I can remember. I've never found out why, but the dictionary definition may provide a clue. It says 'to plonk' is to put down hard, and a 'plonker' is a stupid person. Maybe that's how the men saw us when the phrase was first introduced, although I have always been happy to accept it as a term of endearment rather than a put-down.

When I arrived at West End Central there was a chief plonk, a woman inspector, two corporal plonks called sergeants and a flock of ordinary plonks consisting of about sixteen women constables, of which I was now one. We worked mainly with missing children, aliens (illegal immigrants) and just about everything else where women were concerned. In the daytime we dealt with the regular flow of handbag snatches, teenage runaways and indecent assaults, but by night we doubled up as cell matrons for the toms (prostitutes) and were given a lot of the rotten jobs the men didn't want to touch. But nothing seemed to dampen my spirits, not even slopping out the station cells.

The only blot on my horizon was the woman sergeant who had been briefed to keep an eye on me. That woman gave me hell. She must have lain awake at night devising new ways to make my life a misery and to keep our Chief Superintendent happy. I remember returning from foot patrol five minutes before my shift was due to end, only to be told to go back out onto the streets until my tour of duty was properly completed. If there was some particularly unpleasant task to do, you could bet your last pound note I got it. She really applied the pressure and after six months I nearly resigned because I thought I couldn't stand it any longer. But I had made some excellent friends and they persuaded me to stay.

A rather unusual ally, whom I met on my first visit to Westminster Juvenile Court, turned out to be the court inspector. From the day I arrived, I was warned never to be late for juvenile court or the court inspector would have my guts for garters. Needless to say, on that day, I was late by a matter of minutes for reasons beyond my control. I remember trembling when I was told that Inspector White wanted to see me immediately.

I walked into her office and faced this well-endowed woman with peroxide-blond hair and two pips on her shoulders, who glared at me as if she was about to eat me for breakfast. 'Just where do you think you've been?' she boomed. 'Answer me, girl, what have you got to say for yourself?'

I suddenly remembered something my dad had told me, so I said: 'My name's Bristow, ma'am, and I think you know my father.'

She paused, her face fixed in an icy glare, but then the ice cracked and she broke into a huge grin. 'Bristow? Bristow, you say? You're never Ernie Bristow's little girl!' I smiled in acknowledgement. 'Come here and let me take a look at you.'

From that day on, Police Inspector Edie White (she didn't use 'Jackie' in the police force as she had on the buses) treated me with great kindness. I knew she was the boss, but when she barked I always saw the twinkle in her eye.

I spent an extraordinary amount of time at West End Central trying to avoid doing anything which would give my supervisors a reason to write any adverse comments in my monthly reports, thus incurring the wrath of the Chief Superintendent. I worked like a little navvy. I reckon I spoke to more potential runaways than the rest of the other plonks on my shift put together. On one particular day, when I approached a group of youngsters I suspected of being up to no good, I discovered seven of them were either wanted or reported missing. I herded them back to the station like the Pied Piper of Hamelin. I'm not sure if it was pride or stubbornness, but I insisted on completing all the paperwork myself and dealing with each one at court without any outside assistance. I was going to prove to the Chief Superintendent, the woman sergeant and, most of all, myself that I could do this job and do it well.

My hard work paid off because within a year the woman sergeant was transferred to another station and the Chief Super was posted to Scotland Yard, which meant that they were both finally out of my hair. I imagine they had seen it all as a bit of a giggle but, for my part, I had lived through a hellish existence during that time, trying so hard to prove myself. The experience had such an effect on me that later, when I took on the responsibility of training new probationers, I was determined never to give anyone quite such a difficult time.

My life improved significantly after the two people I thought hated me most had left. But their unremitting bully-boy tactics hadn't all been wasted. Within a few months, I was shocked to discover that – due to my diligence – I had been voted one of the top four women constables in London. Our reward was to be invited to dinner with the Air Vice Marshal and Black Rod at the House of Commons. I felt honoured. It was 8 March 1967 and I can still remember what I chose from the *à la carte* menu – fillet steak and mushrooms, which cost my hosts the grand sum of 12/6*d*. I came back from that dinner puffed up like a Trafalgar Square pigeon. I wanted to tell my old Chief Super and that woman sergeant just where they could stick their oppressive behaviour, but of course they were long gone.

By now, I felt much more comfortable with my supervisors. The powers that be had a clear-out of most of the established female officers at West End Central, moving them on to pastures new. This led to the arrival of a new woman inspector, two new women sergeants and at least two new senior women constables, all of whom actively encouraged me and occasionally picked me out for special tasks.

One of the first was an undercover job set up to try and obtain evidence of drug-dealing in an all-night West End club frequented by youngsters. My brief was to go to the club with a male constable, posing as an ordinary couple and dancing ourselves silly while keeping an eye out for anything dodgy.

Night after night for over a week, PC Paul Bates and I went to this Soho club and danced the night away to Beatles and

Tamla Motown hits, as we watched the dealers dishing out drugs to the kids. The craze was for 'speed' – purple hearts, yellow amphetamines, reds and black bombers. Long before amphetamines and other drugs had all turned to white powder, the pills were every colour of the rainbow. I had never seen anything like it in my life.

We monitored the chief protagonists, took mental notes and carried on dancing to the likes of 'Yellow Submarine' by the Beatles, 'Pretty Flamingo' by Manfred Mann and 'You Can't Hurry Love' by the Supremes. Even now, I can't hear 'Pretty Flamingo' without remembering those long, hot nights.

To protect our methods of detection, Paul and I had to be 'arrested' by our colleagues when the police raid eventually took place, so that no one would suspect we were involved. The officers burst into the club, bang on the dot of 1 a.m. The music stopped, the lights were turned up and a senior detective told the throng that we would all be interviewed and searched before being allowed to leave.

It didn't matter that my colleagues knew exactly who I was when they herded me into the ladies' loo along with the other girls, but I was really miffed when some of them took their instruction to make it look realistic rather too seriously for my liking – particularly during the strip search.

'Get 'em off,' they ordered. There were three of them standing with their arms crossed, staring at me as I stood in a row of young girls.

'What, me?' I asked, surprised.

'Yes, you. Get 'em off.'

'Don't you know who I am?' I whispered, reluctant as ever to reveal my body to anybody, least of all my colleagues.

'Just strip,' came the instruction. I was mortified and my mind flashed back to the police medical as I turned my back on them and let my knickers fall to the floor. Fighting to keep a straight face, they searched me for concealed drugs before letting me go. One of them bumped into me later in the police canteen and, seeing the look on my face, said that if I couldn't take a joke then I should never have joined. She was right, of course, and I comforted myself that we had done a good job and the main dealers were likely to go to prison for some time.

On another operation, one of the Vice Squad superintendents asked me and nine other WPCs to help him carry out a raid on a brothel in Mayfair. It was a beautiful Georgian house, owned by some member of the landed gentry but run by a caretaker who lived in the basement and chose to let out the rooms to prostitutes to entertain their clients. The toms were very active and never short of customers. Our brief was to burst into our allocated rooms with a male constable at the appointed hour and stop whatever activity was taking place. We were not to allow anyone to move, dress or leave, the idea being that the Superintendent would then visit each room, take notes of what he saw and use the evidence to prosecute the caretaker for running a brothel.

When the time came to enter the designated room, my colleague and I burst in to find the tom stark naked in the middle of quite a performance on the bed with her punter. In an adjacent room, another constable found a man, tied to a rack on the wall, being beaten with a leather whip; and further down the corridor a third (male) punter was found dressed in nothing but black tights and a bra. Overcoming our initial shock, we did precisely as we were told and kept the participants in their exact positions until the Superintendent arrived. I was twenty-three years old and had never found it so difficult to keep a straight face in my life.

I felt sorry for the poor sods, in their state of nakedness, with their erections slowly deflating and the disapproving eyes of the law upon them. The punters were never taken to court because they hadn't committed an offence, and all in all they were treated with as much respect as we could muster in the circumstances. But I will never forget their scarlet faces and absolute embarrassment as long as I live.

I was still a rookie with only six months' experience when I dealt with my first rape victim at West End Central. They say nobody ever forgets the first. The CID had contacted my uniformed woman inspector and asked for her help. She in turn summoned me to the matron's office and introduced me to a young woman who had walked into the police station in a state of distress. It was well before the days of specialized rape suites; the one-bar electric fire and the matron's worn armchair were all we had to offer.

The victim was a plain young woman called Janice, who wore a multicoloured kaftan and a fringed sheepskin coat. She was twenty-five, three years older than me, and dreadfully nervous although she held it together pretty well. Getting out the statement sheets, I started to take down the details about how the previous evening her date had forced himself upon her after a meal out.

'He seemed so gentle and kind in the bistro. I didn't think twice about inviting him back for coffee,' she said, tearfully. I imagined this naïve young woman in the little bed-sit she had told me about, innocently turning her back to switch the kettle on before being grabbed viciously from behind by this wolf in sheep's clothing. As she continued her story, she broke down and it was impossible not to feel terribly sorry for her, not least because she was obviously telling the truth.

Unable to offer her any sort of special facilities at the police station, I was forced to listen to her story in the most inappropriate conditions. Sterile and bleak, our surroundings did little to put her at ease. I had managed to find a spare mug to make her some tea but that was the only little luxury. She sipped it gratefully as she continued to tell me what had happened.

I listened intently and passed her a tissue to blow her nose. 'Remember,' my inspector had told me, 'write down *every* detail. We need to know everything that happened, where, when and why.' Well, the poor woman must have thought I was nuts, because as she started to tell me tremulously how her attacker had pinned her down to the sofa-bed I interrupted constantly, asking her everything from the colour of her curtains to the type of carpet and style of wallpaper she had. She must have wondered if I was in the process of redecorating and was looking for tips. But whatever she thought of me – and I suspect she could tell I was incredibly nervous – she never once flinched from giving me every detail, even though the interview took hours and her statement covered several pages.

As I waved her goodbye at the station door (she insisted on walking home) I knew from my brief experience as a police officer that there wasn't a hope in hell of getting a prosecution case going. It was in the days before the term 'date rape' came into being and I knew it would be her word against her attacker's in a court of law. In the mid-sixties, at a time when the media were constantly ranting about the loose morals of the hippies, the offer of coffee in her flat would be regarded as virtually 'asking for it'.

Still, I had her story, chapter and verse, and I sincerely hoped that something might come of it, for her sake. It is no easy matter for a victim to report a rape. It takes a great deal of guts and considerable strength of character; this was even more pronounced in the 60s when victims still faced scepticism and intense police questioning, not to mention considerable fear that the man they were accusing might come back to attack them again or pressurize them into dropping any charges. Janice was so terrified of the man, who knew where she lived, that she moved in with a friend, an address she had begged me to keep secret. Yet she had found the courage to report what had happened in the hope of bringing charges against the man who violated her, and maybe preventing him from doing it again to someone else. I admired her enormously and wondered if I would have been as brave in similar circumstances.

I handed her statement to the inspector, happy that I had taken the necessary care, but she was not at all impressed. Instead of praising me for being so conscientious, she gave me a right earful about the time I had wasted writing down useless information about Janice's taste in house furnishings. 'And what on earth is this?' she asked, pointing to a plan I had drawn up of Janice's home. 'What did you think you were playing at?' She was dead right, of course; I realized I still had a lot to learn.

But the experience had taught me something. It led me to believe that there had to be a better way of treating victims of rape. If only there could have been a quiet place we could have gone to, I thought, somewhere away from the police station where we could have sat comfortably on sofas and chatted in a much more relaxed way, without fear of interruption or distraction.

Later on, when specialized rape suites were introduced and the attitudes of some of my male colleagues to rape softened, I dared to hope that we were entering a whole new era for the victims of sexual assault. But there was never the speedy transition I had hoped for. Even now, despite enormous progress, some of the more old-fashioned detectives and, worse still, the judges find it difficult to overcome their prejudices, leaving me in no doubt that there is still plenty of room for improvement.

In those first few years of my career, however, I was too inexperienced to voice that particular worry, and in any event I was far too busy getting on with the job. Within a year I had my own little bed-sit in Shepherd's Bush, I had made some good and dear friends in the police force and for the first time in my life, or so it seemed, I was standing on my own two feet. I no longer felt useless, I acknowledged to myself, even if my personal life still left a lot to be desired.

When I joined the police I felt convinced that I was sufficiently street-wise to be able to deal with whatever came my way, but in fact I hadn't even scratched the surface. The person who first brought that home to me was Annie, a fifteen-year-old runaway from Glasgow, whom I pulled out of a locked ladies' lavatory in Piccadilly underground station. With her wholesome looks, carrot-ginger hair and freckles, she looked for all the world like the sort of kid the television advertisers would snap up. But she was dirty and frightened. She had run away to London to find happiness only to discover that, for her, it didn't exist. She had been living rough for a month, and was demoralized and famished.

The minute I set eyes on her, my heart melted. She seemed like the kid sister I never had but used to dream about. I took her to the station to get her fed and cleaned up and to find out more about her. Having established that she was under age, and because I had no other choice, I put her in a detention room while I made some calls. In less than thirty minutes, I was summoned to the custody suite to be told that she was screaming for me.

I could hear her sobbing along the corridor and when the sergeant opened the cell door my mouth fell open. This sweet-faced little kid was scrunched up in a corner flailing her hands around in the air, calling out for me with one breath and, in the next, telling me that there were rats on the floor and skeletons coming out of the walls. I had never seen the effects of withdrawal from heroin before and it shocked me rigid.

Her hallucinations were vivid and she begged for my help, her face contorted and red. I raced over to her and held her in my arms while calling for a police doctor to give her something to calm her down, but there was little he could do. She remained in a very bad way for some hours, as I sat helplessly with her. Long after my shift had ended I was still comforting her, and didn't leave until ordered by my sergeant to go home and rest. It wasn't until I was safely inside my room that I allowed myself to cry. I wanted to make Annie better and I wanted to fix her problems. It took me a long time to learn that there was little I could do on either front.

When I reported back for duty early the following morning, Annie's cell was empty. She was, I was told, already on her way to Westminster Juvenile Court for welfare proceedings under the Children and Young Persons Act. I followed her to court and sat in the wings as this trembling, ashen-faced little kid waited to be told what arrangements would be made to take her back to Glasgow. If she didn't go home, she would be placed in local-authority care, in a children's home which specialized in young drug addicts.

Back at the police station, I asked if there was any way I could maintain contact with Annie. I attempted to make the point that I would like to try to help her but a battle-weary sergeant – who must have heard it all before – said: 'Carol, you're going to come across a thousand Annies before long and you can't help them all. Drop it, because it won't help her and it won't help you.'

With less than six months' policing experience under my belt I wanted to save the world, but the reality was that I could hardly help myself. How am I ever going to cope? I thought, and several hours later as I downed my third large Scotch, I was still asking myself the same question.

The 1960s were a fascinating time to be working in central London, which was by then the Mecca of world fashion and music, as well as being the focus for radical politics and free love. It was home to new young models like Twiggy and the Shrimp, and to the psychedelic era heralded by *Sergeant Pepper's Lonely Hearts Club Band*. It became the venue for political protests over anything from foreign wars to the student riots in Paris; for the first time in years angry young people were challenging the previously unquestioned respect for their elders and those in authority.

Despite my age and uncertain political stance, my uniform classified me as one of the latter, and it frightened me to realize that certain members of my own generation saw me as the enemy. On duty during a particularly violent affray outside the American Embassy in Grosvenor Square, I was involved in running scuffles with long-haired, brick-throwing revolutionaries, protesting against ongoing American military involvement in Vietnam.

As tensions rose and the mounted police were drafted in to disperse the crowd, I was put in charge of a band of protesters who had been arrested and herded into one of the fifty-two-seater coaches that had brought in police reinforcements. Seeing that I was on my own while the rest of my colleagues battled it out on the streets, the protesters decided to rock the coach from side to side until the whole thing almost tipped over, with me inside. It took all my very best endeavours to calm them down and stop them wrecking the bus.

Every day was a new experience, and I frequently encountered situations which were a revelation to me. After two years, I completed my probationary training, qualified as a fully fledged constable and wondered what would come next. It was 1967 and the question was very nearly answered for me when I received an extraordinary job offer out of the blue. The Chief Superintendent in charge of the separate women's police department summoned me to her office and indicated that I should sit down.

'We've been invited to help out the Royal Ulster Constabulary,' she told me. 'There have been a series of sectarian murders in Northern Ireland since the Troubles began and they need our help. The Commissioner is sending a team of senior detectives to Belfast and they have asked for volunteers from the uniformed ranks to assist them. They need women constables and I wondered if you might like to be one of them.'

I was amazed and more than a little flattered. I wasn't a detective, after all, and I couldn't work out what use a young and relatively inexperienced WPC like me could be to anyone. The option, I was assured, was entirely voluntary. I wouldn't be put under any pressure to take it up and nothing would be held against me if I refused. 'Go away and think about it,' she said.

As the days passed and I started to think about what hostile responses we Met officers might receive in Northern Ireland, I began to feel very uncomfortable. Every story from the province seemed to leap out at me from the newspapers. They were violent times and bloodshed, bombs and murder seemed to be everyday features. Increasingly I became wary at the thought of crossing the Irish Sea.

Knowing that I had the choice, I decided to decline the offer. To this day, I wonder if I made the right decision. Half of me accepted that it would be a new and exciting challenge for one so young, while the other half recognized that I would probably be scared witless from the time I got up in the morning to the time I went to bed, something I really wasn't ready for.

The offer and my subsequent decision unsettled me for a few weeks, but almost immediately I was fortunate enough to be transferred to Harrow Road Police Station in Paddington. It meant that I would be removed from the rather unreal world of Soho, the West End and Mayfair and be among real people: men, women and children living in ordinary circumstances, the kind of people I had grown up with and those I had originally joined the police force to help.

Harrow Road covered parts of Paddington, Maida Vale, Kensal Rise, Bayswater and Westbourne Grove and was a terrific place to experience residential policing at first hand. It opened new doors, and Northern Ireland with its dangerous attraction was quickly forgotten. My workload became much more varied; I was regularly called out to deal with burglaries, domestic incidents, sexual assaults and cases involving children. As far as I was concerned, Harrow Road was the place to be.

One of the nicest aspects of my new job was the great cama- raderie we built up with the nursing staff next door at Paddington General Hospital (now called St Mary's). The nurses' office at the back of Accident & Emergency was a good place to call in for a cup of hot tea on a cold day and I became friends with many of the girls, who always seemed happy to have a uniformed police officer around.

One week they had a real problem patient, called Archie, who kept arriving at the front desk claiming to have sustained serious internal injuries in some accident or other. Each time, the doctors and nurses examined him and found him to be perfectly healthy, and each time Archie became aggressive and refused to budge until, as he saw it, he was properly treated.

'He's pretty harmless,' one of the nurses told me as I escorted him out of the front door on the first occasion. 'He just wants some love and attention.'

'Don't we all?' I joked, as I helped him shuffle out of the door.

Two days later he was back again, claiming yet another injury, and once again I was called in to see him off the premises. It was about the fifth time he had been into casualty in as many days and the nursing staff had quite enough on their hands without the likes of Archie.

The following afternoon I was in the back of casualty, spong- ing my four o'clock cuppa, when there was a sudden rumpus at the front desk. Putting down my mug, I ran round with some of the nurses to find Archie lying on the floor, moaning and groaning and clutching his stomach. Blood appeared to be pouring from his mouth.

'He just vomited this lot all over the front desk!' a casualty receptionist complained as she tried to mop up vast quantities of blood which now swamped her workspace.

'Good God!' I exclaimed, sorry at not having taken poor old Archie seriously. 'Here, let me give you a hand.' We manhandled the writhing, filthy old tramp into one of the cubicles, and I backed away while the doctors and nurses pulled the curtains around him, desperate to try and stem the bleeding.

Before leaving, I lingered around, certain that poor old Archie was about to breathe his last, particularly as he'd lost so much blood. If only I had been more understanding, I chastised myself. What if he didn't pull through?

An hour later, I called back just as the cubicle curtains were abruptly pulled apart. 'Now get out and stay out!' a senior consultant was scolding a shamefaced Archie. I couldn't understand what was going on and sidelined one of the nurses.

'What's happening?' I asked her. 'I thought he was really ill this time.'

'So did we,' she said, 'until we took a sample of his blood for grouping. That's when we discovered it wasn't the same blood type as the stuff he threw up over the front desk.'

I still didn't understand, so she had to spell it out for me.

'Realizing he wasn't going to get any sympathy from us unless he did something drastic, the stupid idiot stole a bottle of blood from the pathology lab, drank the lot down and then staggered into casualty to throw it up. Can you believe it?'

I almost couldn't. The very thought was so disgusting. 'How could he do that?' I asked. The nurse explained that Archie was suffering from an attention-seeking disorder called Münchausen syndrome, where someone complains of physical symptoms which he or she pretends exist or self-induces. In some cases, the 'sufferers' are so persuasive that they are unnecessarily operated on by surgeons who are deceived into thinking that the patient is seriously ill.

When I looked into Archie's background, I discovered that he had performed the same trick in numerous hospitals all over England. So I felt I had no option but to charge him with stealing the pint of blood and take him to the local magistrates' court. They discharged him conditionally for twelve months' good behaviour and that was the last we saw of him in Harrow

Road – although there was no doubt in my mind that he was off to try and take in some other poor sod somewhere else.

Harrow Road is where I gradually came to realize that all the best jobs in the police force went to the CID. We, the uniforms, might get to nick the bodies (prisoners) but they, the CID, got to do all the interesting investigation and detective work. In many police stations there was very much a 'them and us' atmosphere between the two departments, but not at Harrow Road. The CID fellas really valued their uniformed colleagues, accepting and understanding the need for women officers within their department. The good news was that they sometimes invited me to work alongside them, and when I saw what that entailed I became enthralled.

From then on I wanted to become one of them. When I told my female colleagues, many said I was nuts, because detective work simply wasn't considered women's territory. 'You'll never handle the hours,' they warned. 'Stay in uniform, it's far less aggro.' Not only did I really want to do the work, but the more people said I shouldn't and couldn't do it, the more determined I was to prove them wrong.

So, against all advice, I applied to join the CID, and was over the moon to be accepted almost immediately to train as a detective constable. It would mean a transfer away from my beloved Harrow Road, but that was a small price to pay for being a 'tec' and right in the thick of things. Miss Marple, eat your heart out. This was just the beginning.

The station I was going to be based at was crucial. There wouldn't be much for me to get my teeth into at a suburban nick, so I kept my fingers crossed and prayed for an inner-London posting. All my prayers were answered when I discovered they were sending me to Notting Hill which, with its incredible variety of work, was considered by many to be another of the finest training grounds in the Met for a young, aspiring detective. My father always said that if I fell in a bucket of shit I would come up smelling of roses, and he was right.

I arrived at Notting Hill CID in October 1968 and was given the grand title of Temporary Detective Constable or TDC. The word 'temporary' would only be dropped when I had completed a considerable amount of training, passed several examinations and was considered by the established senior detectives as a suitable candidate to remain within the department. Shortly after my arrival, I was packed off to Detective Training School at Hendon for four months to read law and commit great chunks of legislation to memory. Within a relatively short time, I would be expected to know my police powers in all criminal matters and to be adept at evidence-gathering and presenting the more difficult cases in the law-courts.

There were only two women in my class of twenty-six, me and another girl called Pauline Hobill from south London. We loved every minute of it and religiously tested each other's knowledge to ensure that neither of us could be found wanting. Both of us were gobsmacked to learn that we had achieved second and third places in the final examinations. The man who beat us later became Chief Constable of the City of London Police. At the time, I had no idea what good company I was keeping.

With all the examinations under my belt, and after a trip to Amsterdam with Pauline to celebrate, I felt pretty pleased with myself when I returned to Notting Hill as the only woman in the CID office. I had got thus far without any serious setbacks and certainly without experiencing any of the male chauvinism I had sometimes come across in my civilian life. Most of my colleagues, male and female, were my friends, it seemed, not adversaries.

There were, of course, women who liked to moan about sexual harassment in the force, although I never really agreed with them. My view was and is that they were – generally speaking – women who were oversensitive, who took the jocular, locker-room banter among the male officers far too seriously. I gave as good as I got; if anyone gave me any lip, they could expect some straight back. That's not to say that I would tolerate deliberate rudeness, but I didn't see the point in taking someone to task for an off-the-cuff ribald comment. It was just the way of the world.

Many of these women seemed to me to be their own worst

enemies and in a time of increased sexual equality they became so overprotective of their status that they lost their sense of humour completely. I had little sympathy with any woman who complained about light-hearted sexual innuendo from male colleagues, but I took a very serious view of male behaviour which breached those boundaries.

Not that the other lads in training at Notting Hill didn't put me in my place. Some weren't quite so receptive to the idea of a woman detective as the CID officers at Harrow Road appeared to have been. Although they welcomed me warmly into their drinking circle (where I quickly proved my worth), I felt very much alone when it came to the work side of things.

It was a rough area to police and when the fellas went out on inquiries they generally preferred to pair up with one of the other male TDCs – it was just human nature, I suppose. But at times this made me feel my new career was being overlooked. Time and again when a call came in they grabbed their coats and went flying out of the door. Time and again I was left in the office, answering the phones or waiting for further instructions. To say I was frustrated was the understatement of the year.

Fortunately, one of the senior detective sergeants – a man called Don Brown whose official title was, appropriately, 'First-Class Sergeant' – took me under his wing and used me as his 'bag carrier'. In the days before all the ranks were changed, a first-class sergeant was the rank between second-class (basic) sergeant and inspector. The first-class sergeants in uniform were recognized by the distinctive three stripes on their arms topped by the gold crown (as in *Dixon of Dock Green*). For CID officers not in uniform, there was no such obvious distinction, although everyone who knew DS Brown appreciated that he was more than worthy of his crown.

Everywhere DS Brown went, I went too, with the result that he involved me in some of the most serious investigations that came into the office. It was brilliant, although I couldn't help feeling guilty when I realized that a few of my male colleagues were eyeing me with envy.

I learnt so much from that marvellous 'old-school' detective.

He was a gentleman in the true sense of the word and treated everyone with respect and courtesy. He showed unbelievable compassion, and not just to victims. Whoever you were, you were dealt with in the same even-tempered way. I had been in interview rooms with colleagues plenty of times when suspects had been handled pretty discourteously because of the crimes they were meant to have committed, but DS Brown wasn't like that. Even when he was dealing with the most awful little scumbags, he never once lost his temper.

He introduced me to investigations that ordinarily, due to my inexperience, I wouldn't have been allowed to touch. Through him, I met my first back-street abortionists at the time when abortions were carried out with syringes and buckets of soapy water (before the Abortion Act), and I was involved with several cases of serious sexual assault, all of which he strictly supervised.

Unlike many of his colleagues, DS Brown was way ahead of his time when it came to dealing with victims of rape. Long before the days when they were shown any special kindness, this man put himself out to give them the respect, understanding and support they rightly deserved. Elsewhere, women were quite often subjected to a severe grilling by sceptical male police officers who suggested that either they had made it all up or they had asked for it.

When I saw the results DS Brown's gentle tactics achieved, particularly the way the women responded to his sympathetic approach, I vowed to try to do the same. I wanted to emulate him as much as possible, and I was determined to make my teacher-cum-mentor proud of me.

Like most young detectives in training, I was eager to please and anxious to prove myself to my superiors. I volunteered for just about everything and it was not unusual for me to respond to an emergency call virtually single-handed if the opportunity presented itself. I never stopped hoping for 'the big one' to fall into my lap, the case that would get me noticed. So when an emergency call came in over the airways that a burglary was under way at one of the better houses in Notting Hill, I was ready, willing and raring to go.

Two of us were sitting in the canteen when the 'shout' went up. 'Two male suspects seen at a house in Lansdowne Walk,' our hand-held radios blasted. 'Informant is Mrs Pringle, who lives opposite.' Well, that was it. Lansdowne Walk was just round the corner, so we ran like bats out of hell, down the stairs, out of the nick and across the road. You couldn't see our bums for dust as we shouted our numbers into the handsets and yelled: 'We are responding.'

When we arrived at the four-storey Victorian town house we could tell that it had been recently renovated. The builders had been in, gutted and completely refurbished it. It had been rewired, replumbed and had had a modern central heating system installed. It looked beautiful.

As we ran up the garden path, I shouted back to my colleague: 'I'll look upstairs. You check downstairs.' I didn't give him time to argue as we both charged through the open front door. He ran on through the house towards the back door while I flew up the ornate staircase, taking the treads in twos.

Stopping to catch my breath on the landing, I tried to decide in the few seconds I allowed myself which of the heavy panelled doors I would tackle first. Choosing the one straight in front of me, I burst through the door, eyes blazing, handcuffs at the ready, prepared for every eventuality. Or so I thought.

Unable to slow my momentum, I suddenly found my feet flying through the air. Before I could say, 'You're nicked, sunshine,' everything seemed to go into slow motion. I looked down to find that the floorboards had been removed from the bedroom I had just burst into by the burglars, who had helped themselves to the copper piping and the radiators. Gravity took over as I did a little pirouette in mid-air before crashing heavily through the gaping hole in the floorboards and the newly plastered ceiling below.

Had it not been for a cross-beam which broke my fall, I would have tumbled twelve feet to serious injury on the marble floor of the drawing room below. Saved I might have been, but I was now unceremoniously wedged astride the ceiling joist in a most unladylike fashion and in considerable pain.

My colleague heard the crash and came running into the

drawing room. Looking up through the hole in the ceiling to see my legs dangling above him, he shouted: 'Bloody hell, Carol, you OK?' As he tried unsuccessfully to stifle his laughter and avoid looking up my knickers, he added: 'We missed them. They legged it out the back.' He then climbed the stairs and, in an attempt to be gallant, started to manhandle me out of the hole.

I was not amused. My back was badly jarred, my right knee cut and bleeding, my tights and skirt ripped and split, but most of all my pride was seriously dented. More humiliation followed when some other colleagues arrived. Before I could be prised out each of them eyed me from the ground-floor drawing room and, seeing my little legs wiggling aimlessly through the ceiling, they fell about laughing. So much for getting myself noticed.

Undaunted, and in a bid to improve my standing, I decided to have a crack at the sergeant's exam, a notorious hurdle for many a young constable. In for a penny, in for a pound, I thought. Having qualified as a substantive detective constable by October 1969, I returned to my law books for several more months, studying right through to the following April, when I would have the chance to sit for promotion.

The sergeant's exam had an almost mythical reputation among police officers. Even those who passed have never pretended it was easy. And for the vast majority who failed, it became an obvious barrier to promotion and better pay; it was surely a device dreamt up by someone to keep the underachievers at bay. By the 1970s an average of two thousand constables sat the annual sergeant's promotion exam but probably no more than 15–20 per cent passed. Many failed year after year but still went along for the day out and the possibility of blinding inspiration to give them the answers.

To ensure promotion at the earliest opportunity, a constable not only had to pass, but pass competitively. By the 1990s the whole system of promotion had changed, the most divisive elements of competition had been removed and in recent times as many as 30 per cent have passed. When I sat down and turned over my examination paper, however, I knew that I had to pass in the top one hundred to be assured of speedy promotion, and the thought did nothing for my pre-examination nerves.

Fortunately, I passed joint seventy-seventh that year and all the indications were that I could be promoted after a total of five years' service and a successful passage through the promotion board. In other words, by November 1970 I could be a sergeant.

I was thrilled, although my pleasure was marred somewhat by rules that stated I would have to serve as a uniformed sergeant for at least a year before applying to the CID for re-admission as a detective sergeant. I was really miffed at the thought, because this rule did not apply to my male colleagues who were in the same position as me. The legislation which was to make us equal in terms of pay and conditions had not yet been brought in.

Luckily for me, however, a woman detective sergeant had recently appealed to Sir John Waldron, the Metropolitan Police Commissioner, about the unfairness of the system. She asked to be allowed to take what she saw as her rightful place as a detective inspector (the rule applied to all ranks) without having to go back into uniform first and, amazingly, he granted her wish. From that time on, any woman in the CID could be promoted and remain within the department. Good fortune was on my side once again.

With my promotion only a matter of months away, it was decided that I was needed at Chelsea Police Station, which had an urgent vacancy for a woman detective. So in July 1970, four months before I could officially be called a DS, I said farewell to my friends at Notting Hill and moved across the division to Chelsea as 'acting detective sergeant' to replace a DS who had just left. I was dead chuffed and happily settled into the posting.

Chelsea was like nowhere else on earth. From outrageously daring jewel thefts to 'crime of passion' murders, it offered a fascinating cornucopia of cases to work on and the crimes were as diverse as I had seen anywhere. For a fledgling DS, it was a real eye opener. Rich old ladies used to tip tradesmen with ten-bob notes (the equivalent of a £5 note these days), which seemed to me like a small fortune. Called to homes which had suffered a variety of crimes, I quickly came to appreciate the lavish interiors filled with fine art, furniture and expensive fittings which the residents of Chelsea seemed to take for granted. And the bohemian lifestyles of some of the survivors of the still-swinging 60s filled me with wonder.

Nothing ever seemed straightforward in Chelsea. Even the suicides took on a slightly bizarre tone. Death by hanging seemed to be the preferred method among the Chelsea set, rather than the overdoses which I had become used to at Notting Hill and Harrow Road. The suicides were so regular – almost daily – that we took turns to be the CID 'suicide/ suspicious death officer' for the day, a task none of us relished.

My first Chelsea suicide was that of a twenty-two-year-old nanny who had been working for a professional couple in a beautiful house off the King's Road. Depressed and homesick one morning, she had packed her small charge off to bed after breakfast and strung herself up from the hook in the ceiling used for the baby bouncer. The mother returned home from shopping two hours later and called us out immediately.

My detective inspector quickly ruled out 'foul play', helped enormously by the brief but beautifully written suicide note the nanny had left, saying she couldn't go on. What a waste of a life, I thought. My DI then turned to me. 'Better cut her down,' he said, holding out a kitchen knife and instructing a PC to take the weight of her body as I climbed up to the rope.

Reluctantly, I pulled a chair up to the dangling horror before me and stood on it so that my body was adjacent to hers. The memory of her swollen face and staring eyes so close to my own makes me shudder to this day. When the knife eventually sliced through the rope, the sudden weight of her body on the PC below made him collapse to the floor, and she fell on top of him. I remember shuddering and wanting to be sick.

The sight of death has never sat comfortably with me. I've often felt embarrassed that I couldn't get used to it and, though I tried to laugh it off like some of my colleagues, it has always affected me. I remember once having to take the fingerprints from the corpse of an unidentified woman at Westminster

Mortuary with a young PC who went as green as grass the minute he walked into the room and saw four bodies all laid out in varying stages of post-mortem examination. Sensing his unease, and hiding my own, I picked up the dead woman's ice-cold hand, rolled it into the ink pad and pressed her fingers on to the sheet of paper. 'Come on, miss, don't mess me around, straighten your fingers,' I shouted at the corpse. I think the PC was still trying to smile as he hit the floor.

When we weren't working our socks off dealing with all manner of impossible situations, we were down the pub sharing our experiences, laughing, drinking and winding each other up. Anything was preferable to returning home to an empty bed-sit and dealing with the issues which clouded my personal life. The concept of counselling didn't exist then – there was no one I could turn to to discuss personal problems or concerns arising from the job. To admit anything to a senior officer or even a colleague would have been seen as a sign of weakness, and the very thought would never even have entered my head. The only way I had of working the day's events out of my system was down the pub. That was the only therapy I thought I needed. I didn't seem to notice that increasingly I was the last one left standing at the bar.

3

'I'VE GOT SOME INFORMATION WHICH MIGHT INTEREST YOU,' the voice on the telephone said. 'I think we should meet.' It was George, a man I had been cultivating as a potential police informer and who now looked as if he was coming up trumps. With previous convictions for petty theft and other crimes, he was known to the police as a bit of a drunk, but he seemed to be wanting to tell me something important.

Even in a place like Chelsea it is crucial for police officers to identify and use informants, people who are prepared to 'grass' on the unlawful activities of their friends or colleagues in return for a small fee and the special relationship they can enjoy. I was no exception and when George, now living on the fringes of Chelsea and working as a handyman for some rich employer, called me out of the blue one day, I arranged to meet him.

Over a cup of coffee in a gay bar in the King's Road, George whispered that his boss was dealing in cannabis. 'He entertains young men and gives out cannabis like he's offering sweeties,' he said. I had no reason to doubt him, even though I suspected he was probably only telling me because of some kind of personal grudge. It was not my job as a police officer to question his motives, it was merely my task to examine and act on the information he gave me, which I duly did.

Anxious to get it right, I applied personally to the local

magistrates for a search warrant and rallied the troops I needed to gain entry to the suspect's address.

He lived in a beautiful studio flat over some stables in Reece Mews, off the Brompton Road in South Kensington, and everything seemed very peaceful when I arrived at eight the following morning with sniffer dogs and their handlers. Warning the uniformed officers to keep an eye out round the back, I banged on the door and shouted: 'Open up! This is the police. We have a search warrant.'

There was silence inside for a moment and then I heard shuffling, as someone wearing slippers ambled down the stairs. A bolt was slid across and the door opened a few inches. Wedging my foot into the gap, I showed the dishevelled-looking occupant the warrant for drugs, and he stood there blinking at me.

'Just who do you think you are?' he suddenly asked me in an indignant but impeccable Anglo-Irish accent. I told him exactly who I was and, forcing the door wide open, I brushed on past him, up the stairs and into his little flat, followed closely by the team of dogs, pulling on their leads.

The man followed us upstairs and I could see now that he was wearing a brightly coloured paisley silk dressing gown and pyjamas. He looked thoroughly bemused by the whole event. 'May I call Lord Goodman?' he asked.

'You can call the Queen Mother when we're back at the station,' I told him, unimpressed by the name-dropping. His attempt to intimidate was completely lost on the likes of me.

Taking the flat room by room, we searched every cupboard and drawer, every nook and cranny, looking for the evidence we needed to nick him. 'What exactly are you looking for, sergeant?' he asked me several times.

Finally, I answered: 'Cannabis, sir, I've been told you have some.'

He snorted and then laughed aloud. 'I'm afraid you're completely wasting your time. I don't smoke cannabis. I am an asthmatic.'

Before I could answer, I heard a yell from a bedroom. 'In here, sarge, the dogs are on to something.' I walked into what looked like an artist's studio, covered in canvases and easels, and watched as the dogs' tails wagged furiously by some paint-boxes on the floor. Sure enough, in the bottom of one of them, we uncovered some cannabis wrapped in silver paper. A few minutes later, a twelve-inch pipe stem was found hidden among some clean underwear in a tallboy in another bedroom. Despite the suspect's protestations, I arrested him and took him back to Chelsea nick, well pleased with my morning's work.

I booked him into the custody area and thanked the dog handlers for their help. 'It was a pleasure, sarge,' one of them responded. 'We don't get involved in the big league that often.' I wondered what on earth he meant and thought he was probably being sarcastic. However, when my detective inspector called me into his office the shit hit the fan. 'Do you know who you've just arrested?' he asked me, an agitated expression on his face.

I nodded, confused. 'Of course, sir,' I said. 'He goes by the name of Francis Bacon.' My DI looked at me expectantly, hoping that the penny would drop. It didn't. I was twenty-seven and a philistine. You could write what I knew about the arts on the back of a postage stamp.

'And do you know who Francis Bacon is, DS Bristow?' he asked me, rather impatiently now.

'As a matter of fact, sir,' I said, cautiously, 'the only Francis Bacon I've ever heard of, prior to nicking this one, is dead. All I know about this chap is that he deals in cannabis and entertains young men in his flat.'

The DI sighed. 'He also happens to be one of the world's greatest living artists. His works hang in the Tate, for God's sake. He's a man whose connections go right to the top, a man whose arrest will be plastered all over the newspapers by six o'clock tonight. A man who is about to be legally represented at this police station by Lord Goodman.'

I gulped. I had heard that name before. 'Yes, sir. Mr Bacon asked for him back at his flat. Who is this Lord Goodman?'

The DI shook his head unbelievingly. 'You must have heard of Harold Wilson?' he asked, rather disparagingly I thought.

'Of course, sir. He's the Prime Minister.'

'Too right he's the bloody Prime Minister. Well, Lord Goodman is the Prime Minister's personal solicitor.'

For once I was lost for words. 'What should I do now, sir?' I asked meekly.

'Just carry on as normal,' he instructed. 'But for Christ's sake make sure you dot the Is and cross all the bloody Ts.'

To his credit, the DI gave me every support. Having established that I had acted correctly and entirely within the law, he assured me that he would back me all the way. As I stepped from his office to await the arrival of Lord Goodman and an entourage that would have filled a copy of *Who's Who*, he called after me: 'Be careful out there.'

Well, those big and powerful men frightened the living daylights out of me. They treated me like something they had picked up on the underside of their shoe. Once Lord Goodman had established that I was the 'acting' detective sergeant he demanded that his client be dealt with by the most senior detective on duty, implying that I simply wasn't good enough. My DI stood by me and politely told Lord Goodman that he had every confidence in me. So Muggins here ended up dealing with the lot and I had no idea what I was letting myself in for.

The grilling at the police station was only the start of it. Months later, when Bacon had elected trial by jury, there was a lengthy committal hearing at Marlborough Street Magistrates' Court when his barrister attempted to have the case thrown out before it could reach the Crown Court. The committal, which is a kind of pre-trial examination of the evidence, effectively became a trial in itself, with me in the witness box being cross-examined on every aspect of the case, which really put me under pressure.

Fortunately, the magistrates dismissed Bacon's claims that the cannabis must have belonged to one of his many visitors from the world of the arts, and they committed him for trial before a judge and jury. During the months that followed, there were times when I felt completely strung out at the thought of giving evidence in a case of such media importance. I felt as though I might as well have been giving evidence against the Queen.

When the trial started at the Inner London Crown Court, I found myself in the witness box once again, this time being ruthlessly cross-examined by Basil Wigoder QC, one of the most brilliant criminal barristers in the country and a formidable opponent. It was an experience not to be recommended to the faint-hearted, especially when every word I uttered was faithfully reproduced in the national newspapers. Even when my cross-examination was over, I mentally pressed the rewind button and replayed the whole thing in my mind.

Ann Curnow QC represented the Crown and knew we were up against it. During the trial it emerged that my informant George was an alcoholic ex-con who had worked for Bacon for years, but kept falling out with him. Feeling particularly upset after yet another argument, George had come to me with what the defence described as a 'trumped-up story', born of malice.

George had, the court heard, an unstable mental background and had twice attempted suicide. After one such attempt, when he was being ministered to by medical staff, Bacon had allegedly said: 'Tell the doctor to write him another prescription so he can do the job properly.' I felt all eyes upon me in court as I imagined people criticizing my choice of informant.

Bacon told the court that George was a sick man who had only gone to the police out of spite. The pair had undoubtedly had a very turbulent relationship. 'When he is drunk he feels I don't pay him enough. Sometimes he has broken down my front door and forced his way into my flat. I pay him a regular wage but that doesn't suffice because of his drinking.' The jury looked increasingly sympathetic to his plight.

Faced with the full might of the Prime Minister's personal legal advisers, and George's rather murky past, the jury eventually acquitted Mr Bacon, something he and his agents were hugely relieved about, because a drugs conviction would have prevented him from entering America with his work. After his acquittal, he held a press conference on the steps of the court, telling reporters that he bore no animosity towards either George or me. 'I am just relieved this whole business has cleared my name. It has been a great strain,' he added.

Flushed and feeling more than a little uncomfortable, I watched him climb into a taxi with some of the most influential people in the land and it occurred to me that it wasn't what you knew that mattered, but who you knew. I made a mental note never to tangle with the likes of them again if I could help it.

Two years later I read that George had been found dead sitting on the lavatory of his hotel bedroom in Paris, blood pouring from every orifice after what appeared to be his final, successful, suicide attempt. Bacon had apparently forgiven him for his earlier misdemeanours and had invited him to the opening of a new exhibition of his work at the Grand Palais, an exhibition which included a painting of George sitting on a lavatory. Strange people, the Chelsea set. Very strange indeed.

My brief period in the media spotlight was enough to scare me off reporters for the rest of my life. Fortunately for me, my failure to convict Bacon didn't seem to stand in the way of my promotion prospects. After I was made up to a substantive DS, I was sent to work with my old friends at West End Central for a brief six-month posting before being transferred back to my beloved Harrow Road at the end of May 1971 and straight into the Leslie Perrin Arab terrorist job, where I was to receive even more unsolicited publicity.

The busy first-floor CID office at Harrow Road nick became my second home for six years. Often smelly, dirty and smoky, and littered with case papers, empty spirits and beer bottles and discarded coffee cups, it was the one place I felt truly at ease. My desk sat neat and tidy in the middle of all the chaos, its paperwork and files stacked in an orderly fashion beside the typewriter, telephone and ashtray. To the right, a small green houseplant struggled to survive, the solitary sign of verdant life in the whole room.

The only woman in an office of more than twenty men, and one of the few women detectives in the Met, I had positively skipped through all the examinations and interview boards needed to progress from WPC to DS in just five years. Once there, I had deliberately stalled, without proceeding onwards and upwards to the coveted detective inspector's role, for one reason and one reason only. In spite of all the hard work, the crappy hours and the heavy drinking, I was having the time of my life and I never wanted it to end.

Not only was I regularly drafted in to help out with some very high-profile rape and sexual assault cases, but my caseload was peppered with some amazingly interesting investigations. In spite of the low points, the ones that were driving me increasingly to the bottle, I loved my job and had never felt so fulfilled.

It was at Harrow Road that I felt my happiest and where I had discovered my calling to be a detective. A vibrant and fascinating place to be, the extraordinary nature of the crimes committed within its boundaries never failed to amaze me.

'Could you possibly come down to the front desk, Carol?' the station sergeant whispered into the telephone. 'There's a foreign lady here who has come to report an allegation of rape. I think she's either completely off her trolley or making it up.'

Within a few minutes I had grabbed a bundle of statement sheets and had run down the station stairs where I met an incredibly composed and beautiful young Thai woman whom I led into an interview room.

'Yes, Miss Whon,' I said as we both sat down. 'How can I help?'

She blushed slightly and looked down at her delicately manicured hands, before pulling out a small white card with her name and address printed on it. 'I live at this address,' she answered softly, in an attractive eastern accent. 'And I've come here because I think I have been raped recently.'

I suppressed the urge to raise my right eyebrow. 'You *think* you've been raped, *recently*,' I repeated, writing it down. She nodded hesitantly. 'Well, perhaps you would like to tell me what happened.'

'It was about a week ago,' she said.

'A week ago,' I repeated, my heart sinking.

'I was asleep at my flat and I suddenly woke up and there was a strange man sitting on the end of my bed, smiling at me.'

'Smiling at you,' I dutifully recorded.

'I asked him what he wanted and he said he wanted to watch me.' She lowered her head shyly. 'He said I was beautiful when I was asleep.'

'Then what?' I asked.

'I didn't know what to do so I waited.'

'Waited?'

'To see what he would do.'

'And?'

'After watching me, he said he had this overwhelming desire to make love to me. He also told me he had a knife.'

'A knife? Did you see any knife?' I asked.

'No,' she said. 'But I was frightened.'

'What happened next?'

'Well, he got into bed with me and . . . we made love.'

'You mean he raped you?'

'No. Well, yes. I mean it didn't feel like I was being raped. He made love to me. He said I was beautiful. I didn't realize it was rape until I told a friend about it this morning and she suggested that I come and see you.'

I took down all the details and wondered whether this oriental butterfly was telling me the truth or not. It was her word against whoever's, it was too late for any forensic medical evidence and there were no signs of injury requiring a doctor's examination. When we had finished, I showed her to the door telling her I would do what I could.

Just as she was leaving, I called out, almost as an afterthought: 'By the way, if you happen to see this chap in the street do let me know straight away, won't you? Don't leave it a week.' She walked away, her head bowed.

I filled in a crime report and put a copy in my inspector's in-tray. A few hours later he walked over to my desk with it in his hand. 'What's this load of Enid Blyton all about, Carol? She's dreamt the whole thing up, hasn't she?'

'I honestly don't know what to make of it, sir,' I replied, and carried on typing. 'I'll go through all the usual procedures, but we both know there's not much else I can do.'

Three days later I was sitting at my desk when the telephone rang. It was the station sergeant. 'Someone to see you at the front desk, Carol. It's that Miss Whon again.' I trotted downstairs, and as I entered the reception area she stood up and blurted out: 'He came back. Last night.' I looked at her incredulously.

'Just like before,' she said, as I led her into the interview room. 'I woke up and he was sitting on the end of my bed. He wanted to make love to me again. I did as he asked and now I've come straight to see you.'

I called the police surgeon, who gave Miss Whon a full medical examination and, sure enough, there was evidence of recent sexual intercourse. There was no evidence of any force used, but then she had never suggested that her assailant had been brutal. In fact the opposite was true. He had been as gentle as a lamb, so it seemed. She was completely calm and entirely co-operative and I was still having difficulty deciding where the truth lay.

After the medical, I took her home and got a forensic team to examine her flat with a fine-tooth comb. Miss Whon believed that on both occasions her night-time visitor had entered through an open first-floor bedroom window and, to my utter astonishment, the fingerprints officer found a full set of inverted finger- and palmprints on the bottom of the window, left by our cheeky chappie as he had swung himself in. Fingerprint Branch quickly identified a forty-year-old man known to us as a regular burglar, but who had no known history of sexual offending.

I was determined to nick this bloke myself, so I took a team round to his address straight away. We had no idea what to expect so we arrived heavy-handed in anticipation of him doing a runner. But, to our surprise, he opened the front door himself, a mug of steaming coffee in his hand, and looked as if he knew why we were there.

'I am arresting you on suspicion of rape,' I told him as he stood meekly in front of me. 'You are not obliged to say anything unless you wish to do so, but anything you do say may be written down and given in evidence. Do you understand?'

He put his mug down on the table, stuffed his hands in his pockets and shrugged his shoulders. 'She was just so very beautiful,' he told me, his puppy-dog eyes pleading for sympathy. 'I saw her and fell in love. I had to sleep with her and then, once I had, I had to go back and see her again.'

I wasn't going to fall for it. 'But you still felt it necessary to threaten her with a knife,' I reminded him.

'I know, that was a bloody stupid thing to do,' he agreed. 'But I could never have hurt her in a million years.'

He was the least likely rapist I had ever dealt with and she was the least likely victim. In different circumstances, they might even have been compatible. The man was as good as gold. He admitted everything, never put his victim through the ordeal of a not-guilty plea, and when I went to the Old Bailey to see him sentenced he turned up all spick and span with an overnight bag packed with pyjamas and a toothbrush, ready for the prison sentence we both knew would follow.

The judge, who was as bemused as the rest of us by the case, gave him four years and told him he had taken into consideration his total co-operation and the fact that he had no previous record of sexual offending. The defendant nodded his acceptance as he was taken down to the cells. It never occurred to him that his treatment had been anything but fair.

I went down to the custody suite below the court to see him before he was taken off in a prison van. 'You know something, sarge?' He looked at me coyly. 'I want you to tell Miss Whon how very sorry I am for everything. But four years for two nights with her? It was almost bloody worth it.' He winked as he was led away.

My life at Harrow Road had never been busier. Not only was I still learning the ropes myself, but occasionally I had to take budding young police officers under my wing and hope that they could learn something from me. Every police constable who passes out of training school gets placed on probation for two years, during which time they take more exams and are attached to different departments, to see how they work. My early career had been much the same, and now I was asked by my detective inspector, Iain Darroch, to take charge of a young trainee called WPC Susan Pattison.

'The dips have been giving that bus stop outside the Red Lion in the Bayswater Road a right hammering recently,' he told me in front of her. 'Why don't you take young Susan up there and see if you can catch anyone?' he added, grinning from ear to ear. Susan – who was still getting to know the special language of the police force – hadn't understood a word my DI had said, so I explained.

'Dips are pickpockets. They operate at this particular bus stop because it's used regularly by tourists to get into Oxford Street, people whose wallets are generally stuffed with cash. The reason the DI is grinning like that is because these dips are so slippery they're almost impossible to catch.' Registering the enthusiastic look on her face, I continued: 'Still, we'll give it a go, eh?'

It looked so overcast outside as we left the office that we donned macs and I took a large umbrella with me. At the bus stop, Susan and I joined the end of the large queue, while a colleague, Tom Brazil, stood on the other side of the road, keeping us in view. Almost immediately, a number 12 bus arrived and the tourists clambered aboard.

Another queue quickly formed and Susan and I made our way to the back again, since we had no intention of getting on any bus. At this moment, I looked round to see four smartly dressed men immediately behind us. With their suits and heavy gold jewellery one would have expected them to have had a car. I nudged Susan in an effort to convey my suspicions about these men, when a number 88 bus suddenly pulled in.

Quick as a flash, the men went to work. Two of them ran forward to the front of the queue and barged their way inside – one upstairs and one downstairs. Then, as soon as the passengers had climbed on behind them, the other two men pushed forward from the rear as their two accomplices, already inside the bus, turned and started forcing their way back to the exit. The pressure was so intense that the passengers became as squashed as sardines, enabling the men to dip their hands in and out of handbags, pockets and jackets to remove all their valuables, without the hapless victims even noticing.

As soon as I spotted what they were up to, I signalled to Tom, who came running over. Susan clocked exactly what was happening and grabbed one of the two men on the outside, while I seized the other. Her suspect broke free and the last I saw of her and Tom was their backsides as they legged it down the Bayswater Road after him.

My bloke was in his fifties, probably the oldest of the lot, and not amused. I was clutching his arm as I shouted: 'I'm a police officer and you're nicked.' With that, he whacked me straight round the head with the flat of his hand and tried to run away. I was shaken by his reaction but hung on for dear life, with the result that one of his jacket buttons came off in my hand. As he parted company from the button and started to break away I kicked off my high heels, dropped my handbag and gave chase.

Quickly drawing level with him and holding my umbrella broadside, I rammed into his body so that he was forced backwards and fell on to the pavement, groaning. Just as I went to grab him again, he kicked out with his foot, which made direct and forceful contact with my right kneecap. The pain shot up through my leg and I screamed. As I was thrown backwards, my nylons ripped and my white three-quarter-length mac split right up the central seam.

I climbed back on to my feet and charged at him again as he tried to get up from the pavement. My right fist extended, I punched him hard in the stomach and he groaned, sinking back to the ground. By this time, another number 12 bus had pulled in to the stop and the passengers from both buses formed a circle around the two of us brawling on the floor.

'I'm a police officer. Will someone please help me?' I screamed, but nobody moved. Every time I tried to grapple my suspect to the ground, he lashed out with his feet, connecting with my now throbbing right knee. I punched him repeatedly in the stomach, and so it went on, for what seemed an age.

'Would somebody please call nine-nine-nine!' I pleaded breathlessly to the motionless audience around me. 'I'm a police officer and I need help.' There was no response.

I was almost hoarse with shouting before a woman in the crowd stepped forward and asked me sheepishly: 'Are you *really* a police officer?'

With a hand grabbing my hair and trying to yank my head down, and a foot kicking out at my shins, I managed to answer: 'Yes. Yes, I am! Please go and get help.'

Bless her, she must have done just that, because within

minutes a police car pulled up, sirens blaring, and my man was carted off to Harrow Road, looking very down-hearted.

I rose to my feet rather shakily and stood panting, looking at all the people around me. My clothes were dishevelled and torn, my hair was a mess, my lip was bleeding and my knee was already beginning to swell. I looked a right state.

'OK, the show's over, now where is the lady who helped me?' I asked aloud. The middle-aged woman stepped forward as the rest of the crowd slowly drifted away, the excitement of the day over.

'I'm so sorry,' she told me, as she picked up my now broken umbrella and handed it to me. 'I just thought you were a married couple having an argument and I didn't think I should get involved.'

'But he was old enough to be my father!' I protested. She looked contrite and offered to act as a witness, so I forgave her and took her back to the nick.

At the station I learnt that Susan and Tom had eventually caught up with their suspect, so we had two of the gang in custody. As I was waiting to see the police doctor for my injuries, I drew out their files and found that they had form as long as your arm for pickpocketing and had previously operated with two others, who were probably our missing pair. Later we went to their homes and I identified them as the other dips and arrested the lot.

My injuries were mainly bruises, but as my right kneecap had taken quite a battering I ended up having to walk with a stick for a couple of weeks. It was the same knee that had taken the brunt of the fall when I'd crashed through the ceiling of the house in Notting Hill and, after this beating, it was never quite the same.

Our four suspects all pleaded not guilty to pickpocketing and my attacker denied a further charge of assault. They were taken to Inner London Crown Court for trial, where the woman from the crowd made a fabulous witness. In fact, she couldn't have been more helpful and by the time she'd left the witness box she had described the incident in such glowing terms that you might have thought she was putting me up for the George Medal.

71

The defendants were found guilty and, while three of them were given short terms of porridge, my assailant went down for four years, mainly for attacking me. The judge commended Susan, Tom and me for 'determination and ability leading to the arrest of four men for assault and theft', and the Commissioner supported the judge's comments with personal commendations for each of us. As I nursed my injured leg, I read my commendation and felt the pain had been worthwhile.

Although there was still a good variety of work at Harrow Road, my involvement with victims of sexual assault began to take up more of my time. Reports of sexual offences against women seemed to increase yearly, but I could never work out whether this was because the actual number of crimes was going up, or whether more women were willing to come forward and report the incidents. Either way, I was convinced that the number of cases we dealt with was just the tip of the iceberg.

Some radical changes within the Met had led to a high turnover of some of the most senior officers at Scotland Yard and a mood of growing enlightenment towards the treatment of women, both inside and outside the force. More women were encouraged to join, along with members of minority groups. 'Your country needs you' seemed to be the message. It took a long time to filter through and was very slow to be taken up, but with the passage of the Equal Opportunities Act (I had previously been paid less than my male equivalent) the number of women joining up did start to rise and the load started to be spread more evenly between the sexes.

Not that this was welcomed by all. Many of my female colleagues were positively indignant about equal opportunities. They hadn't joined the police force to do men's work. They hated the idea of being in the front line, and being told to do all that their male colleagues already did. They relished the boundaries between them and most would have quite happily carried on being paid less and doing the tasks they had traditionally been given.

The women of today would be equally outraged if they

couldn't have a crack at the jobs their male counterparts do. It is now quite common for women to do all manner of dangerous surveillance and undercover work, running their own teams of officers, jobs which had previously been a male preserve. I had never felt anything but equal to my male colleagues, but I looked forward to the day when I could welcome some female company into the CID office.

However, until that happened, and with females in the department still something of a rarity, my workload slowly and almost imperceptibly shifted towards sexual offences. I found myself called to help out with investigations into rapes, indecent assaults, buggeries, incest and child-abuse cases by colleagues as far afield as Notting Hill, Paddington, St John's Wood and Gerald Row. I knew I was in demand and I loved the sense of responsibility it gave me.

There was still enough variety for me not to be swamped by the misery that followed some of these investigations and, despite everything, I truly believed that to be working as a female detective sergeant was the finest of all ranks and positions. Very much one of the lads, I was smoking and drinking heavily, often arriving home very late and leaving early for dawn raids and early 'spins' (searches). I seemed permanently knackered and I knew that something was going to have to give sooner or later.

But instead of slowing down or trying to spread the load, like an idiot I began studying again – this time for the rank of detective inspector. I guess I still felt I had something to prove. It meant that I was often dog-tired when I got in and picked up my law books. Completely forgetting the advice my father had given me as a child – about being happy with the eight hours' work I did each day – I drove myself nearly into the ground with the extra strain. God knows how, but I managed to take the exam and pass. This meant I could qualify for promotion in 1974.

I was delighted at first, believing that the best way to prove myself was to be promoted as high as I could as quickly as I could. But here I was, having a ball as a DS, when my father's words hit me. What the bloody hell was I doing? Hadn't I always said that I loved being on the 'shop floor' and that any rank which involved more paperwork would drive me nuts? I could have kicked myself when I suddenly realized that the rank of detective inspector wasn't what I wanted at all. It would be like going back to an office job in my civilian days.

I kept my fingers crossed and sincerely hoped that I would be able to resist any attempts to move me from the rank I loved. The only answer, I thought, was to keep my head down, get on with the work and not complain. And so the cases, the rapes especially, continued to fill my in-tray.

Most of the sexual assaults I dealt with involved people who knew each other and some were of a domestic nature. These attacks were none the less terrible for the women involved. The more violent rapes, however, were usually associated with the much rarer random attacks (representing approximately 7 per cent of the total reported) where the victim had been confronted by her assailant whom she had never met before. Either way, dealing with the victims was often harrowing and almost always sent me straight to the bottle afterwards. The cases became so frequent that regrettably some of the victims' faces began to meld into one in my mind, with the odd exception.

One young woman whose attack stuck in my gullet for months afterwards was Flora, a pretty young girl from Gloucestershire, who came to London for a two-week catering course. After a night out with some fellow-students at the Hammersmith Palais in west London, she accepted a lift home from a man touting as a minicab driver.

Unfamiliar with her surroundings, she asked the driver to take her to her lodgings in Bayswater and didn't realize he wasn't going the right way until they were way out in west London, near Osterley Park, where he stopped the car and suddenly lunged at her.

A virgin, she fought him every step of the way. He was particularly rough with her, gouging the flesh from her thighs with his long fingernails. To stop her screaming, he also punched her hard on the nose, causing it to bleed heavily. She tried to concentrate on the man and the car. Flora noted that he had an Irish accent and that the passenger seat she was on had

74

a sheepskin cover, which became stained with her blood as he savagely abused her.

Having prematurely ejaculated, her attacker asked her where she would like to be dropped off. Sobbing and trembling, she said she wanted to be taken to Bayswater. He drove her back towards central London, but her weeping clearly irritated him, so as they approached Queensway he reached across her while the car was still moving, opened the passenger door and kicked her out with his foot, causing her to roll heavily into the road.

She was found lying in the gutter by a passer-by and taken to Paddington General Hospital. By the time she had been medically examined and patched up, I received an early-morning call to go and interview her.

I drove into town and braced myself for the day ahead. I had had very little sleep and my concentration levels were not good, but I knew from experience that I would be OK after a couple of cups of coffee.

But, despite my best endeavours to put on my bravest face for Flora, I wasn't much use. In the first stages of shock, she was struck dumb, literally, by what had happened. Apart from some incoherent mumbling heard by the nursing staff when she arrived at the casualty department, she could barely string two words together. All she could do was curl up in a ball and cry inconsolably.

The nurse who had initially seen Flora in casualty the night before handed me a piece of paper. 'She wasn't making much sense when she came in,' she said. 'She just kept repeating three letters. I wrote them down in case they were important.' I thanked her and studied the scrap of paper, across which were scrawled the letters NTD, NTD, NTD. It took a long time to get Flora even to turn her face towards me. Her features bruised and swollen, her country-girl innocence lost, she looked at me with those big brown eyes full of tears, wondering what she had done to deserve such treatment. With much cajoling and coaxing, I used all the tricks in my book to get her to tell me even the scantest details. On the point of no return, I gave it my final shot.

'Come on now, Flora,' I told her, squeezing her hand. 'You can't cry about this for ever. If you do, then the man who attacked you has won, hasn't he? Because you'll be allowing him to hurt you for the rest of your life. Help me to help you. Let's try and catch him, eh?' She stopped sobbing and stared at me for a moment. I knew then I had reached her.

Gradually, she was able to tell me that her attacker's car had been reddish-brown and that it had a sheepskin cover on the passenger seat. 'I memorized the first three letters of the car registration,' she sobbed. 'I saw it as I lay in the road after he kicked me out. I didn't see it all, but I think it began with the letters NTD.' I reached for the scrap of paper in my pocket and thanked her. Later, when she felt up to it, one of my colleagues took her to a second-hand car dealer to look over a number of saloon cars in the hopes that she would identify the make which her attacker had driven, but she was unable to pick out any particular model.

Next, I drew the files on every car ever made with the part-registration NTD. There were hundreds of them and I sent telexed messages to officers throughout Greater London, asking them to make discreet enquiries about the registered owners. I knew it might not be regarded as a priority by them, so I labelled my enquiry 'Urgent', and suggested the detectives go round to each address on their patch and examine the vehicles, paying particular attention to any cars that might have a sheep-skin cover on the passenger seat.

I went back to tell Flora what I had done and to see if she could tell me any more, but the hospital told me that her parents had taken her back to Gloucester. I learnt a few days later that, once back in the bosom of her overprotective family, Flora had become very depressed and was in the psychiatric ward of her local hospital. She had suffered a complete mental breakdown and was too sick to see anyone. I felt angry and upset at the news. She and I had been through a great deal together and I was distressed that she was somewhere I couldn't help her any more. Within days she was refusing to communicate and would just sit day after day rocking herself in a corner, crying. I was very worried about her.

It is not unusual for the officer who gets the first ghastly facts down on paper to form a unique relationship with the victim because the hitherto unspeakable truth has been shared and ultimately forced into the light. By telling a virtual stranger the grisly details in such a clinically detached way, the victim is able to dissociate herself further from the events and form a close understanding with the officer involved. This whole painful experience will have been cathartic in that it will have relieved the victim of the burden of 'telling', and the special bonding with the officer will be born out of that extraordinary intimacy. From that point on, the victim can begin to lay down the foundations of her recovery and use the officer in her support system, often relying on her emotionally and psychologically in a way that she would not be able to do with a relative or loved one.

The hunt went on as I waited for that all-important lead. Attempts to find witnesses to Flora's attack or her ejection from the car proved futile. The friends who had watched her go off in the car from Hammersmith Palais hadn't even noticed if the driver was black or white. It was long before the days of closed-circuit television surveillance outside clubs and shopping malls, which might have given me a picture of the minicab, and there was absolutely nothing that could point me in her attacker's direction. My only chance was Flora's description and the part-registration of the car.

The call came a few days later, from Brentford CID on the fringes of west London, not far from Osterley Park. A young detective constable called Brian Greenan phoned and sounded very excited. 'I've been checking those car details you sent us,' he said breathlessly. 'I've found a Ford Cortina, reddish-brown, which belongs to a bloke called Hugh Williams who moonlights as a minicab driver. What's more it's got sheepskin covers.'

This was the best lead I had. Then, putting the cherry on the cake, he added: 'And guess what? The sheepskin on the front passenger seat has been washed, but I swear you can still see faint traces of blood on it.'

I nearly fell off my chair. 'Where the hell is this Williams now?' I screamed down the phone, fit to burst.

'I nicked him for you,' he said almost nonchalantly. 'He's

here now. I'll bring him straight over if you want.' If I could have climbed down the telephone and kissed him, I would have done.

I waited for Williams and his escort to arrive from Brentford, thinking of poor Flora locked away in her psychiatric ward. If Williams was our man then I hoped nothing would foul up the due legal process which would put him behind bars.

As soon as I walked into the interview room and glowered accusingly at Williams he bawled his eyes out and admitted he had attacked Flora. He was a real blubberer, one of those men who cries and complains and gives you every excuse under the sun for what he has done. He was having a bad time with his wife and had just flipped. Listening to men like him, who seemed totally incapable of accepting responsibility for their heinous crimes, often made me very angry, but expressing my anger wouldn't do anyone any good and I had learnt to control it long before.

I heard what he had to say and forced myself to play the good guy in a 'good guy, bad guy' routine. My male colleague – whose nickname was 'Flash' – a huge man who dressed in dark pinstripe suits more befitting someone from the Italian Mafia, pretended to be surly and menacing while I was sweetness itself. The temptation to kick Williams in the balls was enormous, but instead I smiled kindly, patted his shoulder reassuringly when he started to cry, fetched him a cup of coffee and gave him several of my cigarettes.

'I know you've been having a hard time, Hugh,' I told him gently. 'May I call you Hugh? Good. Now I understood what you've just told us about your wife, but how did that lead up to you attacking this poor girl?'

He gave me chapter and verse, telling me everything according to his version of events, which amounted to a confession of attempted rape. He had not, he said, been able to penetrate her because she had put up such a fight. At one point I had to leave the room for a moment to regain my composure. I clenched my fists and kicked the waste-paper basket before returning to the interview room, a well-worn smile glued to my face.

I charged Williams with attempted rape but, because he had

a fixed address and no previous history of sexual offending, I couldn't put up any good arguments to prevent him from getting bail. I also knew that our case against him was weak because if he went back on his confession – which, strictly speaking, was all we had – Flora would never be able to give evidence against him in court.

Would you believe it – at the first opportunity the little toerag did a bunk to southern Ireland and disappeared. We didn't find out about it for a day or two and by then I thought I had lost him for ever, not least because I had no idea where he was exactly and extradition proceedings with Ireland weren't great. It seemed hopeless.

But Hugh Williams had been right about one thing. He was having a bad time with his wife. When I went round to their home to ask her if she knew where he was, she grassed him up and told us where he was staying. After much cajoling on the telephone, I finally persuaded the Garda to go round and nick him. So began my first ever extradition proceedings. We eventually got him back and this time he remained in custody at HM Prison Wandsworth until his trial.

Not surprisingly, he did the dirty on us once again and pleaded not guilty at the first hearing. It seems he was now aware that Flora was too sick to give evidence against him and knew that all he had to do was claim that the police had beaten a confession out of him to stand a reasonable chance of being acquitted by a jury. What a bloody sauce. As always, I had exercised the ultimate self-restraint – for what? So that he could claim we knocked the hell out of him anyway?

Within a few months, Williams' case was listed for trial at the Old Bailey, but Flora was still in a bad way and I knew that without her evidence we had no case. If I wasn't careful, I was going to lose Williams and he would be free to try and rape again. I left it as long as I could, and successfully applied to the Old Bailey to delay the case for another two months, explaining that my chief prosecution witness was very ill. But Williams' lawyers were getting twitchy and I knew I couldn't postpone it indefinitely, so I climbed into the car and drove to Gloucester.

The doctors were not pleased to see me. They told me Flora

had relapsed and still felt unable to talk about what had happened. They were worried that my showing up unannounced on the doorstep might set her back. I begged to be allowed to speak to her. They reluctantly agreed and I was ushered into her room. She was curled up in a corner, her knees clenched tightly to her chest.

'Hello, Flora. It's me, Carol. Remember?' I spoke softly and touched her hand. She looked up, her face pale with sadness. Recognition flickered across her eyes before they filled with tears which tumbled down her cheeks.

'I've come to see how you are and to ask for your help,' I told her. She drew her hand across her face, wiping away the tears while looking at me intently, suddenly taking in everything I had to say. I decided to tell her the truth. 'I've caught the man who reduced you to this,' I said, as gently as I could. 'He's in prison now, awaiting trial. But unless you feel able to appear in court to help me get him convicted, he's going to walk free. Please can't we do this together?'

Her face registered helplessness before she dropped her head into her hands and started rocking again. I reached out and took both her hands in mine, fixing her eyes with my own. 'Now you just listen to me, Flora,' I told her firmly. 'You owe it to yourself to stand up in court and tell them all about him. It was a terrible thing to happen but you are alive and you still have the rest of your life ahead of you. Your recovery will only start the day that you agree to talk about it with people who can help you.'

I told her that I had four weeks before I needed to know her answer. I added, 'If you can't do it, then OK. I know I'm asking a lot. We'll catch him next time he does it, God forbid.'

I put my arms around her, gave her a big hug and kept my fingers crossed that the persuasive drama I had injected into my little speech might do the trick. 'We've got him, Flora. The rest is up to you,' I told her before driving back to London, wondering if I had done any good. On my return, there were two messages waiting for me from Willams' lawyer and I cursed out loud at his impatience.

I have never lost sight of the fact that asking a victim to stand up and be counted in this way is probably expecting far too much of her, not least because the outcome can never be guaranteed and the psychological trauma each of them must go through in the run-up to giving evidence puts untold pressure on them. However, it is my honest belief that, whether an acquittal or a conviction follows the giving of the victim's evidence, the mere fact that she has taken that giant step forward and spoken out against her attacker will unquestionably aid her recovery. I believe it is our secrets that destroy us. Only when the truth is laid out can it be examined, and the telling of it weakens its power to hurt us.

Sadly, so many cases do end in acquittal at the Crown Court, despite the best endeavours of the victim, the police and the lawyers. That need not mean that the victim was not believed, only that there was insufficient corroborative evidence to support what she said. I often tried to take the time to make victims understand this, although I know I haven't always succeeded and they have often left court believing that the jurors thought they were liars. How heartbreaking and potentially devastating it must be for someone like Flora to summon the courage to speak out, only to see her attacker walk free anyway.

Over the next few days I pondered the question I had asked myself a hundred times before. Would I have had the courage to do what I was now expecting of Flora? The truthful answer has always been: I don't know.

Three days later, the hospital rang to tell me the good news. Flora had improved dramatically. She had started talking and wanted me to know that she would be giving her evidence in court. I went out that night and had a bloody good drink with the lads to celebrate.

Flora gave her evidence beautifully at the Old Bailey. Like many victims before her, she somehow detached herself from the incident and spoke as though she were telling the story in the third person. She presented the jury with exactly the right mix of vulnerability and strength. They could see she was shattered by what had happened, and they recognized the enormous courage it took for her to tell them her story. She was one of the best witnesses I have ever had the privilege of listening to.

I heard her evidence and thought: Fantastic, we've got him, but then Williams came into the witness box and was horribly convincing. I could see the jury dithering, being swayed by this personable young Irishman who told them that Flora got into his minicab willingly, flirted with him and encouraged sex. I prayed to God they wouldn't believe him, after all I had said to Flora.

The clincher came when the barrister for the prosecution cross-examined Williams in the witness box. Handing him Flora's ripped tights and knickers, he instructed him to hold them up high for the whole court to see. In doing so, it became very obvious just how shredded and bloodstained the garments were. The jury was visibly shocked and I imagined that they were finding it difficult to comprehend how Flora could have consented to Williams' sexual advances as he would have led them to believe.

The scientific evidence provided the last nail in his coffin. It was before the days when we could identify an assailant by his 'genetic fingerprints', a profile of his unique physical make-up from DNA left at the scene, but the bloodstains that Williams had tried so hard to wash off the sheepskin cover were still enough for the forensic boys to match exactly to Flora's blood type. The jury convicted him unanimously, and the judge sent him down for three years.

This was the 70s and we were lucky if we got a sentence of three years for attempted rape. Some said you were given more for beating your dog than for sexual assault. I never failed to be disappointed at the sentencing in sexual assault cases, but I tried to convince myself that three years was just, even knowing that it actually meant substantially less with time off for good behaviour. After taking into consideration the time Williams had served inside awaiting trial, he would be out in a little over a year. Still, as my dad would have said, be grateful for small mercies.

The law provides that a person found guilty of rape or attempted rape is liable to a maximum sentence of life imprisonment, which means he can get anything from zero to an indefinite term. I couldn't help asking myself how bad a rape had to be before a realistic sentence was imposed. When would some members of the judiciary stop bringing their own prejudices into the courtroom? Over the years I had accumulated a file of newspaper clippings citing dozens of cases where judges had allowed their views to get in the way of justice for the victims. Like the judge who expressed his 'considerable sympathy' for the thirty-five-year-old builder who had sex with a seven-year-old girl, adding: 'It strikes me as one of the kinds of accidents which could almost happen to anyone.'

In another case, a judge jailed a rapist for eighteen months after saying that his assault on a fifteen-year-old girl was 'reckless', not malicious, despite the fact that he had dragged her into a derelict garage and battered her face with a nailed piece of wood before raping her. In a further case, a judge gave a reduced sentence of eight years to a rapist with a history of sexual assault because he pleaded guilty, despite having beaten his victim so badly that her own parents didn't recognize her.

If I could speak personally to the judges who hand out such inappropriate sentences I would ask them to put themselves in the victim's shoes or imagine their own feelings were it their wife, mother or daughter who came staggering home battered and bruised. I would ask them to state their expectations then in relation to sentencing such an attacker. Given that scenario, I wonder how many of those judges would express contrition?

Two decades on – and thanks mainly to the increased awareness of the trauma caused by rape – sentencing across the board has vastly improved. But for young victims like Flora the seeming inequality of the punishment to the crime would never leave them with the sense of justice they should have felt as their attackers were led away to the cells. How many women have walked away from court asking themselves if it was worth all the hassle – the intrusive medical examination, the police probing and the anxiety of the trial – given that the sentence so rarely fits the crime?

Happily, I was right about Flora. Giving evidence that day

was the beginning of her recovery. Almost a year to the day after I first saw her curled up in a ball in hospital, a transformed young woman stood in front of me in the ornate marble lobby of the Old Bailey and thanked me for persuading her to stand up and be counted. 'I was absolutely terrified of seeing him again and having to give evidence against him but, afterwards, it was the best feeling ever and I am so glad you encouraged me to do it,' she said, smiling, before giving me a warm hug.

As I watched her walk away on the arms of her parents, I knew that she would eventually learn to live with her experience and adapt her life accordingly. Mindful of the fact that no victim ever completely recovers from the nightmare of a serious sexual assault, I was grateful at least that Flora had no physical scars to remind her of the experience every time she looked in the mirror, as some unfortunately do. The attack had undoubtedly marked her life and I wondered if she would ever be able to trust a man again, but she was still young and I sincerely hoped the years would be kind to her.

4

I WALKED IN THE FRONT DOOR AND KICKED OFF MY SHOES.
Dropping my briefcase and coat, I headed straight for the
double-fronted cabinet, unscrewed the cap on a half-full bottle
of Scotch and poured myself a large drink. Slumping into an
armchair, I glanced at the clock. It was 1.15 a.m. and I was due
back in the office for an early spin at 6 a.m. Hardly time for a
bath, let alone a decent night's sleep. I closed my eyes and
gulped from the glass, holding the bottle in my other hand.

The next time I looked at the clock it was 3.45 a.m. I was
still in my armchair, only the bottle was nearly empty. I knew I
was on duty in a couple of hours, so I stood up unsteadily
and headed for the bathroom. Splashing my face with soap and
water and reaching for a towel, I glanced in the mirror
and didn't much like what I saw.

I peered at a woman in her mid-thirties, single and very much
alone in the world. It had been nearly twenty years since I had
met my best friend Booze and it had been love at first sight. We
had certainly been inseparable ever since. I had started drinking
as a fifteen-year-old working in my friend's father's bar, trying
to make some sense of my life. It was bravado initially. I drank
because then I could pretend to be like all the other kids in the
neighbourhood. And yet I was so very different.

I had a hidden torment that I was unable to share with

anyone, a torment which had become worse through my un-exciting and uncomfortable early sexual experiences and proposals of marriage. Unsure of my own sexuality from an early age and yet desperate to grow up 'normally', I was a bundle of neuroses and insecurities. I first realized how different I was at the age of thirteen. I didn't have the least fancy for boys, but every decent girlfriend I had I ended up wanting to be near. I didn't yearn to do anything rude with them, I just needed to be by their side.

As I grew older, these urges became stronger and I became sick with worry about them. The only way I knew how to obliterate the shame of my disgraceful ideas was through alcohol. With enough drink inside me, I could be the person I wanted to be and fulfil the pretence to the point of almost fooling myself.

I have absolutely no idea what determines the sexuality of any individual, whether heterosexual, bisexual or homosexual. There was no significant difference in my upbringing from my brother Pete's, yet he is wholeheartedly heterosexual and I am not. Who knows why we turn out the way we do?

All I knew was that it never made sense to me until I was well into my forties. As a kid, I just wanted to be like all my friends. I knew I wanted to be married and have four children one day but, feeling as I did, I had absolutely no idea how on earth I was going to achieve that. Had I done something terribly wrong and upset God? I knew it was wicked to swear and I had sworn a few times to impress the other kids, so I stopped immediately, hoping that the 'other thing' would go away. I was terrified that someone would see me for what I was and tell my parents.

When I first heard the word 'queer' and understood that it might refer to people like me, I felt so ashamed. According to my friend's mother, 'queers' were sickos who molested children and should be drowned at birth. A big woman, she said she would have no problems killing anyone she found out to be 'queer'. She would like to follow them down a dark alley and make sure that they really suffered. As a kid coming up to my fourteenth birthday, I believed every word she said and I bit my lip so hard that it bled.

All my girlfriends seemed to have steady boyfriends and took great delight in comparing notes about their sexual experiences. I was terribly jealous, because all I wanted was to be with them on my own. That is when drink started to come into play. It made life so much easier to bear.

I worked every weekend in that pub for five years and every weekend I drank too much. I didn't always get plastered, but I put away far too much for the teenager that I was. The emotional turmoil I felt inside because of my particular inclination was often unbearable and I had no one to share my terrible secret with, except Booze.

My father, who was tactile by nature, had taught me that it was OK to tell people that you loved them and wanted to hug them. Through him, I inherited a wonderful ability to express love, which made it a million times more difficult to know that whatever I felt would have to be suppressed. It looked as if I was going to lead a monastic life and the resentment of that began to eat away at me.

Self-pity overwhelmed me and I wanted to scream, 'It isn't fair! I didn't ask to be like this.' Painfully aware that the revelation of my sexual identity would have destroyed my mother, I smothered the urge to say anything. I prayed at Sunday school for God to take all my bad feelings away, to cleanse me and make me normal. When He didn't, I eventually stopped communicating and lost my faith. I told myself that if God didn't want me then I didn't need Him. Three decades passed before I realized I could have a spirited relationship with a benevolent God of my own understanding.

So, pretence was the name of the game. I could pretend to be everything I wasn't with a drink inside me. Drink became my means of survival. I had taken to it like a duck to water and where, I asked myself, was the harm? I look back on that terrified teenager who found solace in a bottle because she believed herself to be a freak, and I feel so very sad for her.

By the time I was twenty, when I was set to emigrate or join the services, I was merely trying to escape from the real me.

Already I had the unenviable reputation of being a young woman with hollow legs. High on booze, I could be the life and soul of the party. Sober, I frequently felt depressed. It was only when I joined the police that, for the very first time, I was able to concentrate my mind on helping others in their misery, instead of constantly focusing on my own.

As a young DS at Harrow Road, I doubtless appeared to be a capable, self-sufficient professional who was in control, but in truth I was an emotional mess. No matter how much I involved myself with the people who really mattered, no matter how I tried to emulate my father and be all things to all people, the great irony was that I was still unable to help myself.

Having finally found something via the job that made some sense of my life, I was terrified of losing it, of being found out and ejected from the force (both homosexuality and alcoholism were, in certain circumstances, disciplinary matters for which I could have been sacked). But it was alcohol that took away the rawness of the situation and made the razor-sharp edges blunt.

I was about thirty when I became a daily drinker and crossed the line from heavy social drinking to solitary alcoholism without even noticing that it had happened. I drank for a thousand and one reasons, but always because I couldn't do without it. I saw it as my saviour. I comforted myself with the thought that anyone, in my circumstances and doing my job, would take a drink. I drank to celebrate, I drank to commiserate. I drank at weddings, I drank at funerals. I drank when the sun shone, I drank when it poured with rain. I drank at the sight and stench of death but, most of all, I drank when I felt the anger, frustration, inadequacy and utter helplessness at being unable to help the victims of rape and other crimes that I came across. I owned these feelings, they lived with me night and day. How many times had I held a victim's hand as they wept and so keenly shared the pain of their ordeal? I drank for every one of them and excused myself time and again for having to reach for the bottle.

I was a functioning alcoholic who never got sloshed on duty, who never got caught for being out of order, and who worked all the hours God sent because I felt I deserved nothing less. I got punched, kicked and spat on and took it all on the chin with little complaint. I never turned work away and frequently took on more than I felt able to cope with. Yet I was still a drunk and I knew it.

If my colleagues recognized my alcoholism, none of them spelt it out for me and I had got the pretence down to a fine art. Worried that they might start to smell whisky on my breath, I interchanged with vodka – that colourless, odourless answer to an alcoholic's prayers. My friends and colleagues gave me their love and their loyalty and I did my best for all of them and for the people we were working with, but I always rewarded myself with a good drink.

To many I must have appeared a hard-faced workaholic who had resigned herself to a solitary, celibate life devoted to the police force, and to those who guessed my secret I must have been a real enigma. They knew I lived alone and many must have wondered about my personal life, although they never asked; any relationships I did have were deliberately kept secret. There had been the odd fling and a couple of fairly serious encounters, including a brief affair with a married man when I was pretending to be someone I wasn't, but none of them ever had happy endings.

During this time, I had lost the love of someone very dear to me who had proved – for the first time – that my feelings about my sexuality were not unique. Her own fears and uncertainties sadly drove her from our brief liaison straight into the arms of the first man who showed her any affection. It all but broke my heart, because I loved her very much.

I now had no doubts about who I was. I had loved another woman with an intensity I had not experienced before and I felt unable to reject the word 'homosexual' any longer, although I hated the consequences of my private acceptance of it, for with it came the most terrible feelings of shame and self-loathing. My misery was entirely self-inflicted and all stemmed from my deep-rooted insecurities. There was no law against female homosexuality, but I was absolutely terrified that others would use it as a reason to treat me like the leper I believed myself to be.

Work and booze were the only antidotes to my malady, I believed, and for the most part it was a successful combination.

I could focus my energies on getting stuck in and leave behind what I didn't like and didn't understand for the time being. If I couldn't help others, then I was nothing. I thought about neither the possible long-term consequences nor the physical side effects of excessive drinking which soon began to rear their ugly heads.

I was in my early thirties when I started to suffer regularly from dry heaving, nausea, hot sweats and a feeling of detached disorientation. Imagine the panicky emotions associated with the sensation of choking on your food, or walking on legs so unstable that they make you feel as though you are about to fall over, or believing that you have the power to control your heartbeat so that, if you wanted to, you could make it stop. It reached the point where I felt so helplessly out of control with these feelings that I went to see my doctor. I told him, in no uncertain terms, that I thought I was going 'mental'. I described all my symptoms in great detail and said I thought I must be in need of psychiatric help. I failed to mention that I was drinking a half-bottle of whisky or vodka a day and that I had some severe emotional problems to deal with.

Concerned, he sent me to a psychologist who carried out various tests. The two doctors conferred and between them they concluded that I was someone who worked incredible hours in a stressful job and didn't know how to relax. I never raised the question of alcohol and they never asked. I was far too embarrassed to talk about anything that personal and, for their parts, I simply don't think it occurred to them to enquire.

Much later on, after experiencing still further problems, I was diagnosed as suffering from acute panic attacks, brought on by stress, and was prescribed a course of tranquillizers. The lethal cocktail of alcohol and 'tranqs' is well documented. Not surprisingly, the combination virtually comatosed me and, realizing that one part of the equation had to go, I flushed the pills down the lavatory. I might have lost my handle on booze, but at least I knew that I was still in control when it came to drugs.

And that was to be the pattern of my life for several years to come. When I wasn't drinking, I found myself prone to panic attacks, which I knew would be put right with a slug of alcohol.

Drink, I convinced myself, was my saviour. It never occurred to me that if I stopped drinking then I wouldn't suffer the terrors of those panic attacks in the first place. That was far too complicated for my addled brain to reason out. I was on a merry-go round. Get through this day any bloody way you can, Carol, and when tomorrow comes try again. The days just kept coming and nothing changed.

The doctor's words followed me through the heavy double doors leading to the private ward. 'Her name is Renata Chandler, officer, and I am afraid she's in a pretty bad way. She's been badly beaten.'

That was, unfortunately, all too common in the many rape cases I had previously dealt with. But it was his final words that filled me with rage as I walked towards the young woman's bedside. 'One other thing. When her attacker couldn't kill her by crushing her windpipe, the bastard tried to cut her right hand off and he damn well nearly succeeded.'

I'd spun round to look at him, my head swimming. Long ago I'd acquired the unenviable ability of putting myself, mentally, in the place of the victim. I shuddered and stamped my half-smoked cigarette into the floor.

It was nearly dawn, about four o'clock on a June morning in 1976, and the room was lit only by a small swivel lamp poised above her bedside. I swallowed hard, steeling myself for that first glimpse of her face and the haunted look I had come to expect.

In the pool of light, I could see that her features were swollen and bruised, yet I was still able to tell that this was the face of a beautiful young woman. Her right hand lay heavily bandaged on a raised platform placed at her side. Across her neck I could make out the angry red marks left by her attacker's fingers as he pressed them into her throat in an attempt to stifle her.

She turned her head slowly towards me as I fought to control the anger welling up from the pit of my stomach. Her face was ravaged by a combination of shock and fistwork. Her shoulder-length blond hair was plastered to her scalp with blood and sweat. Her eyes peered at me from deep within their sockets. They had seen what no woman should ever be forced to see.

I wanted to cry out loud, to scream my fury at the man who had done this. No matter how many times I walked into rooms like hers and saw the handiwork of the men I spent much of my life pursuing, the shock of that first sight never failed to ignite me. I was raging inside and my eyes were stinging with tears. Suddenly my well-rehearsed speech of introduction seemed inadequate. All I could say, in a whisper that almost matched Renata's own hoarse attempts at speech, was: 'I am so very, very sorry.'

A woman I correctly assumed to be Renata's mother sat at the other side of the bed, her eyes glassy. All she could do was stroke her twenty-three-year-old daughter's hand and take the odd trembling sip from a tumbler. There was a half-bottle of whisky on the metal cabinet beside her. Looking up at me with a mixture of relief and apprehension, Mrs Chandler's attempts at some sort of controlled composure appeared to be on the point of collapse. I focused my attention on her daughter once again.

Controlling the pitch of my voice, I steadied myself for the task ahead. I'd had plenty of time to learn my lines, I'd been playing the same scene for years. Now was not the time for stage fright. 'My name is Carol Bristow. I'm a detective and I'm afraid I'm going to have to ask you some pretty detailed questions about how you came to be attacked.' I paused. 'Would you like your mother to stay or wait outside?'

Renata sensed that the questions would be tough enough without the added pressure of her mother by her side, so she asked her to leave in a voice which was no more than a whisper. The immaculately dressed woman stood up carefully, kissed her daughter on the cheek and thankfully left the room, the whisky bottle neatly slipped into her black leather handbag. I moved round to the hard plastic chair on which she had been sitting and held Renata's uninjured hand in my own.

Alone with her now, the stage was set. The problem was that I was the only one who knew how to act out the parts. Renata looked as frightened as a rabbit caught in the headlights and I knew that it was my job to calm her down and prepare her for what lay ahead.

'I am truly sorry that this has happened to you and that we have to meet under these circumstances,' I told her, speaking as softly and slowly as I could. 'You've been through the most dreadful experience and I'll do all I can to try and catch the man who did this, but I need your help. OK?'

She tried to nod and smile, but her facial injuries wouldn't allow it. I could tell from her eyes that she was dreading my questions. We both knew that, in their own way, they would be a violation. I went as gently as I could.

'I'm sure there must be a million things that you want to ask me, and one of them must be how quickly are we going to catch this man. But to capture him I need you to tell me in your own words what has happened. I'm afraid that means going into every single detail, but I can assure you that, once I'm finished, you'll never be asked that sort of question again by me or by another police officer. All right?'

She seemed somewhat reassured and I could tell I was winning her round. With some victims I would not have got this far this quickly, but I sensed from her remarkable composure that I was dealing with an intelligent young woman whose determination to do all she could to bring her attacker to justice would be one of the overriding factors in her eventual recovery.

Swallowing painfully, she whispered: 'It's OK. I understand what has to be done. My father is a lawyer. I'll help you all I can. I'm sure it can't be any worse than the medical examination I just had.' Her eyes widened as she remembered what seemed to many victims like a second rape.

Wishing for the thousandth time that there could be some better way for the forensic evidence to be collected from rape victims, I slowly tried to explain the reasons for the police doctor's examination, so that she would understand the need for every prod and poke, every swab and sample she had endured. I sincerely hoped that the doctor had been one of the better ones, who understood how extremely distressing their role in the police investigation could be and who treated their patients with gentle courtesy and kindness. At that time, the large majority of police doctors – known as forensic medical examiners or FMEs – were men, and understandably victims were distressed by the idea of a man conducting the most intimate medical examination of their lives so soon after they had been brutalized.

One or two of the doctors I had worked with had staggered me through their complete insensitivity about what their patients must be feeling. The problem was that they had examined so many rape victims that they had lost sight of the horror of it all from the victim's point of view. The worst case I came across was a doctor who actually told a woman: 'For Christ's sake, open your legs wider. How am I supposed to take a swab if you won't let me in?' When she winced as he poked and prodded around, he snapped: 'Stop whining. I know you've had worse than this.' It didn't help the victim to know that the doctor was having a bad day or had been on call since 6 a.m. When I was told what he had said by a junior officer immediately after the examination, I was speechless with indignation on the victim's behalf. I reported the incident and the doctor's services were dispensed with. Thankfully, due to specialist training, those callous attitudes no longer exist.

When Renata told me she had been examined by Dr John Shanahan, a family GP and one of the best FMEs around, I was relieved. He was a good and kind man who I knew would have treated her as well as he could in the circumstances. I explained to Renata the urgency of it all, the need for such a thorough medical examination so soon after the event, which did not allow time for a dignified pause or the opportunity for a bath. I told her that the human cells left in an assailant's bodily fluids, which may eventually identify him, deteriorate within six hours and that, where possible, all victims should be deterred from washing away any vital evidence before being seen by a police doctor.

Many victims not as seriously injured as Renata will go home, have a bath, talk about the rape to a friend and then finally come to the police to report the matter a day or two after the event. They are then shocked and distressed to realize that they have washed away viable prosecution evidence which may have been used to identify their attacker.

In cases where the victim hasn't washed, three vaginal swabs are taken, at varying depths. The swabs look like cotton buds and are swivelled at the entrance to the vagina, half-way up and against the cervix. Rape is provable only when a man has unlawful sexual intercourse with a woman without her consent. To constitute an offence of rape, there must be some penetration of the vagina by the penis. There does not need to be proof of ejaculation and full penetration does not have to take place.

The science of DNA profiling or 'genetic fingerprinting' – where the unique make-up of an individual can be identified from deoxyribonucleic acid in saliva, blood and semen samples – had not been established as a means of forensic evidence when Renata was attacked, but we could still identify blood groups from semen samples. It would be eleven years before the first conviction based on the DNA technique was achieved.

I explained to Renata the importance of examining her body intimately and removing all extraneous matter which might eventually identify her assailant. The examination would have included taking samples of her head and pubic hair and saliva from her mouth. She would have been asked to give a tiny sample of blood for grouping and her fingernails would have been clipped to see if any traces of her attacker's skin, hair or microscopically small fibres from his clothing had been caught under them in her struggle to fight him off.

Finally, and perhaps worst of all, I explained the need for the anal swabs which are sometimes taken. Many victims who have been buggered during a sexual assault either block it from their minds completely or are too embarrassed or distressed to tell police officers about that part of the attack. The swabs, if taken, may provide additional evidence of semen even without the act of buggery.

I told Renata, as gently as I could, that a pregnancy test was available to her as a matter of course, and that she shouldn't worry unduly. The concept of becoming pregnant by rape is often too terrible for victims to contemplate and can tip them mentally over the edge. Strangely, in my experience, pregnancy by rape is an extremely rare event and I always try to reassure victims of that. I promised Renata that when she was up to it I would also take her to see a woman doctor friend who would check her for any sexually transmitted diseases. This was long before the fear of contracting HIV had added a further dimension to the trauma suffered by rape victims, but the prospect of gonorrhoea, syphilis or herpes was also terrifying.

Before she had too much time to let the full horror of all I had said sink in, I asked Renata if she felt up to taking a friendly 'grilling' from me and she managed to smile her consent, but asked me to check on her mother before we began. 'She's taken this pretty hard,' she whispered. 'I'm worried about her.'

I wandered out into the corridor and lit a cigarette. I caught the eye of the fresh-faced young doctor working on some papers at a desk opposite. He smiled at me sympathetically. I remembered my days as a naïve uniformed WPC and how I envied and admired the detectives doing the 'real' work. Well, this was real all right, so real it was frightening, and I couldn't imagine anyone envying the position I was now in.

Renata's mother sat further up the corridor, sipping coffee from a plastic cup and staring at the floor. The poor woman looked shattered, caught as she was between anger and grief. I had seen that look so many times before. It is a dreadful bereavement for parents, seeing a daughter so violated. It is the death of innocence in the true sense of the word, a child lost to the ultimate evil when they, as parents, weren't there to save her. Mrs Chandler glanced up at me briefly, her moist eyes seeking some kind of reassurance, but I could only half smile and nod. I had seen so many relatives of rape victims go to pieces at times like this, but I sincerely hoped that this well-bred woman would keep it together when her daughter needed her most.

In my experience the mothers weren't too bad, it was the husbands and boyfriends who were the worst. They either backed away completely or seemed to need to know every last detail, as if they couldn't help mentally torturing themselves and the victim. Their 'possession' had been contaminated somehow and they found it very difficult to handle. With many there was a tremendous sense of personal guilt that they were not there to protect, and with a few the fearful, sick suspicion in the pit of their stomach that, in some way, the victim may have asked for what happened or, worse still, even enjoyed it.

At such a traumatic time, men find it extremely difficult to deal with such feelings and few stay the course. Those who do are real gems, priceless to the victims and their eventual recovery. Renata only had her mother around at this stage and I was grateful for the absence of an over-anxious partner or a harrowed father. Like the boyfriends and husbands, few fathers can cope with seeing a beloved daughter so defiled and none I had ever met really came to terms with it. Rape was and is such a destructive act. Its consequences send tremors of shock, pain and guilt through families and friends far beyond its turbulent epicentre.

I spent the rest of that night and much of the next day with Renata in the side ward of St Charles's Hospital in Notting Hill. I held her hand as I helped her piece together the events of the previous night. From time to time I stood out in the corridor, angry as hell, smoking a cigarette and wishing more than anything that I could pour myself a large Scotch from her mother's now empty bottle. On one such occasion, I collected a steaming plastic cup of coffee for myself from the vending machine and pushed through the doors for the next round. Registering the sympathetic look on the face of the young doctor still on duty, I shrugged my shoulders. 'I've no one but myself to blame,' I quipped. 'I could have been a housewife.' He smiled hesitantly.

From our very first meeting, I knew that Renata was a remarkable young woman and someone who was extremely lucky to be alive. Barely able to talk, she whispered her answers through her battered windpipe. There was pain each time she tried to speak, swallow or move her neck, but she was determined to help me in every way she could. Deliberate in her answers, she responded carefully to all my questions.

Amazingly composed despite what she had been through, she

never once broke down and cried. Not then, anyway. Still in the numbing early stages of shock, and yet quite clear in her recollection of all that had happened, she made me increasingly aware that the man who had attacked her was evil and had neither intended nor expected her to survive. She told me right from the outset that she had memorized every detail so that she would be able to recount it to the police if she escaped.

'I will never forget him as long as I live,' she said. 'I don't want to forget him. I want to be able to say to you: "That's the man who raped and tried to kill me." '

I scribbled down everything she said in my notebook, trying to blot the revulsion of it from my mind and keep my feelings locked away. I read and re-read her statement back to her and we worked on it together for several hours, adding details and adjusting others until she was certain that it was an exact account of the attack. She could not sign it because of the damage to her hand, but for now the signature was unimportant. I folded the twenty-page statement carefully and placed it in my briefcase, relieved that the ordeal was over but reluctant to leave her side just yet.

At twenty-three, Renata was ten years younger than me. From a wealthy, well adjusted middle-class family, her background made her an excellent witness. I felt as if I had relived every word of her statement and I knew even as I put it away that its appalling contents were now indelibly etched on my mind.

She lived with a girlfriend in a flat in a terraced three-storey town house not far from Ladbroke Grove underground station in west London. The previous evening, 9 June, she had gone out for a drink in nearby Notting Hill with a childhood friend, a man who had called her out of the blue. Returning alone at about 11.15 p.m., she parked her white Renault 6 outside her house; she was happy but ready for bed.

Just as she was about to attach the Krooklok anti-theft device to the steering wheel she heard a man's voice asking her the time, which made her jump. Her window was slightly open and peering through it was a large Afro-Caribbean, his face inches from her own. As she looked at her wristwatch, the man yanked open the car door and pointed a five-inch, narrow-bladed knife at her lower body.

'Move over, don't make a noise or you'll get this.' He forced her across into the passenger seat before swinging his enormous bulk into the small car beside her, suffocating her with his presence. He wore dark trousers and a sports top with a white stripe on the collar, sleeve and hem. She noticed his massive biceps under the short sleeves of his shirt.

'Don't do anything silly and you won't get hurt,' he said. 'Give me the car keys . . . now.' Dropping the Krooklok at her feet, she handed him the keys and watched, dumbstruck, as he fumbled for the ignition and started up the engine. He asked where first gear was and, when she pointed out the unusual arrangement of the gearstick, he pulled out jerkily into the passing traffic, almost colliding with a lorry which had to brake suddenly behind them. He drove her away from the main Portobello Road towards a maze of streets bordered by the Grand Union Canal.

'Where are we going?' she asked him, trying to control the fear in her voice.

'I want to talk,' was all he said.

She told him she had some money and offered him the £5 she had in her handbag. There was more in her bank account and she could write him a cheque. He ignored her.

'Please don't take me too far,' she pleaded. 'Can't we talk here?'

'No. It's too well lit.'

The car eventually stopped in a quiet area near an open space but, as they parked, a woman and child walked past.

'This is ludicrous, I could shout to that woman,' she said, to herself as much as to him. 'I could ask her to help me.'

'Don't be silly, I'll knife you, then her, and then the little girl,' he threatened, pulling her into his huge arms as if they were lovers. When the woman and child had passed, he maintained his grip on her, his huge bulk pressed against her small frame, and started to fumble clumsily between her legs under her dress.

'Oh no, not that,' she said, the sudden realization of what

was happening chilling her heart. 'Please, not that, please stop.'

'Shut up, bitch,' he said as he leant his enormous body towards hers. 'It's OK, I'm not going to hurt you, I just want to have a little feel.'

She tensed, praying he would stop and wondering how she could get away.

'I'm going to screw you,' he told her. 'Do you know anywhere we could go?'

She was overwhelmed with fear, but tried to keep calm. Intending to run away as soon as she had the chance, she said in a tremulous voice, 'Let's get out here and do it over by those railings,' pointing to some houses across the road.

He shook his head. 'I know a nice place in Hammersmith.'

'Please, just let me go now. I won't say anything to anyone,' she pleaded. 'Please don't take me anywhere else. I don't want to go to someone else's house.'

He stopped mauling her and reached for a rag on the floor, ripping it effortlessly into strips and binding her hands and wrists tightly with them. Setting off at speed, he drove her to Southern Row, a dimly lit cul-de-sac in Notting Hill, and parked at the far end where the street was flanked by tall Georgian houses, largely boarded or bricked up. A network of alleyways which ran between the scruffy tenements was deserted. Renata knew she was utterly alone.

In the struggle to maintain her sanity and in the hope of early escape, she almost resigned herself to the fact that she was going to be raped. She tried to memorize her assailant's features as she stared at his face. Suddenly he reached across her, his hot breath on her neck, and turned the ratchet-wheel to recline her seat.

'I mustn't get these messed up,' he said, as he methodically removed his trousers, folded them carefully and put them on the back seat. As she half lay, half sat, frozen with terror, he pulled off her knickers and placed them neatly in the glove compartment in front of her. He then lifted up her light cotton dress, lay on top of her and raped her.

She could taste his mint-flavoured chewing gum as he kissed

her full on the mouth. Concentrating hard on every detail as he abused her, she registered that she could not detect either alcohol or cigarettes. She could smell his skin, but there was no stale body odour. As he became more and more aroused, she could feel his sweat running down her face.

'There's my baby, there's my baby,' he said to her, over and over again.

'Please, please don't make me pregnant,' she whispered tearfully, and registering her concern he ejaculated outside her. When he had finished he slid his body back into the driver's seat. As he did so, she noticed an unusual-shaped scar on his neck, just below the left side of his jaw.

After he had re-dressed he checked her wrists, pulling the bindings even tighter, as she lay shivering beside him, still reclined on the seat. Suddenly he started talking to himself, a monologue which was to last for over an hour.

'Oh, Johnny, what have you done? Was it worth it? You should never have done it,' he recited, still sweating profusely and wiping his thick-rimmed glasses on her dress.

'Is that your name? Johnny?' she questioned quietly.

'Why do you want to know?'

He asked her name and age and she told him, remembering some advice she had once heard about winning an attacker's confidence by talking. But just as their conversation seemed to take an easier tone, he uttered something which chilled her to the marrow.

'If I let you go, you'll go to the police.'

'No, I won't, honestly, I won't.' Panic rose from deep within her. 'I'll sign a statement saying I agreed to have sex with you. No one will ever know.'

He shook his head. 'I know you'll go to the police. There's only one way out, I'm going to have to kill you.'

Her heart froze. Her mind raced with the possibilities for escape. She wriggled to free her wrists from their bonds but they were too tight. She looked wildly around at the desolate spot and realized, once again, that she was completely alone.

'Please, no,' she begged. 'You can't kill me. I mean, you couldn't. What about my family, my parents? It would destroy

101

them. What about your family? What would they say? Please, think about what it would mean.'

In a bizarre exchange, they discussed the pros and cons of his murdering her. For every argument she put forward, he countered that he would be arrested and imprisoned if he didn't. She felt that time was running out.

The conversation stopped abruptly when he lurched towards her. Sweating now and shivering, she stared at him wide-eyed as he started stroking her hair. 'You're too beautiful to die,' he whispered softly. 'You're only twenty-three. I thought I could hurt you whites, but now I know I can't kill you.' Her mind swam. Did this mean a reprieve? She knew she had to seize the opportunity and act on it.

'That's right, you can't kill me. I knew you couldn't,' she said, trying to smile. 'If you'll only let me go, I promise I won't go to the police. My flatmate'll already have called them. She'll be worried about me by now, but I promise I won't say anything.'

'How would you describe me to the police?' he asked her abruptly, his huge hand still stroking her hair and face.

'I wouldn't, I wouldn't say anything,' she sobbed. 'But if I did, I would just say you were black and wore glasses. I wouldn't say any more than that, honestly I wouldn't.'

He seemed upset. 'I can't go home after what I've done. I'll have to do this.' When she looked up at him fearfully, he added: 'Don't look at me! Do you hear me, don't look at me!' She turned her face away, her whole body trembling. 'It's so easy to kill someone, you just cut their wrists,' she heard him say quietly. She turned and stared at him with horror. 'But now I'm going to screw you again,' he added, and calmly undressed.

'Then can I go?' she asked weakly.

He didn't answer but forced her to engage in oral sex. His huge body towered over her and seemed to fill the tiny space within her car. Roughly turning her over on to all fours and lifting up her dress, he raped her a second time from behind, causing her considerable pain. Her head was repeatedly banged against the driver's door and this time he ejaculated inside her, the possibility of pregnancy forgotten. When he had finished, he dressed and then untied her hands.

Am I free now? she thought. Is it over? She was losing strength and felt the end was near. She had a chance to speak and if she didn't seize the opportunity she knew she might never have another one.

'Please will you take me home,' she begged.

'I can't do that. I'm going to have to kill you,' was all he said.

'Please, no, you can't, no.' Tears splashed her cheeks. 'It'll be far worse.' She tried to summon up the nerve to argue with him once again. She struggled to maintain a clear head.

Turning to her, he said simply: 'It's my life or yours . . . Kiss me.' She leant towards him, sobbing softly, but as he kissed her his hands grasped her neck. She threw her head back to give herself more air, but he was too strong for her. His hands tightened around her throat, his thumbs pressing deep into her windpipe, blocking the flow of air. She felt herself gradually slipping away, losing her senses. Close to death as saliva bubbled from her mouth, she could do nothing but wait for the moment of extinction. It seemed only seconds away when he momentarily lessened his hold and stopped to stare at her face.

'Are you feeling OK?' he asked, smiling at her almost benignly.

She gasped for air and started sobbing as the blood and oxygen rushed to her brain. Believing this to be her last chance, she screamed as loudly as she could, thrashing her arms and legs about to kick and push him off. She scratched him and tried to punch him in the testicles, but as he grabbed her neck once more and dug his thumbs into her windpipe, she lost all strength and began to lose consciousness again.

'Why don't you die?' she heard him say through the foggy confusion of semi-consciousness, as his hands slipped from her neck. Her body jerked and then went completely limp as he struck her several hard blows across her windpipe, chopping it with the side of his huge hand.

Stupefied and slumped over, she was suddenly aware of a sharp slashing sensation to her right wrist, and opened her eyes just enough to see that he was sawing through the veins and tendons with his knife. When the blade reached the bone, the excruciating pain jerked her back into consciousness.

'Die, you white bitch, die!' he shouted. She saw blood spurting from her main artery, dripping down the inside of the windscreen. She felt it saturating her dress and as she lay back, fighting for breath, her eyes squeezed tightly shut, she waited, half expecting him to finish her off by stabbing her in the chest or throat.

Instead, she heard the driver's door creak as it was pushed open. The little car shook as the door slammed shut. Then, as mysteriously as he had arrived, her attacker disappeared into the night.

She sat stock-still, convinced that she'd hear him return or open the passenger door. She could hear nothing but a strange rasping sound. Realizing it was coming from her own mouth, she blinked hard for a minute, fighting to clear her eyes and her mind, and then slowly pulled herself up.

She could hardly see out of the car for the blood, and as she peered through the windows hesitantly, she expected to see him standing in front of her with the knife. When she finally appreciated she was alone, the sudden flood of adrenalin to her brain jerked her into action. With her left hand she grabbed the rags that had previously bound her and pressed them into the gaping wound on her right wrist. She felt no pain and a bolt of energy surged through her as she saw the car keys dangling from the ignition.

Summoning up remarkable reserves of strength, she held her right arm up in the air to try to stem the flow of blood and slid herself across into the driver's seat. Starting the engine, she somehow managed to turn the car around one-handed and drive back through Notting Hill towards her flat. Determined to get home, she ignored all the other road users as she sped through traffic lights and across junctions before screeching to a halt outside the familiar building where she lived.

Leaning heavily on her damaged arm, she pushed open the driver's door weakly and tried to call for help, her strength failing her now. No clear sound emerged from her crushed throat as she staggered to the front window of the basement flat. Once there, she managed to alert the attention of the couple who lived inside. As they emerged cautiously in their nightclothes, wondering who had woken them up in the small hours, she collapsed blood-soaked and semi-conscious into their arms. They called an ambulance and the police. It was 1 a.m., just two hours since she had first been abducted.

5

BY THE TIME RENATA ARRIVED AT ST CHARLES'S HOSPITAL, DR
Mark Zupan, the night duty casualty officer, had called for
surgical assistance. A cursory examination of the battered
young woman told him all he needed to know. She was severely
traumatized, both her eyes had been blackened, her neck was
badly bruised and her thighs were covered with dried blood.
There were cuts and grazes to her face and body, but her right
wrist was his chief concern. Packed with rags and bandaged
tightly by paramedics, it was still bleeding heavily and
demanded immediate attention.

Surgeon Alnadhir Sherif had been bleeped and within minutes
Renata was in the operating theatre, while detectives waited
anxiously outside. Mr Sherif had to work quickly to stem
the flow of blood and repair the damage to her artery and
tendons. He would do all he could to save her hand, even
though it had almost been severed. She would probably require
further surgery later on, but for now his task was to limit the
damage as best he could and replace the blood that she had
lost.

Lying in her hospital bed just a few hours after surgery,
Renata insisted that she was well enough to be interviewed by
the police. She said she was determined to help detectives all
she could, as her family's legal background had taught her the

importance of co-operation and of making a speedy statement. I found it remarkable that she was able to tell me with such detached deliberation about the man who had earlier raped and tried to kill her.

He had, she said, enormous strength and physique, wore square-shaped spectacles and bore a scar on his neck. He was about five feet eight to five feet ten inches tall, aged thirty-five to forty-five, wore dark trousers and a dark T-shirt with the distinctive white stripe. 'He spoke well, as if he had been educated and lived in this country for a long time. When we were arguing about him taking my life, he seemed very logical,' she whispered.

Her statement was clear and precise, the telling of it the first step on her long road to recovery. I listened with a mixture of horror and revulsion. I was staggered by the brutality of the man who had attacked her, but hugely impressed by Renata's courage. Rarely had I seen a rape victim so unwavering in her resolve to see a case through to the bitter end, so clear in her demand for justice. But I also knew all that could change. There was still so much she had to face.

During the days and nights ahead, she would relive her ordeal continuously. She would never be able to erase the contamination of her attacker's touch. Her mind would play tricks, blanking out whole sections of the incident, leaving her numb and devoid of emotion. It would be a long time, if ever, before her right hand would function fully again. The doctors had saved it, but every time it failed her in the years to come, she would be forced to remember that night, 9 June 1976. The tidal wave of memory would rush back, engulfing her.

Hard on the heels would come the guilt, the nagging doubt that maybe she could have done more to prevent what had happened, the questions every victim thinks everyone around them is wanting to ask. Why didn't I lock myself in the car? Why didn't I scream out at the beginning, or jump out of the other door while I still had the chance? All the What ifs become Why didn'ts. The factual, logical explanations that he had threatened her with a knife, that she was stunned into submission, transfixed by fear, helpless in the presence of someone so much larger and so menacing, would seem inadequate.

Renata still had all of this to go through, and my questioning, however insensitive it might have appeared, my involvement with her, would become part of the recovery programme she would need in order to survive. The doctors would do all they could for her physically but there was little anyone could do to heal her mental scars.

It would take superhuman stamina to begin to recover from such a harrowing ordeal. The process she had started to go through, an initial dissociation from the event so that she could focus on the evidence and tell me many of the gruesome facts so dispassionately, is a common psychological phenomenon in rape victims. How much easier it is during the act to concentrate on minutiae – a scar on the neck, the smell of mint on the breath – than to accept the full horror of what is happening or, worse still, what may be about to happen.

That narrowing of perception continues at the hospital or police station, with victims describing their experiences as if they are watching them happen to another person. They focus on something else and temporarily lock away all the feelings of shock, hysteria, anger and finally guilt which are yet to overwhelm them. Rape is one of the few crimes where the victim ends up feeling guilty and ashamed. It was part of my job to help them overcome that, whether I was up to it or not.

Renata's attack had not even occurred on my patch. I was stationed at Harrow Road, not Notting Hill, but it had seemed common sense to call me as I was so local. Even then, back in the dark ages, the Met had appreciated the need for women detectives when taking statements from rape victims. If a woman detective couldn't be found then a WPC would be given the task, even though she would not have had any specialized training. It was years later that the need was recognized and SOIT (sexual offences investigative techniques) courses were set up for women officers across the board to receive instruction on these very complex matters.

Right from the outset, I was aware that my role in the investigation of Renata's attack – however important – would be transitory. As was so often the way, I would only be asked to 'top and tail' her evidence – make the first contact by taking her statement, and then maybe spend some time with her prior to court proceedings (which could have been several months, if not years later) if her attacker was ever caught. I would not be expected to contact her in the intervening period, the time when she probably needed me the most, and she would only have limited access to me, even if she rang me, because of my own heavy workload.

There was still no true concept of proper care for rape victims within the police force. It was slowly changing for the better, and had greatly improved even from the days when I had started as a rookie, but it was a very long way from being anything like good enough. There was nothing like the widespread support systems that are in place today, for either the victims or the police officers involved.

From my point of view, I was generally happy to be called out to help on these jobs. It meant that I was right in at the sharp end, sleeves rolled up, on the front line, which was one of the reasons why I had been attracted to the police force in the first place. Taking an accurate witness statement from a victim (the emphasis being on accurate) was probably one of the most important parts of any police investigation because, taken properly, it could yield new clues which might help catch a suspect before he could strike again. I could count on one hand the number of female detectives employed in west London and felt proud when I was called off my patch to help colleagues elsewhere.

As I sat with Renata for those first few hours at the hospital, encouraging her to remember more, my colleagues at Notting Hill were out hunting. The area where she lived and the place where the attack happened were saturated with police officers for the following forty-eight hours. Detective Chief Inspector Peter Boorman, an experienced detective who had served with the Flying Squad and the Regional Crime Squad, was rung at home and alerted to the serious rape and attempted murder which had occurred on his patch. Within hours, a team of investigators had been identified and told to set up shop in the rabbit warren of narrow corridors and small offices that made up the CID office on the first floor of the Victorian-fronted Notting Hill Police Station.

Small and stockily built, DCI Boorman did not look much like a detective. He had previously specialized in undercover work and most famously had been instrumental in arresting members of the notorious Richardson gang for operating a massive car-park fraud at Heathrow Airport. Now in charge of a case which had shocked even him, he was determined to get a result, and get it quickly. 'This man must be caught,' he told his team in the hastily set-up incident room. 'Who knows when he will strike again?' Quietly confident that Renata would be able to provide a good photofit of her attacker, with a clear description of the scar on his neck and other features, DCI Boorman hoped that his plans for an early arrest would not be thwarted.

Within a few hours of Renata's neighbours making that 999 call, he was supervising officers from the uniform side and his own CID as they interviewed local residents and any other possible witnesses to the abduction and rape. Most people claimed to have been in bed asleep at the time, as the attack had happened late at night in the middle of a working week. Most people denied seeing anything that could assist police. One woman, however, whose house backed on to Southern Row, later admitted hearing screams at about 1 a.m., but said she hadn't called anyone because she had assumed it was kids mucking about.

As the foot soldiers attempted to gather any clues from witnesses, the scientific side of the investigation was also well under way. Renata's car and the scene of the crime were captured on film by a police photographer from Scotland Yard before being assiduously searched by a team of forensic experts from the Metropolitan Police Forensic Science Laboratory in Lambeth, south London. After being examined *in situ*, the little Renault was loaded on to a trailer and ferried to the car park of Notting Hill Police Station for further examination.

It was clear to anyone who saw inside the car that it had been the site of a savage and brutal attack. A semen-stained rag was found on the floor, and blood was spattered all over the inside of the vehicle. Swabs of still-fresh blood were taken from the passenger-door handle and floor, while fibres, hairs and dust particles were collected by means of sticky-backed tape.

These were compared to fibres and samples taken from Renata's blood-soaked clothes, which had been carefully removed from her by the police doctor and sent to the Forensic Science Laboratory for analysis and examination. The body fluid samples were examined microscopically and the experts said the semen found was from a man with an A-secretor blood group, which occurs in approximately 33 per cent of the population and just over 20 per cent of Afro-Caribbeans. In the absence of DNA testing, nothing more would specifically identify the rapist.

Renata's injuries were photographed so that her cuts, bruises and the deep wound to her wrist could be shown in colour to any jury asked to judge the severity of her attack long after the scars had healed. Finally, the statement I had taken in my best handwriting was typed up and photocopied by a clerical worker before being circulated to the team of Notting Hill detectives entrusted with the task of trying to apprehend her attacker before he struck again.

My part in the investigation was over by lunchtime the next day. Despite my reluctance to leave Renata and my sense of foreboding as to how she would cope with her parents and her own delayed reaction, I couldn't wait to drive home and take my first shower in more than twenty-four hours. My head throbbed, my stomach trembled and my back ached from being bent forward, hunched over my notebook, trying to catch the whispered answers. There would be precious little time to unwind after such a mammoth session. I would be expected back on duty at Harrow Road the following morning to take up the enormous workload I had waiting for me, or maybe I would have to go through the whole process again with some other poor victim.

At Harrow Road about twenty of us dealt with around three thousand cases a year. Subject to the availability of officers, that could work out at an average of three to four cases each a week

111

– sometimes one a day – and that constant pressure, together with follow-up enquiries, court preparation, paperwork and what little victim support we could give, left no time to take on other divisions' work. However much I wanted to take part in the hunt for Renata's attacker, and however much it might have made sense to keep the continuity and the rapport between the two of us going, I just couldn't afford to help out with rapes in other areas even if the rules allowed it. Despite the fact that I had taken on a psychological responsibility when I accepted that early-morning call to see Renata, there was nothing I could do now but make a mental note to stay in touch with her when I could and keep an eye on the case from afar.

As I stood up to leave, I noted the resistance in her eyes and wished there was more that I could do or say to help. But there was little to add. She had to come to terms with what had happened in her own way now. I couldn't be there to hold her hand for ever and, even if it were possible, it would mean that I wouldn't be there for the next one and the countless others that would follow. There was also the question of how much I could allow myself to give. It was not so much what you took away with you from those meetings, but how much of you got left behind; if you kept on giving away little pieces of yourself, in the end there would be nothing left.

Renata, like me, needed to sleep. She was understandably drained after all my questions and the doctors urged that she should be allowed to rest before she helped the police Identikit expert compile a likeness of her attacker. The story of her rape was about to hit the national newspapers and the police wanted the media to carry a picture of the attacker which could only be compiled with the help of the specially trained officer. He, too, would spend a long time at her bedside, piecing together sections of a face to make up the features of the man she would never forget.

When the story appeared later in the *Daily Mirror*, Renata's ninety-five-minute ordeal was overshadowed by the latest development in the story of Jeremy Thorpe, the Liberal leader, who was implicated in a scandal with a male model. It was condensed to four paragraphs on page ten. Under the headline

GIRL IN KNIFE RAPE ORDEAL, the story said a huge police search was under way for the attacker, who would have been covered in blood as he ran away. An unnamed senior detective was quoted as saying: 'I am certain he will kill if he is not caught.'

As I put my coat on and stood up to leave the room, I turned for a last look at the young woman whose story had so appalled me. I couldn't help feeling that something about her and the man who had attacked her would remain with me for the rest of my days. It had been the worst case of rape and attempted murder I and many of my colleagues had ever dealt with and I had felt an immediate bond with her. The painful extraction of the events whispered from her split and swollen lips had left as much of a mark on my mind as the scars would on her wrist. I prayed to God that the man who did this to her would be caught, and caught soon.

By the time I arrived home, standing under the hot-water jets of the shower, allowing them to sting my face and head until they hurt, I felt almost as exhausted as her. Slumping into an armchair in my dressing gown, my hair still wet, I gulped down the first of several large Scotches in an attempt to wash away the foul taste that recent events had left in my mouth.

Grateful once again for the solitude my single, celibate existence allowed me, I stared into the bottom of the glass and thanked my lucky stars I didn't have to make polite small talk to any house guest or demanding partner. How much easier it was to live my life alone and entirely self-contained. I could come in when I wanted, drink as much as I liked, and never have to try to explain to anyone what my working day had been like. Where on earth would I have started talking about Renata?

Clicking on the remote control of the television set, I winced as assorted images of sex and violence flickered in front of me. Even something as innocuous as a gentle grope between two consenting adults had begun to offend me. I changed channels from a film about teenage sex, billed as 'first love', to a sinister thriller with men lurking in the shadows. Nauseated, I switched the television off and poured myself another large drink. There was only one route to oblivion and I had discovered long ago that this was it.

The following day did indeed bring a list of tasks and a pile of paperwork that was to swamp me for several weeks.

The calls never stopped coming. One, which came in from the police at Heathrow Airport, told us the intriguing story of a young Parisian girl who had arrived at the airport to fly home, when she collapsed on the plane and was found to be haemorrhaging internally.

Tearfully, she pleaded with the air hostesses to be allowed to travel. There was a slight delay while they attended to her, but – in consultation with the authorities – they did allow her to fly, although not before establishing that she had just had an abortion. She named the doctor who had operated on her as a GP working out of an address in Porchester Road, Paddington.

It was the mid-1970s and the law allowing abortions in Britain was relatively new, having been passed in 1968. The Act permitted abortions in certain cases but only with the approval of a second doctor and at a few registered clinics. Needless to say our chappie's tiny surgery was not one of them. The one registered clinic in London was the Langham.

In France abortions, and the right to travel abroad for one, were illegal. This explained the young girl's determination not to cause a fuss. Had her plight become known to the French authorities, she would probably have been detained at Orly Airport.

The police at Heathrow called the Home Office and then us to pass on the information the girl had given them about the doctor in Porchester Road. My boss called me in and asked me to investigate his background and see if we could build a case against him.

Not long after I started on the case, we had another call from the Home Office. A young farmer in Totnes, Devon, had made his girlfriend pregnant and then had an argument with her. In the heat of the exchange, she told him she was going to

114

London to have an abortion. He allowed her to rush off, but changed his mind after she had left for the station. He called the Langham to tell them that when she turned up they were not to allow her to go ahead with the termination. The Langham told him that they had never heard of the girl, and called the Home Office. Someone then put two and two together and thought that the same doctor I was watching might just be involved.

The Home Office contacted the farmer and asked him to let them know when his girlfriend returned. He did and told them that she claimed to have had a *bona fide* abortion carried out by a doctor in Paddington, after being referred to him by someone she had met at Victoria Station.

I did every check imaginable and confirmed he was an established GP, but could find nothing to suggest he was anything other than an excellent family doctor. Back-street abortions were still fairly commonplace because of the newness of the Act, but the concept of a real-life qualified doctor operating outside the law, risking being struck off the Medical Register for a few extra pounds, was a whole new ballgame.

I was duly dispatched to Totnes with a male colleague to take a statement from the farmer's girlfriend. We eventually arrived at the filthy, muddy farm and saw the woman and frankly she couldn't have cared a toss, making it abundantly clear that she resented our presence. It took me four days to obtain her statement because she insisted on carrying on with her farm-work – feeding the ducks, milking the cows and so on – and all she would give me was snatches of conversation in between.

She told me that when she had arrived at Victoria Station and spotted an on-site medical centre, she went in and asked where she could have a legal abortion. A woman there told her that if she couldn't afford the Langham, she knew a cheaper place where it would be done by a professional doctor. She took down the address and went to Porchester Road where she had the operation. The only time she ever showed any emotion was when she described what had physically happened. Her face wrinkled as she told me it was a horrible experience, painful and not very sterile.

After I had taken her statement, I returned to London and told my boss all I knew and he referred it to the Detective Chief Superintendent. Before I knew it, some senior officers suddenly began to get twitchy about nicking a pukka GP and were clearly concerned about any possible repercussions. I was very disappointed.

My DI, however, had a lot of bottle and between us we agreed that, as we only had the evidence of the girl in Totnes, it might be worth our while watching the surgery for a while before I actually felt the doctor's collar. That was good enough for me. I got out the obbo (observation) van and we parked it in Porchester Road and waited.

It wasn't a prolonged observation. The morning surgery was between 9.30 and 11.30 and, sitting in the back of the van watching through the blacked-out windows, I clocked everyone going in and out, registering them on my clipboard. Just before 11.30 two young women arrived – it was obvious they were the last patients of the day – and half an hour later only one of the women came out. At that moment, the Venetian blinds in the surgery were pulled down and I resolved to watch and wait.

Two hours later, the first woman came back and went inside. After ten minutes she emerged with the second woman, who, looking absolutely dreadful, was clearly having difficulty walking. The two of them hailed a black cab and were driven off.

My colleague and I, who had been watching through binoculars from the back of the van, both dived for the driver's seat. I got there first and attempted to turn the cumbersome obbo van around so that we could give chase. As was often the case, however, we were so tightly jammed in between vehicles that it seemed – short of shunting the cars front and rear – impossible to get the van out into the road. Fearing we'd lose the two women, I leapt out on to the pavement, hailed another black taxi and for the first and only time in my career shouted: 'Police officer. Follow that cab!'

As the first vehicle began to disappear from sight, my cabbie gave chase with the enthusiasm of a young Stirling Moss.

Breaking all speed limits, he drove up Inverness Terrace, along the Bayswater Road and right into Park Lane where, because of the volume of traffic, he was reluctantly forced to slow down. Seeing that the first taxi was now only about six vehicles in front, I took my life in my hands, dived out into the traffic and wove my way past motorbikes and cars until I drew level with the cab, which had just stopped at some traffic lights. Pulling open the door, I stepped in and faced two frightened women who were sitting clutching each other on the back seat.

'I am a police officer,' I puffed, trying to catch my breath, 'and I need to ask you both some questions about your reason for going to see the doctor in Porchester Road.'

They looked at each other quizzically. 'Qu'est-ce qu'elle a dit?' the paler one said to her friend. They were French and didn't speak a word of English. For several minutes, I tried to explain who I was and what I was saying. Defeated, I told the cab driver to take us to Harrow Road Police Station, where I hoped to find someone who spoke French. As we pulled up outside the nick and the women realized where I was taking them, the one who looked ill broke down completely. She was clearly very distressed, and it didn't take a genius to work out why.

I took her straight round to casualty at Paddington General Hospital and told them what I thought had happened. Within fifteen minutes they confirmed that she had recently undergone an incomplete termination and they took her away to give her a D&C (dilation and curettage) which they assured me would stop the bleeding and clear out the debris the abortion doctor had left behind. I returned to the nick to collect my colleagues and made plans to arrest the doctor.

Five of us drove to Porchester Road, and walked in through the front door to be met by the doctor and his assistant. 'I am a police officer and I have reason to believe that you have just carried out an illegal abortion,' I told him.

To my surprise, he was entirely co-operative, and said: 'You mean the young Frenchwoman? Yes, that's right.' He led me into his surgery and showed me the remains of a recently aborted foetus in a dish and the bloodied gown the woman had been wearing. Laid out on a steel trolley next to the operating table was the most archaic equipment I have ever seen, huge metal instruments all still covered in blood, waiting to be washed.

We took him to the nick and he came as clean as a whistle, not just about the three girls we knew about, but at least twenty others he had operated on in recent times. He then took us to his beautiful house in Ealing, west London, where he opened his safe and handed over bundles of foreign currency, which constituted payments from the innocents abroad. Making light of the huge amounts of money he was making, the doctor said that he believed abortion should be available on demand to any woman who wanted it. 'Women', he announced, 'should not have to go through the ignominy of having to plead for something that I believe is their right.' I thanked him for his speech and arrested him.

We charged him with four specimen counts as it was clear he had flagrantly disregarded the law on abortion. He appeared at Marylebone Magistrates' Court at once and was due to be committed for trial at the Old Bailey at a later date, which was reported in all the papers because it was so unusual for a doctor to be prosecuted. On the day of the committal, the court was full of journalists waiting to record every word, but the doctor never showed up. I was furious. I remember thinking: The bastard's done a bunk.

I applied for an arrest warrant and went round to his surgery, fully expecting him to be long gone, and I was right. The doctor's assistant was in tears as she told me her employer had had a heart attack and died just as he was leaving for court.

The Frenchwoman, who would now not have to give evidence, was delighted. The ancient surgical tools the doctor had used to abort the foetus went on display in a glass cabinet at Detective Training School and became an historic visual aid to the instructor who lectured on the subject.

* * *

I kept in touch with Renata's case as best I could, but the months passed and there was still no news. No matter how I tried, I could not erase the horror of her attack from my mind. Having heard nothing positive about the case for three months, I decided to visit the officers hunting her attacker to see how they were getting along.

As is traditional at most of the London nicks I had ever known, the first-floor CID offices were buried somewhere in a labyrinth of corridors and rooms. As I picked my way through Notting Hill Police Station in search of a friendly face, I came across Ted, an old mate from West End Central, who had recently been transferred. I asked him how DCI Boorman, now in charge of a diminishing number of officers investigating Renata's case, had fared since the attack.

Ted poured me out some coffee and filled me in, gloomily. House-to-house enquiries in the area where Renata was abducted had proved utterly fruitless. No one had seen anything suspicious either there or, perhaps less surprisingly, in Southern Row, the scene of the attack. A television appeal on Shaw Taylor's *Police 5* programme had shown the Identikit picture Renata had helped devise, but there had been no significant public response.

DCI Boorman had carried out all the normal police routines and had compiled a list of possible suspects in the area. Anyone with a conviction for anything from flashing to murder had been looked at. At first there had seemed to be no obvious candidates but, looking once again through the hundreds of names, a detective on his team had come up with a convicted rapist who had seemed to favour the same MO (*modus operandi*, literally 'method of operation'). The man was a West Indian and his name was David Ronald Lashley.

Digging out his criminal record and examining his previous convictions, Boorman's memory was suddenly jogged. He remembered this investigation. It had been carried out by a colleague seven years earlier after a series of sex attacks on women in small cars in and around west and south-west London. The attacker, dubbed the 'Beast of Shepherd's Bush' by the press, was presumed to have committed more than twenty rapes and sexual assaults. On every occasion, the victim was a young woman returning home alone in a car in the early hours of the morning.

'By now we were pretty excited by the similarities in MO and the attack on Renata,' Ted told me, 'so we checked Lashley's files to see if he was in or out of prison at the time of Renata's attack. We discovered that in 1970 he was sentenced to twelve years' imprisonment, and I thought, He surely can't be out already? But then a few phone calls later we discovered he was released early, in March 1976, three months before the attack on Renata, which put him right in the frame.'

Next, Ted said, they needed to check his blood group. He was an A secretor, which matched the foreign fluids found on Renata's swabs. But without the certainty of DNA profiling, that simply made him one of the 20 per cent of the Afro-Caribbean population who could have been responsible. The officers needed more to go on.

Looking into his prison background and the reason for his premature release, Boorman's team discovered that Lashley had been given early parole because he had gone to the aid of a prison officer who was being attacked by an inmate. His records showed that during the course of the ensuing fight Lashley had been cut on the neck by another prisoner. The excitement in the incident room had been electric.

'But then came the bad news,' added Ted. 'We didn't want to make any direct contact with Lashley until we had to, so we asked prison and probation officers about any scars on his neck. The answers weren't the ones we were looking for. Lashley did have scars, but not where Renata had described. The left side of his neck, we were told, was definitely clear. They also said Lashley had grown facial hair in recent years and had been sporting a beard at the time of the attack.'

Hopeful anyway, Boorman had a series of photographs of male offenders shown to Renata, including an old one of Lashley. She failed to pick him out. As the temperatures in the summer of '76 reached record levels, the trail for her attacker went cold.

I was deeply troubled by what Ted had told me, and much

more so when nothing new had turned up by Christmas, but suddenly I no longer had time to think about anything. Out of the blue I was summoned to the office of my DCI and asked to sit down.

'I don't know if you're going to thank me for this or not, Carol,' he told me, smiling. 'But I know you'll never regret it.' I swallowed hard and asked him what he was talking about. 'A few weeks ago I recommended you for the Flying Squad,' he said. 'And I heard just now that you have been accepted.'

I could hardly believe my ears. I didn't honestly know whether to laugh or cry. Known throughout the Met as the Sweeney, the Flying Squad was one of the most coveted postings in the whole of the force. I didn't think you could get on to it unless you were a man first and a Freemason second.

I was to be one of the twelve officers on Team Ten, which was among the top four squads specializing in the detection of high-profile armed robberies. The timing of my posting coincided almost exactly with an Act of Parliament making working women equal, so I was not only about to start a fantastic new job, I was finally going to get a man's wage for doing so.

As I closed the DCI's door behind me, I cried: 'Whoopee!' and leapt into the air. All thoughts of Renata and the man who attacked her would have to go on hold for a while, I thought, as I went to clear my desk and pack away my pot plant. I would never allow myself to forget her, but suddenly it seemed to me that I had bigger fish to fry.

The Flying Squad was, and still is, the tops. Created in 1919 and so named because of the 'flying squads of picked detectives . . . ready to go anywhere at any time', it was designed as the country's élite detective force against professional armed robbery, and those admitted to its ranks were hand-picked for their proven track record in divisional or central CID policing.

Originally, the Squad consisted of twelve detectives borrowed from divisional police stations, who had to make do with two horse-drawn covered wagons. It was regarded very much as a loose cannon, roaming across London, investigating whatever crimes took its fancy and without any real external supervision.

Detective Inspector Walter Hambrook, one of the original founders of the Squad, wrote in the 1920s:

> The work of a Flying Squad officer demands many qualities of a high order. He must, of course, be thoroughly acquainted with criminals and their ways and have an unerring knowledge of criminal law and police procedure, but beyond that he must have an unbounded love and unflagging enthusiasm for the work, be patient to endure many hours of silent watching and waiting, ever alert, stout-hearted, agile and cool in the presence of danger.

The philosophy was much the same sixty years later, and the attitude within the Met was that it was a tremendous privilege to be part of the Squad and God help anyone who complained.

It was January 1977 and from the moment I walked into New Scotland Yard in Broadway, off Victoria Street, wearing my smartest suit – a green wool jacket and skirt – briefcase in hand, my feet didn't touch the ground. I was about to join the *crème de la crème*, the squad known then at the Yard by its branch code C8 and identified by its swooping-eagle crest. As well as its tremendous kudos, it had an illustrious history of success, including the conviction of the gang who carried out the Great Train Robbery, not to mention the arrest of the Kray brothers.

But, lest I forget, it was also this particular team which had never before employed a woman detective sergeant. I was to be the very first, accompanied only by two other women, both detective constables. Of the 144 officers, 141 were men, and as I took the lift to the fourth floor, my palms sweaty, I half expected the lot of them to be standing on the other side of the sliding doors, arms folded, waiting for me. The truth was, of course, very different.

I walked into a near-empty office, as all the officers were out on operations. The familiar sight of discarded coffee cups, overflowing ashtrays, littered files and scattered newspapers heartened me and as I put my briefcase to one side and smoothed down my skirt ready to report to my new detective inspector, I suddenly felt much more at ease.

My new boss was called Ezra Pritchard and rumour had it he had never worked with a woman detective in his twenty-year career in the Metropolitan Police. He was an old-school police officer, very much a man's man, and from the way he looked at me through his thick-rimmed spectacles I was not sure he liked the idea one little bit.

'So, Bristow. How does it feel to be the first woman DS on my team?' he asked in his lilting Welsh accent.

'Terrifying, sir,' I responded truthfully, and he half smiled.

'Well, in the spirit of equal opportunities, I'd like to welcome you into the fold and, as you'll be taking an equal share of the workload, I've nominated you to become a trained shot. You do want to be authorized to carry a firearm, don't you, Bristow?' He waited for the colour to return to my face.

'Yes, sir,' I spluttered, my voice tremulous.

'Good,' he said, as he straightened some papers on his desk. 'Only all our shots are volunteers and I wouldn't like you to think you were being put under any pressure, so speak up if you've changed your mind. I'm not about to bite your head off. Do you understand?'

'Yes, sir,' I said, not entirely sure of the veracity of his last words.

'Excellent,' he grinned. 'You'll have a week to get acquainted with your new desk before reporting to the police firing range at Holborn Police Station next Monday morning.' As he walked off, leaving me shivering and asking myself exactly what I had 'volunteered' for, I sensed he was chuckling quietly to himself.

My firearms training began with what was called the 'basic course'. It lasted a week and took place in the bowels of Holborn Police Station, where there is a dedicated firearms range. I was the only woman on the course with five men and I had never felt so out of place in my life. But of course, yours truly, Dead Eye Dick, was never going to let the rest of them know that.

The first time I had ever held a gun in my life was when my

training instructor handed me the Model 10 Smith & Wesson .38 Special, a standard-issue revolver. It felt peculiar to the touch, lighter than I expected and warmer than the cold steel it was made from. I glanced around at the rest of my class and none of them looked as if they were giving the weapon a second thought, so I straightened my neck, cleared my throat and paid attention to what the instructor was telling us.

'It's all about safety,' he said, 'and there's no limit to the level of care needed when handling a gun. Always make sure the nose of the weapon is pointing in the right direction and however accustomed you become to handling a weapon, and many of you will carry them regularly, you must never forget the enormous responsibility you bear every time you leave the police station armed.' I found myself nodding in total agreement. 'As long as you know what you are doing and you always follow the safety procedures, you will never unnecessarily endanger yourself or anyone else around you. The saying "Better safe than sorry" is never more appropriate than when handling a weapon.'

For hours on end we were taught loading, unloading and safety procedures. It was a frustrating and stressful task, not made any easier by the competitive nature of the men. I was determined not to be the last to get it right each time. Fortunately for me, there were a couple of real butterfingers in the class, and my smaller hands seemed to work faster than a lot of the blokes'.

Initially we were given dummy bullets, known as drill rounds, to practise with, and were directed to our individual spots at the end of a long row of target ranges, all set up like bowling alleys. Kitted out with goggles and padded headphones to protect our eyes and ears, we all looked very professional but none of us could yet envisage how the 'real thing' would eventually feel.

Using drill rounds I became familiar with handling the revolver and was looking forward to competing against my fellow-pupils on the range. At that stage it all felt like a bit of a game. As I closed one eye and aimed my weapon at the traditional bull's-eye targets, I couldn't relate it to any real-life experiences where I, as a police officer, might be required to use a weapon, because I simply hadn't been through any of that yet. This was just like being on the shooting alley at the funfair where, if I hit enough of the little yellow ducks, I might win a cuddly toy. *Click, click, click*, the gun went as I pulled the trigger.

But when they gave me live bullets, it was a completely different ballgame. Taking that much more care, it felt as though I was now acting in slow motion and, instead of feeling confident and relaxed, I was suddenly aware that I was holding something which I had to treat with enormous respect and which made me very nervous. With a loaded weapon, I felt transformed, and it scared the hell out of me. My new target, pasted on to a board, was a black and white image of a 'criminal' in sunglasses, pointing a handgun at me. The board span round so that the target was suddenly facing me and, levelling my fully loaded revolver at him, I had to fire quickly in groups of two. The noise and the smell of the ammunition being propelled from the chamber permeated my senses and ricocheted around inside my head.

When I looked up and saw that the bullet had left its mark in the target's chest, I breathed the words 'Bloody hell!' and suddenly wanted to laugh. God forbid I ever have to fire this thing for real, I thought.

The terminology used for this type of training was typically long-winded and mind-bogglingly convoluted: 'Sense of direction shooting geared to close confrontation'. In other words, my role on the Flying Squad was likely to bring me into face-to-face contact with armed villains on the street and at such close quarters there would not be enough time to aim before shooting. 'Don't waste time,' the instructor said. 'Just fire at his bulk and STOP him. Remember you must act quickly to protect innocent members of the public.'

The word 'kill' was never spoken by the instructors, and it failed to crop up in any of the terminology. But the operative word 'stop' was used time and again. We were specifically told not to fire at the extremities, like the head, arms or hands, because of the possibility that we would miss, thus giving the villain a good chance to shoot at us instead. 'Go for the chest or the middle of the trunk,' we were told. In other words, aim for the heart. I shuddered at the thought.

The instructor told us he wanted to see clear groupings of paired shots in the upper trunk of the target but, as I looked up and saw a neat array of holes where bullets fired by others intended for the trunk had found their way into the ceiling, I grinned. At least I had managed to shoot in roughly the right direction.

I was also trained in 'aim shooting', but this was secondary to the training I received for 'close-quarter confrontation'. My instructor was anxious to remind me that training women was particularly difficult because, according to him, we lack aggression. He was forever telling me to grip the gun, not fondle it. 'Women's hands are too small for good gun control,' he said dismissively. Despite what he saw as my inherent weaknesses, I somehow qualified and was issued with a pink authorization card, which was proof of my ability to use firearms. It also meant that I had scored at least 7 out of 10 in my final test. Not bad for a woman.

After learning the basic techniques on the range, we were taken by coach to the open-air range at Lippitts Hill, Loughton, Essex, where, we were told, the real fun started. In a specially set-up outdoor area surrounded by sandbags, a dozen or so wooden boards similar to those that had previously been pasted with target criminals were ready and waiting for us, only this time they were all facing away. I had been taught to adopt the classic 'Starsky and Hutch' stance and with the gun pointing directly out in front of me I ran through the range, ready to fire paired shots (two quick rounds) directly into the torso of any villain who suddenly turned on his board to face me.

As I ducked and dived between the boards, I heard the distinctive noise they made as their remote-controlled catches were released and they span round, vibrating slightly with the motion. Turning to face them, I fired my weapon directly at their hearts. Just to make life interesting, the range controller sometimes released the catch on a board showing a woman holding a baby in her arms. God knows how many young mums I accidentally 'killed' before I finally got my man, but I certainly learnt a salutary lesson.

After that it was on to search and rescue techniques. Dispatched to the door of a mock house, we learnt how to burst in through the front door in groups of threes, one on his belly on the floor providing cover, one through the door after he or she (and in my case it was invariably she) had kicked it in and one, back against the wall, ready to fire and follow the door kicker through. It was all classic, adrenalin-pumping stuff, and once we were in we had to try and locate our 'gunman' and any hostages he was holding, and conclude the whole operation quickly and cleanly. It beat typing out invoices any day.

The final stage was something called 'familiarization in cross weapon training', which was a fancy way of saying we were taught how to use a whole range of weapons in case one of our colleagues was injured or killed and we had to take over where they had left off. What a thought. Among those weapons was a Heckler & Koch MP5 sub-machine gun, the most menacing piece of machinery I have ever held in my hands. When my finger exerted the slightest pressure on the trigger, the noise it made was incredible and the vibration from the rounds as they powered out of the weapon rattled the fillings in my teeth.

Once my training was complete, I was sent back to Scotland Yard, the first woman 'shot' on the Flying Squad. This meant that from now on, God help me, I could be called upon in any situation where it was thought that firearms might be used against the public or the police. Whenever I presented my pink card, I would be handed a weapon and live ammunition, and within minutes could be facing a real-life high-street bank robber, with a real-life young mum standing behind him. I prayed that I would never be called.

My prayers were not answered; I hardly had time to introduce myself to my new colleagues before rushing out on 'operations'. So many times I seemed to be up at dawn, then was left to sit in the back of vans for hours on end, waiting for the 'job' to come off. The anticipation was indescribable and, if I was one of the unfortunate shots chosen for that day, then I would feel like a wound-up spring until I had safely returned my Smith & Wesson to the armoury. The adrenalin would start pumping the minute I picked up the weapon and wouldn't stop until I signed it back in.

There weren't any holster belts small enough to fit around my waist – the ones that did exist invariably flapped around by my knees, which was no good to anyone and made me look more than a little obvious. So I was given the smallest holster available and punched some extra holes in the leather so that it could be done up tight around my middle.

Another shot would be paired up with me, and we sat side by side in the back of an unmarked Transit van, ready to be first out of the doors if we spotted the armed robbers we had all been trailing for weeks. If the job looked like it was on, it would be 'Go! Go! Go!' and no turning back.

As I flew out of the doors and across the street, seeking out my targets and hoping to hell that they wouldn't fire at me, I would take in every detail of the scene in those first few seconds out of the darkened Transit. It was always a scary time, with my eyes darting left and right to try and identify the robbers and distinguish them from any innocent passers-by.

Once spotted, I had to focus my attention on the man in my sights, watching his every move, trying to assess whether or not he was going to draw his weapon and fire. Hoping fervently that he wasn't going to do anything stupid and that I wasn't going to have to shoot at him, I would hear my own voice reciting again and again in my head: 'Stop. Armed police. Put down your weapon.' It would take a few more seconds before I realized that the drum beating in my ears would have drowned out any answer.

When a suspect gave up the fight, the relief was tangible. To see him surrender was the sweetest of feelings. After all those hours of tensed nerve and muscle, all those days of watching and waiting, it was over. The job was done. And, thankfully, I was still alive and in one piece. Wound up beyond reason and ready to look death or serious injury in the eye, it would take me an age to come down from that point and start to feel the pressure loosen its hold.

By the time I handed my gun in, I would be fit to burst and the only way I knew how to release myself from that level of tension was to have a bloody good drink. I had come to accept alcohol as the only answer and I didn't need asking twice.

6

IN THE EARLY HOURS OF A FILTHY WET FEBRUARY MORNING IN
1977 I was sitting in the fifth-floor canteen at Scotland Yard. I
would have given my eye teeth to have been tucked up in bed.
Dropping two sweeteners into my mug of coffee, I swung my
weary legs on to a small table and yawned noisily. After
my first few weeks with the Flying Squad, I could hardly
keep my eyes open due to the number of late nights and early
mornings I was doing. I began to wonder what I had let myself
in for. My spirit was willing but my flesh was showing definite
signs of weakness.

Sitting opposite me was Detective Constable Maureen
Dennison, known to all as 'Mo', an old friend and colleague
who had taught me beats as my parent constable when I first
joined the force and was now teaching me the ropes all over
again as one of the two women DCs on the Flying Squad. 'So,
remind me, what strings did you pull to get up here?' she asked,
a smile tugging at the corners of her mouth.

'Believe it or not, none; I was asked if I wanted this posting,'
I answered truthfully. 'And let's have a bit of respect. Remember, I'm meant to be the senior officer here, Dennison.' I
grinned and lit a cigarette, carefully creating a large smoke
ring. Mo hadn't changed a bit. She was about ten years my
senior and a legend in her own right. A cracking copper by

anybody's standards, it was great to be working with her again.

'Still a *Daily Telegraph* reader, then?' she derided, pointing at my newspaper. 'Have you got to grips with the big words yet, or do you just buy it to look intelligent?'

I snatched the newspaper from the table and opened it in front of her, deliberately holding it up between us as I read. She picked up her *Daily Mail* and we sat in silence for a while.

The papers were full of details of the forthcoming celebrations for the Queen's Silver Jubilee, and the police were celebrating success at having found an IRA bomb factory in Liverpool, a week after seven terrorist bombs had exploded in London's West End. Amnesty International were reporting that during Idi Amin's reign of terror thousands had been executed.

As I turned the pages, my eye was caught by a photograph of a pretty young blonde. My mouth smiled involuntarily at her carefree face, suntanned and beaming with promise. What a beauty. But my heart sank as I read the headline alongside it: CRICKETER'S GIRLFRIEND VANISHES.

The article continued:

Scotland Yard's Murder Squad joined the search yesterday for Miss Rosemary Jane Shepherd, 24, girlfriend of Middlesex cricketer and Old Etonian Roderick Kinkead-Weekes. Miss Shepherd, an attractive blonde who was born in Melbourne, and has been living with her cousin in Clifton Hill, St John's Wood, has been in England for six years. She works for an art dealer, the Caelt Gallery in Westbourne Grove.

She left home at 8.40 p.m. on Friday and called at a delicatessen in Queensway to pick up some smoked trout and other things for a meal she was to prepare for herself and Mr Roderick Kinkead-Weekes. She never reached the house and Mr Kinkead-Weekes, who recently returned from an MCC tour, raised the alarm.

Her blue Mini, KGM 300P, which had been cleaned on Thursday, was found on Tuesday parked in Elgin Crescent, a turning off Westbourne Grove. There was a considerable quantity of mud inside the car and mud on the outside which police were examining yesterday.

Miss Shepherd is described as 5ft 5in tall, an attractive blonde who was wearing blue jeans tucked into brown Cossack-type boots, a man's shirt of light colour over a pale polo-neck jumper and was carrying a red soft-leather hand-bag with a shoulder strap.

She wore a gold chain necklet with a gold replica of the cartoon character 'Woodstock' as the pendant, a Gucci watch in modern style set in a grey wristband, a variety of gold rings and a heavy gold-coloured bangle.

Police are particularly anxious to trace any witnesses who saw the car being parked in Elgin Crescent or at any other time. They also want any friends of Miss Shepherd to get in touch with them. Chief Supt Henry Mooney of Scotland Yard is in charge of investigations. People whom the police have spoken to so far say Miss Shepherd's unexplained dis-appearance is completely alien to her character.

'Shit!' I said, as the cigarette I was holding burnt down to my fingers. I dropped the butt on the floor and stamped on it. Mo looked up. I glanced across to the front page of her newspaper and saw the same photograph, staring at me from the other side of the table. I snatched the paper from her hand, tearing a corner as I did so.

'What's got into you?' Mo cried, grumpily.

'Have you seen this?' I said, pointing to the story.

'Yes, another poor kid's gone missing,' she replied. 'So what?'

'Not what but who,' I said. 'I bet I know the bad bastard who did this.'

'Know him?' She was interested now.

'Well, not exactly know him, but you remember that woman Renata I told you about, at Notting Hill? This could have been her. It is all too bloody similar to be a coincidence.' Mo asked me to explain. I grabbed a paper napkin and reached for a pen in my pocket. 'Look at this area,' I said, drawing a line. 'This is Ladbroke Grove and this is where Renata was abducted. There is Queensway, just to the east, and here,' I drew a curved line, 'is Elgin Crescent, where Rosemary Shepherd's Mini was found abandoned. They're right on top of each other.'

'But just because these incidents occurred close to each other doesn't mean it's the same man. We don't even know what happened to this woman,' said Mo, pointing to my newspaper. 'Don't you think you're jumping the gun a little bit?'

'It isn't just the area,' I said, desperate not to lose faith in my hunch. 'It's the car, a small car, and the victim, an attractive young blonde. Look,' I said, grabbing the newspaper and pointing to the photograph, 'this could have been Renata.'

Mo picked up the paper and studied the story more carefully. She smiled. 'You see who's investigating this?'

'I know,' I said sheepishly. 'Henry Mooney. It might as well be God.'

Chief Superintendent Henry Mooney had a formidable reputation at Scotland Yard. Working alongside the legendary 'Nipper' Read (the famous detective who apprehended the gang responsible for the Great Train Robbery), he played a major role in locking up the Kray twins for the murder of George Cornell in the Blind Beggar pub. He was, on his own admission, 'no stranger to strange death' and brought considerable authority and expertise to a perplexing case.

'Well, you'll just have to go and see him, Carol,' Mo told me.

'Mooney?' I exclaimed. 'What on earth would I say to him? And why would he listen to me? He'd laugh me out of the room.'

'Quite possibly, but now you've made a tentative link, you know you'll have to follow it through. At least you'll have done your bit.'

I realized what she was saying was true, but I suddenly felt very tired and wanted nothing more than to go home, have a hot bath and a drink. 'I'll think about it,' I said, reaching across the table for her Benson & Hedges.

'No, you won't,' she answered, grabbing them back before I could take one. 'You'll go and see him, and you'll go and see him now.' I found myself wondering again which one of us was the sergeant, me or Mo. But she was right and we both knew it.

The incident room at Paddington Green nick was still being

set up on 10 February 1977. It was only six days after Miss Shepherd had been reported missing and officers were coming and going, furniture was being moved in and telephone lines installed. I recognized a young detective from Marylebone Lane thumping the old photocopier in frustration. The air was thick with cigarette smoke as I picked my way through the noise and fog towards him.

'Hiya, Pete,' I said, uneasily.

'Carol. Hi. What are you doing back over this way? I thought you were with the Sweeney now, kicking down doors.'

'I am. I just, er, well, I need to speak to Mr Mooney.'

His left eyebrow arched. He studied my obvious discomfort and decided not to add to it. 'First on the left through the double doors,' he said, pointing down the corridor behind me. 'And, good luck.'

I stuffed my hands in my blazer pockets and wandered down the corridor, looking for nameplates on the doors. Just past the gents' loo, a wood-veneer door with the letters DCS came up on the left. I hesitated and then knocked.

'Come,' a deep voice bellowed from within. I turned the aluminium handle and stepped inside.

Henry Mooney was standing at a dirty window in the cluttered office, slipping some papers into the top drawer of a filing cabinet. Taller and slimmer than I imagined, with a balding, domed head, immaculately dressed in a mud-brown suit with a cream shirt and brown brogues, he looked like a country squire filing away his milk quotas. He carried on with his task, and without turning round said: 'Yes?' in a deep Irish brogue.

I stood in front of his desk, shuffled from foot to foot and coughed. Mooney turned and peered at me over his large owlish spectacles.

'Yes?' he queried, more impatiently now. His reputation for being a direct, blunt Irishman was well known.

'Sorry, sir, DS Carol Bristow, Flying Squad, sir. I'm sorry to bother you but I just wanted a quick word. It's about Rosemary Shepherd.'

'Janie,' he said.

'Sir?'

'She was known as Janie,' he continued, as if explaining something to a child.

'Sorry, sir. Janie Shepherd.'

'Well, what is it?'

I folded and unfolded my hands in front of me, trying to find the right way of telling him what I suspected without wasting his time. Eventually, I blurted out: 'I think I may have interviewed his last victim, sir.'

'Whose?' He stood staring at me as if I had just landed from outer space.

'The man who abducted Rosemary, sorry Janie, Shepherd, sir.'

'We don't even know if she was abducted yet,' he replied, sitting at his desk and taking off his glasses to examine me better.

'Well, yes, I know, sir, only, well, I think she may be dead, don't you? And everything about her is very similar to this other woman I met last year, sir, Renata Chandler, who was attacked in her car less than half a mile from where Janie's abandoned Mini was found, sir.'

I had his attention. 'Go on,' he said.

I told him all that I knew, how I had spent hours interviewing Renata and how similar she looked to Janie. I spoke about the car, the rape and the attempted murder. I expressed the fear I had felt then that this man would attack again, and I said that although Notting Hill hadn't found Renata's attacker yet, if he spoke to them he might get a lead on the Janie Shepherd case.

Half-way through my hurried speech, he started taking notes. I saw him write 'Notting Hill', 'Renata Chandler' and the date of her attack. When I had finished speaking, he stared down at the piece of paper for a moment and, without looking up, murmured: 'Yes, thank you.'

I stood uneasily, wondering what to do. He just sat and studied his notes.

'Thank you very much,' he said, suddenly looking up. I knew it was time to leave and I backed out of his room, shutting the door behind me. Just before it clicked shut, I heard him lift the telephone receiver. 'Pauline? Get me Notting Hill.'

I returned to Scotland Yard light of step and full of hope. Mo had been right. I was glad I had gone to see Mooney. Even if nothing came of it, I knew I had played my part. I had been true to myself and to Renata, the woman whose bruised and battered face still haunted my dreams. Despite such a brief meeting, I trusted Mr Mooney, and even if my hunch was wrong, I felt sure from the way he reacted that he would do all he could to check it out.

When I got back to my office I decided to speak to Renata. I wondered how she would feel, reading about Janie Shepherd, and I wanted to offer her my support. She sounded remarkably well, if still a little wobbly. 'I just phoned to see how you are,' I said.

'That's very kind. I'm much better, thank you, and getting stronger by the day.'

We exchanged pleasantries and I finished with: 'Well, if there is anything you need, anything at all that you want me to do, please call and I'll do whatever I can.' She promised she would and asked me if there was any news about the hunt for her attacker. I wondered if she had been reading the newspapers.

'No, nothing yet, but that doesn't mean we won't get him. You just concentrate on getting better and let us take care of the business end.' I couldn't help wishing, as I put the phone down, that Janie Shepherd had had such a lucky escape.

I followed the Shepherd case very closely for the next few weeks, watching every news bulletin and reading every article as the hunt for her abductor continued. Her family and friends initially feared she had been kidnapped because of her wealthy family background, and waited for a ransom demand from the kidnappers, but it never came. Within days, her boyfriend, Mr Kinkead-Weekes, told the *Sun*: 'I fear she is dead.'

Her mother, Angela Darling, and stepfather, John Darling, chairman of BP Australia, flew to London and appealed to Metropolitan Police Commissioner Robert Mark. DCS Mooney took them to one side and warned them to prepare for the worst. Mrs Darling gave an interview to a number of papers about her fears. 'The days have merged into one,' she said, chain-smoking. 'I tell the difference between night and day only by the sun. I face the very worst, most unpleasant facts, then the shutter comes down and persuades me she is alive. I don't permit myself to think about Janie as a person, as the daughter I last saw in France laughing in the snow.' I tried to imagine Janie in a ski suit, but could only see her as she had smiled at me from that first newspaper photograph.

When journalists discovered her family background, Janie was elevated from being the girlfriend of a Middlesex cricketer to an Australian heiress. Theories continued to abound about her being kidnapped but, like Henry Mooney, I never doubted for one moment that she had been raped and murdered.

I learnt a great deal about this young woman I had never been fortunate enough to meet. Janie Shepherd's middle-class upbringing in Australia had been filled with happiness and security until her father's untimely death from a massive heart attack, when she was just eleven years old. Anthony Shepherd, the head of the Australian Rootes car empire, was in his early fifties when he dropped dead after a round of golf.

Janie did not excel academically, but had a wide circle of friends and was immensely popular. Charming and sophisticated, astonishingly good-looking, she – like so many Australians before her – was consumed by the urge to travel. Fiercely independent, she eventually decided to strike out on her own and in the summer of 1971, aged just nineteen, she arrived in London to stay with her cousin Camilla and her husband Alistair Sampson, an antiques dealer, at their palatial home in St John's Wood. For Janie, it was a time of unbridled happiness and the start of a love affair with London that never waned.

Seven years after losing her husband, Janie's mother Angela married into one of the wealthiest and most influential families in Australia. John Darling IV was an old family friend and they settled into a magnificent ten-bedroom sandstone house with several thousand acres, just west of Sydney.

Angela Darling missed her daughter terribly and, when Janie returned to Australia for what was planned as a short Christmas holiday in the winter of 1972, she persuaded her to stay on for several months. Mrs Darling and her new husband offered her a fantastic new job opportunity, selling Middle Eastern rugs and carpets from a small boutique, and Janie jumped at the chance of such an exciting business venture.

But London was never far from Janie's thoughts and in early 1974 she returned to England, accepting an offer to live with friends in a shared rented flat. It was a wonderful time for her. She worked hard and moved happily among the circle of friends who made up the smart set of Chelsea. But Angela Darling still missed her daughter and, at the end of that year, she and her husband came to England for a holiday, and persuaded Janie to go home with them for a few months.

By February 1975, Janie was back in London living with the Sampsons. Still in love with London life, she decided to stay. She had inherited a small annuity from her late father but, unlike many girls in her position, Janie chose to work and got herself a job as a bookkeeper and general factotum in the Caelt Art Gallery in Westbourne Grove, earning £45 a week.

According to her friends and relatives, Janie was an open-faced, friendly girl, who adored swimming, liked to play tennis and loved to dance. She was great fun to be with and her family described her as the sort of girl who would sit with a tramp in the park, strike up a conversation with him, get to know all about him and then, if it was appropriate, she would press some money into his hand.

She later met and fell in love with Roddy Kinkead-Weekes, a solicitor who lived in a flat in Lennox Gardens, Chelsea. They made a handsome couple and were soon inseparable, sharing a love of the good things in life and a passion for cricket. Roddy had asked Janie to marry him and she had hinted that she might say yes later that year. Her life fell into a pleasant daily routine: working at the gallery, driving to Camilla's home in St John's Wood to change before leaving to spend the night with Roddy at his flat in Chelsea, and then in the morning travelling on to work.

There had been nothing unusual about her movements on the evening of Friday 4 February 1977 except that she disappeared. It was raining and before leaving Camilla's Janie had telephoned Roddy to tell him she would pick up some wine, cheese and smoked trout from one of the late-night supermarkets on her way over to see him. She left the house in St John's Wood at 8.40 p.m. after having a 'bubbly conversation' with Alistair and Camilla, whom she regarded as bosom buddies, telling them: 'I

138

must dash, I'm late.' The last they saw of her was as she drove off in her shiny, recently valeted, dark-blue Mini 1275 GT with its FOR SALE sign in the rear window, planning to stop at the Europa Foodstore in Queensway. She was never seen again.

When she had not arrived by 9 p.m., Roddy began to worry and called her home. The maid answered and confirmed that Janie had left at eight-forty. By ten he feared the worst and, assuming she must have been involved in a road accident, began phoning hospitals and St John's Wood Police Station. Alistair and Camilla Sampson arrived home from the cinema later that night to discover that their beloved Janie was missing. They too began ringing round friends and acquaintances, and eventually joined Roddy at his flat in the hope that she would turn up and give them some reasonable excuse for her unexplained delay.

When Roddy was satisfied that Janie hadn't been involved in an accident, he went to Chelsea Police Station at 3.45 a.m. on Saturday 5 February and officially reported her missing. The police transferred the case back to St John's Wood and circulated her description and that of her car after following up Roddy's calls to the hospitals without success.

Official enquiries could not find anyone who could be certain of seeing Janie with someone else, although a caretaker at a synagogue in Bank Place, Paddington, had reported seeing a young blonde girl and a dark-skinned man sitting in a Mini that night in the building's dimly lit car park with the radio turned up very loudly. When he had approached the car and asked them to move on, the man had driven off at high speed.

It was also discovered that someone had attempted to use Janie's cash card at the cashpoint at National Westminster Bank in the Brompton Road that night, but to no avail. The machine had swallowed her card which was later found by bank staff.

After a description of her car had been circulated to traffic wardens and police, it was found four days later in Elgin Crescent, Notting Hill, fifty yards from Ladbroke Grove. Parked at an unusual angle, it was caked in thick mud. Local residents said the car had been there since the early hours of 5 February, the morning after Janie disappeared.

The mud-splattered Mini was taken to the Metropolitan

Police Forensic Science Laboratory and carefully examined. Anyone looking inside realized that something dreadful had taken place. The cloth sunroof had two parallel knife slashes in it, the seat belt had been sliced clean through and the indicator arm on the steering column forcibly bent backwards. Clothes were strewn around the car, including the calf-length brown boots Janie had been wearing when she left home, and some of the provisions Janie had bought *en route* had been partially eaten and scattered in neighbouring gardens.

Forensic scientists who examined the composition of the shredded leaves and thick mud in the footwell of the Mini said her car had been driven out of London to a site with light chalky soil where beech, oak trees and hawthorn bushes grew. Palaeontologists from London University and mineralogists from ICI were asked to examine a minute fossil found in the soil samples on the car mats, to see if it belonged to a specific Home Counties area. This particular type of chalky mud was found in the region which stretched from Marlborough in the west to Bishops Stortford in the north-east. Police then tried to calculate the number of miles the Mini had travelled and initially favoured the Chilterns as the most likely area to which Janie's car had been driven. This speculation became a near-certainty when it was confirmed that the geological and botanical features of the area, coupled with the accessibility to the M40 motorway, fitted into the equation perfectly. Helicopters were sent up over the Thames Valley, Hertfordshire and elsewhere to look for signs of a freshly dug grave.

Her mother and stepfather were determined to do all they could to help. They bought Ordnance Survey maps of the Home Counties areas and for sixty-five days they travelled little-used country lanes and searched fields and hedgerows, copses and ditches, looking for the very discovery they dreaded most. Mrs Darling told reporters: 'Where is Janie? I know she was raped . . . I know she was murdered. It is so futile to look but I must do something.'

Numerous well-meaning people, who fell into the category of dowsers and clairvoyants, began to contact the police with information, all of which was investigated. An eighty-seven-year-old woman from Switzerland rang to say that when she lived in Notting Hill in 1914 a murder had taken place which had never been solved. She felt sure the same man was responsible, and gave a graphic description of events to a senior detective.

I telephoned my mate Pete at Paddington Green to see exactly what evidence had been found. He told me that Janie had probably changed, or been forced to change, into the spare set of clothes she had taken in her car to wear the following day. Police had also found chewing-gum wrappers and peanut shells in the car, but they knew that Janie did not eat either. A single negroid hair had also been found in the car and a suspicious knife recovered from a garden nearby.

As clear proof of sexual assault, Pete said the seats were covered in semen that showed that the attacker had an A-secretor blood group. Officers also found a discarded, recently used tampon on the floor of the car. Poor girl, I thought, shuddering and remembering Renata. Nobody who looked inside that car could possibly have believed that Janie was still alive. Henry Mooney told reporters that one look at the interior showed him that 'something outlandish' had taken place. But, dead or alive, where was she?

The weeks and months flew by. I was busier than ever on the Flying Squad, kicking in doors and lying in obbo vans watching robbers and thieves at work; a hard core of professionals, who toted sawn-off shotguns as tools of their trade and regarded arrest and imprisonment as little more than an occupational hazard.

Unfortunately for them, however, it was the era of the 'supergrass', the bank robbers caught red-handed who then shopped all their mates in the hope of getting a minimal sentence. Bertie Smalls, an overweight north Londoner in his mid-thirties, with a Mexican-style moustache and a weakness for gambling and booze, was the first to do it in 1973. He and four others had carried out a textbook robbery on a branch of Barclays Bank in Wembley, getting away with £138,000. Smalls went to Torremolinos in Spain to sun himself after the raid, but was arrested on his return and made it clear from the outset that he was keen to reach some sort of deal with the police.

Once he had started the ball rolling by offering to betray all his past criminal associates and testify against them in exchange for his immunity, we had some difficulty stopping the rest of them from following suit. It was a vicious circle. With the help of these supergrasses and others, our arrest rate shot through the roof. Smalls confessed to over twenty robberies netting a total of £1.5 million and named more than thirty individuals. The more robbers we arrested, the more they decided to talk, which led to even more arrests – and so it went on.

The Commissioner was delighted because all of a sudden several of the so-called 'untouchable' London gangsters were being arrested and imprisoned for very long terms. But the work it created for us was phenomenal. If all 144 of us had worked twenty-four hours a day, seven days a week, we would still never have kept up. I couldn't have chosen a better time to be on the Flying Squad.

Not only were we watching and waiting to catch all the buggers in the act, but once they had been caught and persuaded to turn Queen's evidence we had to protect them day and night because the blokes they had grassed up would have paid handsomely to have them topped. It was a very exciting time. Within a very short period, many of the biggest names in the underworld were behind bars and the annual rate of armed robberies in the Metropolitan Police area remained static for the first time in years.

Among those that I had direct contact with was Maurice O'Mahoney, arrested in connection with a £17,000 armed robbery near Heathrow Airport. He later confessed to his part in over a hundred crimes – including thirteen robberies – involving the total theft of more than £200,000, in return for a new identity and a reduced sentence.

My colleagues and I took it in turns to guard O'Mahoney while he was in custody at Chiswick Police Station. Every effort had been made to keep him as comfortable as possible in the circumstances, with a small bed-sit-type room in which he could play cards, smoke, drink and eat what he liked.

We sometimes escorted him on visits home to his family, or

to other places outside the police station, but mostly a couple of us would sit and play crib with him for hours on end and laugh our socks off at some of the stories he told us about his exploits. Whatever else he was, he was one of the most amusing men I have ever met and some of the capers he told us about were like scenes from the *Keystone Cops*.

It wasn't all gun-toting, high-danger stuff. On one occasion Mo and I were sent to protect a group of toms who had asked for our help after suffering from a number of violent robberies in the west London area. The thieves presumably believed that the prostitutes wouldn't dream of calling in the Old Bill, so they felt they were on to some easy pickings. But they were wrong. Whatever one thought about their way of life, the toms had their own moral code when it came to violent robbery and they were having none of it.

Mo Dennison and I were mobile, in that we were authorized to drive our own specially equipped motor cars on duty. Some officers had to rely on squad cars for transport, but as our vehicles had been fitted out with police radios she and I could be off at a moment's notice and operate looking like pretty ordinary women in a very ordinary car. My call sign was 'Central 822' and I was mighty proud of it.

At very short notice, we were dispatched to a basement flat in Kensington to guard Roxanne, one of the women in question, and keep an eye out for the thieves. While we sat waiting, hoping to catch the thugs in the act, Roxanne carried on with her normal business and we became surprisingly good friends. She told us her tragic life story – how she was sexually abused when very young and had to work the streets as a single parent to pay for the upkeep of her children – as well as some pretty amazing tales about what she got up to with her clients. I have been wary of cucumbers ever since.

One afternoon I was drinking a cup of tea with her when there was a ring on the doorbell and Roxanne – dressed in a see-through coffee-coloured chiffon négligée over bra and panties – answered the door. As I lurked behind it, peering through the crack, I could see, to my amazement, a red-faced young man with his exposed penis in his hand. He stood there and stuttered that he was prepared to pay her £20 for touching her intimately in the open doorway. 'I j-j-j-just want to t-t-t-t-touch you,' he told her. 'N-n-n-n-no sex, j-j-just a f-f-f-eel.' His face was bright scarlet by now. Roxanne knew she was on to a good thing and quickly got the measure of this poor lad, who was quite obviously a virgin.

'You don't want to do that, not here and now,' she said. 'I've got a much better idea. Give me another tenner and you can take off my underwear and nightie – they're both still warm – and take them home with you.' The boy – who could clearly have been persuaded into anything by this vision of loveliness – handed over £30 and fumblingly removed her clothing before running off up the stairs, clutching them to his chest.

Bold as brass and in broad daylight, she had allowed him to strip her in the basement doorway. She then wandered back inside, stark naked, counting her money with a huge grin on her face. 'Well, I certainly hope he comes back,' she said as she closed the door. 'The whole lot cost me less than a fiver from a stall in the market.'

I was as happy and fulfilled as I had ever been on the Flying Squad, but my mind was never far from Janie Shepherd. Out of the blue, I got a call from Ted at Notting Hill who phoned to tell me that they had arrested a man in connection with the Renata Chandler case.

'Henry Mooney moved in on the investigation and took over from Boorman,' Ted said. 'He looked again at David Lashley, the man I told you about, only this time he went round and nicked him personally. He doesn't exactly hang about, does he?'

Ted told me that Renata had picked Lashley out of eleven men on an ID parade at Harrow Road. All the men were black, given identical dark-framed glasses to wear and were similar in appearance and build. Renata was so terrified of seeing her attacker again that she wore a scarf round her head so that only her eyes were showing. Mooney reported to his senior officers that the horror of her experience was still so 'vivid in her mind' eight months after the attack that she was very 'apprehensive for her safety' and liable to 'burst into tears' with stress.

Renata had been shown into the room where all the men were seated. One by one, they were asked to stand and say: 'Hello, how are you,' before sitting down again. Renata identified Lashley like a shot and placed her hand on his shoulder from behind. The minute she heard him speak, she told officers, she was positive that he was the man who attacked her. She was led from the room in tears.

'Word is that Mooney thinks he is responsible for abducting and killing Janie Shepherd,' said Ted. 'He asked him what he was doing the night she disappeared and he claimed he was at home in bed. But they searched his car, and guess what they found? Chewing-gum wrappers and peanut shells. The guy eats them all day long. He is also an A secretor and the hair found in Janie's car is similar, if not identical, to his.'

'But, Ted,' I said, confused, 'Lashley was ruled out earlier because he didn't have the scar on his neck that Renata described.'

'That's right,' Ted responded. 'It seems we were badly misled. Lashley has the scar on his neck exactly where Renata described it.'

As bad bastards go, David Ronald Lashley was about as bad as you could get. Born on 2 September 1939 in Barbados, he was one of the most violent misogynists the Metropolitan Police had ever come across, and I never really found out why.

Nearly all the rapists I have ever dealt with have had a dysfunctional childhood of some description or other, quite often with domineering mothers, but I never uncovered enough about Lashley's past to understand fully the reasons he hated women, and white women in particular. All I was ever able to establish was that he was brought up alone by his mother in Barbados in very reasonable conditions.

His mother apparently ran a shop and Lashley left school at fourteen to help out with the family income. Working as a car sprayer, he prided himself on his physique and clean appearance, was an amateur boxer and spent much of his spare time weight training. It was a cruel twist of fate that Lashley sprayed cars for the Rootes Motor Company in Bridgetown, Barbados – the same company Janie's late father ran in Australia.

In 1961 he moved to England, looking for a better life. Settling in Southall with relatives, he worked first as a labourer and then as a coach sprayer, but was sacked for aggressive conduct to other (white) workers. He found another job as a car sprayer but was sacked again for fighting at work. He then took up employment as a driver for the London Electricity Board, based in Notting Hill Gate.

Not long after his arrival he met Jean Holland, a nineteen-year-old white woman, who was three years his junior and came from Wigan, Lancashire. She was pregnant by a former boyfriend and emotionally very vulnerable. Soon after the birth of her child, a son called Michael, she and Lashley set up home together and in April 1962 they were married. Lashley was kind and tender to his new family at first, but when Jean got pregnant by him his mood changed. He started to complain about young Michael and 'working for another man's son' and insisted that Jean place her first-born, then aged two, in a children's home. Jean, of course, refused, but as the arguments became more violent, she became a regular visitor to the local hospital with broken limbs and bruises (all of which she claimed had been caused by accidents in the home). Fearing for her safety, she capitulated and Michael was moved by the local authority to the National Children's Home in Harpenden, Herts. The same year Jean bore Lashley a baby girl.

Racked with guilt, Jean vowed to keep in touch with her son, and Lashley drove her to Harpenden once a month to visit him. They would have taken the B651 from west London, passing Nomansland Common in Wheathampstead, where Lashley stopped occasionally to give Jean driving lessons.

Not long afterwards Jean gave birth to their second child, a son named Mark. The following year, in 1965, when she realized she was pregnant again, Lashley told her he could not afford any more children and literally dragged her to a back-street abortionist, who bungled the operation. The baby, a little girl, was born but died nine days later. Lashley showed no compassion and refused to attend the funeral. After that, with her heart all but broken, Jean virtually ignored him.

By 1969 their marriage was in serious trouble and Lashley

was looking elsewhere for sexual gratification, often staying out late. His violence towards his wife had increased, as had his hatred for white women. He started to bring home stolen ladies' underwear and one night Jean returned home to find that he had forced himself upon their babysitter.

Between the months of April and November that year, the media dubbed him the 'Beast of Shepherd's Bush', as he cruised around west London at night, looking for attractive women driving home alone. Months passed before police identified the 'Beast' as Lashley. He would always follow the same routine: tailing his victims in his own vehicle, stopping only when they pulled up outside their homes. As they made to leave the car, Lashley would pounce, confront and terrorize them. He favoured those in small cars such as Hillman Imps or Minis and would approach as the women parked their vehicles, when he would threaten them with violence, indecent assault or rape.

By November 1969 the attacks had become so violent that detectives feared for the safety of all women in the area. Some of those Lashley assaulted only avoided rape by chance. One girl frightened him off by sounding her car horn, another went limp as he knelt over her, which scared him so he ran off. Another was saved because her pet dog, locked alone in the house, heard her screams and barked. But each time Lashley failed, he went on to rape someone else.

An actress was assaulted in a Mini, after Lashley had approached her asking her the time. Another woman, a twenty-two-year-old physiotherapist, was raped in the back of her Morris Minor in the parking bay below her flat. The poor woman became pregnant from the rape and had to have an abortion. At least one of his victims told police that, because she fought desperately to fend off her attacker, he bound her hands together with strips of material.

The most recent assault was on an assistant librarian aged twenty-six who was brutalized on the night of 15 November. She arrived at her home in Stamford Brook after visiting friends and was parking her car when her attacker suddenly got into it and forced her on to the back seat. Her mother, who was reading as she waited up for her, was unaware as she lay in bed

147

that her daughter was involved in a dreadful struggle with her assailant outside in her car.

The victim described the getaway car as a white Ford Anglia and she remembered part of its registration number. After a massive police investigation involving dozens of officers at Shepherd's Bush nick (the station adjacent to mine at the time), David Lashley was arrested the following day, 16 November 1969. At his home, police found pornographic literature, sex aids and indecent photographs.

Detective Inspector Peter Cornish, who was appointed the investigating officer after Lashley's arrest, at first couldn't believe that the suspect could fit his enormous muscular body into the women's small cars. But using a police officer of similar build he proved both that it was possible and that, once inside, he could completely dominate and intimidate anyone else in the vehicle. It was clear that Lashley deliberately chose small cars because the confined space gave him total control over his victims. DI Cornish, who had a distinguished police career and went on to become Commandant of the Hendon training school, knew long before Lashley was identified that he was dealing with a very dangerous man.

After a half-hearted attempt to slash his wrists in custody, using a broken metal spoon, Lashley confessed to offences against a total of seven women, including one of whom the police were previously unaware. He told police: 'I'm sorry I did it. I don't understand why I did. I was depressed. I sometimes go with a prostitute because I like white girls. My wife is white.'

Five months later, on 16 April 1970, at the Old Bailey, thirty-one-year-old Lashley was convicted of three rapes, two indecent assaults and a robbery. Other sexual assaults on women were not proceeded with but were ordered to lie on file. He denied all the charges in court and claimed that the confession he made in police custody had been beaten out of him. His denial meant that all his victims had to go through the second ordeal of giving evidence against him in open court. The jury were unanimous in their guilty verdicts.

Sentencing him to a total of twelve years' imprisonment, Judge Mervin Griffiths-Jones told him: 'I don't suppose in the whole history of this court there has ever been so dreadful a case of rape. Certainly there has been no worse than this. You have behaved like an animal without thought of the damage physically and psychologically that you might do to the young ladies whom you attacked. There does not appear to be any reason to suppose that given the opportunity you would not continue to behave in that way again.'

Once I looked Lashley up in the files, I recalled reading about the arrest and imprisonment of the 'Beast of Shepherd's Bush' in the newspapers at the time, but I had no more involvement than that and his name had certainly not registered with me. His victims had all lived off my patch and I had more than my own fair share of rapes, indecent assaults and other crimes to deal with.

It was impossible to keep track of everything going on in other divisions. I was aware there had been another murder or rape, but it was rare to know any of the details unless they happened to touch on one of my cases, or someone started chatting about it over a drink in the pub. I was happy to keep my nose out of their investigations, and just bloody grateful that their bad bastard wasn't my bad bastard.

Lashley's wife Jean was so disgusted by what he had done that she divorced him while he was in prison, something for which it appears Lashley never forgave her and which fuelled his hatred of white women even more. He was released on parole on 1 March 1976, less than six years after he was sentenced to twelve years. With nowhere to live, he moved back in with his aunt and uncle in Southall, west London.

On 9 June, just fourteen weeks after his release from prison, he had almost certainly carried out the unprovoked and brutal attack on Renata Chandler. His compulsion to assault and ravage seemed unstoppable and increasingly murderous.

Mooney and his team had done everything within their power to find anyone who might have seen Janie with her abductor, but to no avail. More than six thousand people had been interviewed, television and newspaper coverage had reached saturation point and yet no one, not one single person, had come forward to give them the lead they desperately needed.

149

Approximately six hundred files were examined, each one belonging to a known sexual offender, and this inevitably threw up a large number of possible suspects in the Notting Hill and Chelsea areas. All of them were interviewed and eliminated from the inquiry once they had established alibis for the time of Janie's disappearance.

Lashley was still the best bet by far, and he could be linked to her Mini by the fact that mud found in his Vauxhall Victor car was similar to that discovered in hers. His body hair also closely resembled that which was found in the vehicle; he ate peanuts, chewed gum, and was an A-secretor blood group, which married up nicely with the semen samples.

But the most positive piece of circumstantial evidence concerned an oddly shaped white-handled knife which had been found stuck in the flower border of a garden near to Janie's abandoned Mini. When police took it to the canteen of the removals company where Lashley had been working, it was immediately identified by the manageress as the knife she had used as a potato peeler. Not only was she able to identify its unusual features, but she claimed it had gone missing from a drawer in the canteen immediately prior to Janie Shepherd's disappearance, on 4 February 1977. Lashley was a regular visitor to the kitchens, she told Mr Mooney.

During interviews, DCS Mooney asked Lashley: 'Come on, David, we know the score. Why not tell me where you hid her so we can give her a decent burial?'

Lashley smiled and said to the senior policeman: 'You are very clever,' but he would offer no more.

Like DCS Mooney, I did not need convincing that Lashley was responsible, but with scant evidence and no body, Mooney was unable to take the matter any further. He once described motiveless murder without a body as 'looking down the wrong end of a telescope'. It felt as if he was conducting an investigation in reverse, where the smallest detail could not be taken for granted. He was also painfully aware that the longer Janie's body lay undiscovered, the less likely it was to yield clues that could link Lashley to it.

7

ON 18 APRIL 1977, TWO YOUNG BOYS PLAYING ON NOMANSLAND Common, near Wheathampstead, Hertfordshire, came across the putrefied body of a young woman. The discovery was made just a few days after Janie's exhausted parents, Angela and John Darling, abandoned their vigil and flew back to Australia. Their ten-week search of fields and hedgerows had taken them to within a few miles of where their daughter's body had lain.

Janie's body was discovered on the very day that David Lashley appeared in a London magistrates' court and was committed in custody to a higher court for trial for the abduction, rape and attempted murder of Renata Chandler. The barristers and police, magistrates and clerks sifted through mounds of paperwork, witness statements and exhibits, deciding which of them should be sent on to the Old Bailey, where Lashley would face a judge and jury.

Just over ten weeks after Janie's disappearance, her sad remains were found twenty yards off the B651 St Albans-to-Wheathampstead road, two miles north of the cathedral city. Her body was covered with leaf mould and twigs and hidden in a small copse in a natural depression in the ground known locally as Devil's Dyke.

The two boys, Dean James, aged eleven, and Neil Gardiner,

aged ten, were on their Easter school holidays and were cycling home after a day out when they discovered what they first thought was nothing more than a bundle of rags. Examining the unusual mound of clothing, their hands came into contact with a human foot.

Shaken, they dropped their bikes and ran. Trying to convince each other not to be silly and telling themselves that they must have found a mannequin, they crept back to the scene to take another look. This time they saw blond hair and pedalled home as fast as they could, too frightened to stop and tell anyone what they had unearthed. It was dusk before Dean finally blurted out what he had seen to his father Peter. The local police were called and the boys, accompanied by their fathers, led detectives back to the scene.

Janie had suffered a terrible death. Her upper arms had been strapped across her chest with strips of sheeting. Her feet had been similarly tied. Her windpipe had been crushed and what was left of her body showed signs of mutilation with some sharp weapon, including what looked like the carving of the initial L into her left buttock. She had suffered extensive bruising and bore other signs of violence, although decomposition was too advanced to say categorically that she had been raped. It also meant that she could only be identified from dental records, her contact lenses and the distinctive jewellery she was wearing, including the Woodstock charm necklace and Gucci watch.

Detective Chief Superintendent Henry Mooney was alerted to the discovery at ten o'clock that night. Taking three of his senior detectives with him, he drove to the remote spot immediately, only to find that the body had already been moved to the mortuary for examination by Home Office pathologist Professor Cameron. Its removal denied him the opportunity to examine it *in situ*.

But what followed was even more of a blow. When he arrived at St Albans Police Station he was informed that DCS Ronald Harvey, head of Hertfordshire CID, was claiming the body – and the high-profile investigation – as his own.

Under Home Office rules at the time, it was the prerogative

of the constabulary responsible for the area in which a body was found to claim the investigation as their own, even if it meant – as in this case – that Mooney and his team would be effectively barred from any further involvement, despite their ten weeks' work.

The bureaucratic procedures, ludicrous to my mind, meant that Mooney would have to surrender every piece of evidence, every bit of helpful material, to the new investigators for them to begin again. In recent years these rules have changed, allowing discretion to be exercised in similar circumstances.

After putting forward all the arguments he could muster for why the case should remain with the team who had spent over two months investigating it, Henry Mooney, distinguished senior detective of twenty-eight years' standing, had little option but to accept the situation. A true professional, he never showed one iota of bitterness at the decision but, feeling that the time was right, he resigned from the Metropolitan Police within the week, taking early retirement to concentrate on his ambition to practise law. Now it was up to DCS Harvey to try to ascertain who was responsible for the abduction and murder of Janie Shepherd.

The next few months were full of frustrations and false leads for the officers investigating the case. Countless boxes of statements, documents and files had been transported by lorry from Paddington Green to St Albans Police Station and Mooney's team was disbanded before its members were allowed to reap the fruits of their labours.

The newly formed murder squad put their heart and soul into the investigation, reinterviewing all the chief witnesses and re-reading all the statements, but they achieved little more than had already been established. DCS Harvey re-examined all the evidence before him and went to see Lashley in custody. Henry Mooney, patient as ever, had managed to build up quite a rapport with Lashley, something which had taken him weeks to cultivate. When Harvey went to see Lashley, however, it was a different story. He simply denied everything, dug his heels in and refused to co-operate on any level.

DCS Harvey appealed for help from the public in his search

for clues and he asked the media to maintain their interest until the killer was caught. He disclosed the fact that Janie had been forced to change her clothing before she was killed, and that her original outfit had never been found. He said that when she was driven to Hertfordshire from west London she may have been sitting or propped upright in the front seat of her car.

A newly married couple who had driven behind Janie's Mini near Kings Langley, Herts, on the night she disappeared came forward and told police that they remembered seeing it because the number plate was similar to the husband's initials. They had laughed about the occupants because they thought the blond woman passenger was drunk. 'Every time the car turned or veered, she leant or fell sideways with the motion,' they said. Detectives hoped and prayed for Janie's sake that this meant she was already dead by this stage and that her murderer was just looking for somewhere quiet to dump her body.

The post mortem by Professor Cameron and the dental examination by expert Bernard Sims took more than four hours. It established that Janie had been killed by compression of the throat after putting up a courageous fight. There were multiple bruises and stab wounds to her body, as well as tiny pinprick injuries across her chest which Professor Cameron initially thought had been caused by the tip of a knife. He later realized they were caused by Janie's fingernails, dug into her own flesh as she lay face down, presumably being raped or tortured.

At the inquest into Janie's death on 24 October 1977, six months after her body was unearthed, the jury at St Albans Coroner's Court listened intently to all the evidence and returned the only verdict it could in the circumstances, that Janie Shepherd had been killed 'by a person or persons unknown'.

Later that afternoon she was cremated at Garston Crematorium near Watford, during a simple service attended by Angela and John Darling, Roddy Kinkead-Weekes and a few close friends. Her ashes were then taken home to Australia with her mother and stepfather.

In the absence of anything more than circumstantial evidence linking Lashley with Janie's body or car, a decision was made to wind down the Janie Shepherd murder inquiry. Lashley could rest easy, it seemed, for the time being. He had got away with murder and no one seemed able to achieve justice for poor Janie.

The team broke up, and the detectives who had given the case their best shot were transferred to more pressing duties. It was left to a handful of CID officers at St Albans to keep fielding the regular telephone calls from Janie's mother in her attempt to keep track of the investigation and encourage further action. As so often happens with murder investigations, and perhaps especially in Janie's case, the detectives had become personally involved and were bitterly disappointed that they had not been able to effect a just conclusion. They had spent an intensive period of their lives examining the minutest details of Janie's life and felt they had come to know her.

Her photograph, the same one I had first seen in the newspaper, had smiled out at them from the walls of each incident room. One of the officers on the case told me: 'There was something about her face, the way she looked, that made us all fall a little bit in love with her.' I knew exactly what he meant.

Disappointment was tempered only by the knowledge that the man everyone believed was responsible for Janie's brutal death was, at least, in custody and – they sincerely hoped – would stay there for a very long time. They would have to entrust justice to the Old Bailey judge and jury who would later try David Lashley for the attempted murder, rape and wounding of Renata Chandler. It would be up to those twelve men and women to make sure that he was removed from society and for the judge to pass adequate sentence never to allow him to hurt another woman again.

'Has the jury reached a verdict or verdicts upon which you are all agreed?' The bewigged court clerk was facing the jury at one of the more intimate courts at the Old Bailey on the final day of Lashley's three-week trial.

'We have,' replied the foreman, a stocky middle-aged man with bushy eyebrows and an earnest look.

It was 13 December 1977, eight months after Janie's body had been found and eighteen months after I had sat with

Renata for a day and a night in hospital, taking her statement. Now I stood alone in the wings of the court, watching and waiting. Renata had done her bit. She had given her evidence softly and in near-perfect composure at the trial. Under intensive cross-examination by the defence, who suggested that she must have been mistaken when she identified the man who attacked her, she had not faltered once. Giving every ghastly detail of her horrific sexual attack and reliving each second of the two hours she spent pleading for her life in her tiny car, she described coolly and calmly how the man in the dock had attempted to snuff out her life.

Only once did her eyes meet those of the man who attacked her. With a hint of a smile Lashley held her sad gaze, but she looked quickly away, vowing never again to set eyes on the man who had ruined her life.

Her career as a secretary was over, the court was told. The injury to her writing hand meant that she could no longer take notes or perform the duties required of her. Her employers had been very understanding; her family had, she said, been 'wonderful'; and her friends stoical in their support. But it wasn't enough. Nearly two years on, I could see she was still struggling, still trying to come to terms with the past. David Lashley had opened a door in her mind which could never be closed.

Apart from feeling a sense of duty, and needing to see the man responsible for her dreadful injuries, I secretly wanted to see Henry Mooney in action. I had been told that he always made a very good witness, but nobody had warned me just how brilliant he would be.

He was a natural. From the minute he walked up those few steps into the witness box, and stood stiff as a ramrod holding the Bible in his right hand as he repeated the oath in a theatrical boom, he captured the attention of every single person in that court. It was like watching a performance by Sir Laurence Olivier, as Mooney used his remarkable physical presence and resonant voice to describe to the jury exactly what the man in the dock had done to Renata. Lashley wasn't the only one who couldn't take his eyes off him. Any rapport the two men had prior to this was destroyed as, brick by brick, he slowly dismantled the wall of Lashley's defence that his lawyers had tried to build around him. The cornerstone of that wall was that Renata was mistaken, that Lashley was the victim of misidentification, an innocent man caught up in the nightmare of being wrongly accused of rape and attempted murder. But following so hard on the heels of Renata's damning evidence and the sympathy that had welled up in the hearts of everyone in the courtroom, Mooney's authoritative testimony drove home the final nails in Lashley's coffin.

That was the hour in which Lashley's hatred for Mooney really took seed – a hatred that was to endure and become so intense that several years later he would describe how he planned on his release to go to Mooney's house, lie in wait for him, rape and murder his wife in front of him and then slit his throat.

From where I was standing at the side of the court I could only see the shoulders, head and neck of Lashley, but it was enough to gauge his huge physique. His neck and head had no separate definition, they appeared as one large block of muscle and sinew.

As the trial drew to a close, the judge summed up the facts of the case and sent the jury out to consider their verdict. I wanted to scream 'Guilty!' at them as they closed the door of the deliberating room. All of us knew that the waiting – which would soon have us pacing around the floor – was the worst part.

I must have smoked forty cigarettes in the time it took them to come to a decision. I remember I had to send out for a new packet rather than go myself, for fear of missing their return. My hands were tightly clasped together as the ten men and two women jurors filed back into the jury box after four hours and the foreman rose to address the court. No matter how many times I have sat waiting for verdicts, the tension and the sense of moment never fail to set off the butterflies in my stomach; this was no exception. Please, if there is a God up there, let them have made the right decision, I prayed.

'On count one, the attempted murder of Renata Chandler. Do you find the defendant David Ronald Lashley guilty or not guilty?' I held my breath as the court clerk asked the foreman for the answer we all wanted to hear.

'Guilty.'

I exhaled loudly, along with several others in the court. I wanted to jump up and shout, 'Yes!' across the courtroom, but I stopped myself. I watched Lashley's huge shoulder muscles tense as the four prison officers in the dock each took one step closer.

'On count two, the rape of Renata Chandler. Do you find the defendant guilty or not guilty?'

'Guilty.'

I clapped my hands together. The clerk read out the four further charges against Lashley, the second rape, so callous in its execution; the indecent assault; wounding with intent to cause grievous bodily harm; and possession of an offensive weapon, the knife with which he had tried to amputate her hand.

'Guilty. Guilty. Guilty. Guilty.' The words rang out across the silent courtroom. The thick rope of muscles across Lashley's back twisted and tightened. A general hubbub filled the court as the legal profession and members of the public shifted in their seats and released the tension in their shoulders. Then silence fell across the room like a heavy velvet curtain.

Judge Bernard Gillis eyed the defendant and cleared his throat. Leaning forward to stress the seriousness of his words, he said: 'You are, without doubt, the most evil sex attacker ever to set foot in the Old Bailey. Your appalling attack on this woman was a carbon copy of your previous crimes when you preyed on women in Shepherd's Bush and Notting Hill.

'It is clear to this court, not only because of the outrageous character of this crime, but in the interest and for the safety of the public, that a heavy sentence must follow. For attempted murder, I sentence you to eighteen years,' he pronounced. Then, cataloguing the other crimes and sentencing accordingly, he said: 'Take him down.'

As Lashley turned in the dock to be led down to the cells below the courts, his eyes met mine for a moment. I had wanted to smile, to show the triumph on my face for Renata and Janie and all the other women he had attacked, but I found myself utterly transfixed. It is said the eyes are the windows to the soul; in that second or two before he disappeared from my gaze, I felt as if I were looking into the soul of the devil himself.

I couldn't get Lashley's eyes out of my mind for weeks after the trial. Nor could I stop myself thinking about what he had done to the lovely Janie. But life, as ever, went on and mine had become an endless roller-coaster of a ride on the Flying Squad. I was regularly working fourteen- and sixteen-hour days, and for a short time Mo and I had resorted to buying disposable underwear because we were never home for long enough to put a load in the washing machine.

I loved my work, I really embraced it. I seemed permanently exhausted but I enjoyed it. In many ways it was a tremendous relief to get away from the intensive and destructive nature of constantly dealing with victims of sexual offences, which had already started to exact its toll on my personal life. But, no matter how much I occupied my mind, the name 'David Lashley' was never far from my lips.

When I heard through the grapevine that he was appealing against his conviction for the Renata Chandler attack, I shivered. I asked my mates at Notting Hill to keep me informed. They told me that the application for leave to appeal, which was to be heard in the Criminal Division of the Court of Appeal in 1980, was to be made largely on the basis that a probation officer who could have helped Lashley's defence case was never called.

The man, a Mr Donald Scarlett, had allegedly made a statement claiming that at the time of the attack Lashley was bearded and a heavy smoker, something Renata had said could not be possible. The man who attacked her, she said, had been clean-shaven and did not taste or smell of smoke.

The 'beard' the probation officer talked about was in fact 'slight growth' or stubble, and the over-emphasis on this information deeply misled DCI Boorman in the initial stages of his investigation when he was trying to establish whether or not Lashley could be considered a suspect.

Lashley also refuted claims that he had admitted Renata's attack to Mr Mooney and other police officers after his arrest, something that had been mentioned at his trial. He said his so-called confession had been ambiguous and had been mis-interpreted by the police.

He further alleged his defence counsel had advised him that he would not be calling Mr Scarlett as he could prejudice his case in other ways. Lashley now accused his barrister of acting in an 'immoderate, misguided and highly prejudicial' way and of making insinuations which were 'unfounded and unfair'. On counsel's advice, Lashley said, he had read a prepared statement from the dock rather than giving evidence from the witness box, a factor which he now believed had contributed to his conviction.

As a final element of his desperate appeal, Lashley cast doubt over the fact that the woman who identified him at the police station, wearing a scarf around her head and face, was indeed Renata Chandler. He said her identity and selection should have been challenged by his solicitor and never was, although he admitted that at his trial his counsel had suggested the parade was a 'set-up' and claimed that it was 'dishonest and sinister'. All in all, he claimed, his conviction was 'unsafe and unsound'.

Thankfully, the Appeal Court judges who met in chambers disagreed and ordered his continued incarceration. Lashley would stay in prison and continue to serve his sentence. 'Thank God for that,' I sighed when I heard. I felt as if a huge weight had been lifted off my shoulders, and I wasn't the only one to feel that way.

Not that being on the Flying Squad didn't have its own stresses and strains. Quite apart from the heavy caseload and the unreasonably long hours, on average I was having to take a gun out of the armoury once a week in anticipation of con-fronting the hoodlums and gangsters we seemed to be forever chasing, and that did little for my stress levels.

Sadly, I got precious little moral support from my family. 'It's all very well being a career girl, but what about a husband and children?' my mother chided. Her attitude towards me, I concluded, had not changed one iota since I was a teenage typist.

My dad never let me see his unhappiness, but I sensed it was there. Pete, of course, had got married, had kids and was running his own successful engineering company. He could do no wrong, but if my mother's opinion was anything to go on I was a big disappointment. I actually became so used to it that it ceased to get me down, and my dad, especially, remained very close. His love was constant and I appreciated that.

They still lived in the same house. Dad was shortly to retire and they seemed to be settled. Most of all, they were happy and continued to be tremendously fond of each other. I couldn't really complain. If my mother was cold towards me, she certainly made up for it with my dad, whom she adored. And she was still capable of surprising us all.

On his sixtieth birthday, Dad was as shocked as the rest of us when he opened her card and found a receipt inside from a local Ford garage. He looked up at her quizzically. In his confusion, he thought she had bought him a new battery for his beloved old banger. But when he saw her eyes glistening and heard her tell him to look again, his mouth fell open as he took in the precise details.

My mother had bought him a brand-new Ford Cortina, something which he had only ever dreamt about. As the tears started to spill down his cheeks, my mother slung her arms around his neck and hugged him. All those years she had been scrimping and saving, all those little packets with money inside them for the bills, all that time my mother had kept another little tin, one which none of us knew about, marked CAR, into which she put the leftover cash from the sewing jobs she took in. It had taken her nigh on twenty years, but she had finally saved up enough to buy my dad the finest birthday present he could ever hope for.

The gleaming white car was in the local garage, waiting for him to pick it up. I have never seen a happier man drive home, showing off his new toy to just about anyone he could find. That car became my dad's pride and joy and he didn't stop talking about it for months, or so it seemed. He sounded like a twenty year old, going on sixty. I was thrilled for him because I knew it gave him enormous pleasure.

In July 1978 he finally retired and in September, just two months later, Dad – who had always been a very fit man – complained of pains in his stomach and collapsed. He was admitted to hospital, where the surgeons, believing him to have a perforated ulcer, operated immediately. Mum and I visited him within an hour of surgery but before we could enter his ward a nurse stopped and asked us both to step into her office and speak to the doctor.

It was the worst possible news. Dad had inoperable cancer of the pancreas and the liver and was not expected to live beyond Christmas. My mother, who worshipped the very ground he walked on, was inconsolable.

The hospital discharged him and my mother stoically nursed him at home through the terrible weeks of illness that left him a pale shadow of the man we all knew. To her enormous credit she rarely broke down or failed him but spent the next three months making his life as comfortable as she possibly could. Her jaw set to help suppress her emotions, she administered to the only man she had ever loved, finally weakening towards the end, when he became so delirious that he had to be readmitted to hospital.

I remember sitting at his bedside that night stroking his hand and trying not to cry. I sensed a glimmer of acknowledgement in his eyes as he tried to place who I was, but communication was out of the question because of the heavy sedation he was under. All I could see was a sadness in the eyes of an old man as he lapsed in and out of consciousness, for he had aged beyond recognition. I held his hand and kissed his forehead and told him I loved him. Then I left.

I went home, poured myself a large Scotch and, without removing my heavy outer jacket, flopped into an armchair. The living room was warm and cosy and within minutes I was fast asleep, my feet up on the pouffe in front of me. The day had taken its toll long before I had gone to sit with my dad.

The phone rang at about 11 p.m. and woke me with a jolt. 'Miss Bristow? This is Nurse Jarvis on your father's ward. I'm afraid I'm calling to tell you that he's fading fast.'

It was a miracle that I was sober when I received the call, for on numerous previous occasions I would have been completely out of it. Peter had taken Mum home with him and I rang him immediately to tell him the news. He said that, for the first time in months, Mum was fast asleep and he didn't want to wake her. She had endured so many disturbed nights over Dad, it seemed kinder to let her sleep on.

I rang the hospital back to tell them I would be there as soon as possible because I wanted to be near Dad, but Nurse Jarvis told me, in the kindest way possible, that he had – that very minute – died. I was too late. It was 16 December 1978, the saddest day of my life. I had lost the best friend I had ever known. My father had timed his death to coincide almost exactly with the date the doctors had given him.

My mother slept a full ten hours that night, her first good sleep in ages. Peter broke the news to her when she woke up. She didn't cry, she just stared straight ahead of her, fixing her eyes somewhere in space. She held fast like that until his funeral.

After the service, a few friends and relatives came back to Mum's house for tea and sandwiches. I knew I just wanted to be alone, to blot it all out in the only way I knew how. I sank a large Scotch, made my excuses and left. I found the oblivion I sought in the contents of a bottle at home, feeling thoroughly ashamed that I needed to do it in quite that fashion on such a solemn day. I didn't cry, nor did I fully mourn his death until years later. I simply refused to accept what I was feeling because it hurt too much.

As with so much in my life, I simply blocked the pain out. My special combination of long hours and alcohol had successfully numbed everything else in my life, so why not this, the most painful thing of all? I took my 'medicine', doubling the dose to be sure, and it worked.

My mother had a different way of coping. From the moment my father breathed his last, she literally gave up the fight. Her spirit began to leave her body and she was never, ever the same. It took ten years for her body to deteriorate, but Pete and I knew her mind had already gone.

I don't remember much about the Christmas that followed. I

took two weeks off to sort out the funeral and help my mother as best I could, but no more than that. Afraid of what I might do if I sat alone at home, I never asked for any more leave.

And so life, and the job, went on. There was no ignoring that. The London underworld certainly showed no respect for personal loss. I was doing what I wanted to do. It was the only thing I knew that could make any sense of my life.

There was plenty to keep me occupied, not least an armed robbery on a security guard who was delivering wages to the London Transport Offices at Northfields underground station between Ealing and Brentford. Two young thugs, armed with that most vicious of weapons, the sawn-off shotgun, ran up to John Potter, the guard, and shot him at point-blank range. The bastardized barrel of the gun was in contact with his side when they pulled the trigger and literally blew up his body – no exit wound, no visible mess, just the internal destruction of every major organ in his body. He died instantly. The robbers then calmly unclipped the security chain from his waist and made off with the bag full of cash.

We had received no tip-off about the robbery and knew nothing until it happened, but once the news broke the newspapers were full of how this poor sod had been so callously murdered for just a few quid. There were calls for action and for the men to be brought to justice. The Deputy Assistant Commissioner 'Crime', a man called David Powis, known in police circles as 'Crazy Horse', took a special interest in the case, and liaised daily with my boss and Commander Jimmy Sewell of the Flying Squad to establish what progress we were making. Everyone appeared to be demanding and expecting an early arrest.

We set up an incident room at Acton Police Station and our team of twelve was broken up into pairs of two. Working night and day, we used all the tricks of our trade to try and identify the perpetrators. Yours truly was paired up with a super bloke called Brian Crouch, a good DS with a brilliant sense of humour. The secret weapon in his armoury was that he looked just like a smaller version of the Greek singer Demis Roussos and nothing like a copper on the Flying Squad, which meant that he could mix unobtrusively with just about anyone.

Brian and I, along with the rest of the office, checked numerous addresses in the hope of identifying our suspects and the small armoury we collected *en route* was incredible, yet not one of the weapons could be connected to the security robbery. After a lot of dead-end leads and some no-hope tip-offs, we turned over the house of one particular villain – someone known to Brian – who, faced with possible charges for unlawful possession of firearms and the serious implications attached, pointed to a local man called David Ewin for the murder. In fact this information was backed up by two other sources, which made it all sound rather hopeful.

Being identified by some grass isn't good enough. There are plenty of people with a grudge in the underworld and if we went round nicking everyone named we would become embroiled in so many civil suits for unlawful arrest there would be no money left in the Commissioner's coffers. But, after some ferreting around, we finally found good circumstantial evidence which pointed to the fact that Ewin had been one of the two armed robbers.

My boss was delighted with our work and asked me to summarize in writing the exact nature of the evidence we had against Ewin. I have never been the least bit fazed by paperwork and managed to type it all out, chapter and verse, using the secretarial skills I had learnt at school. I presented my report to the Commander and, later, DAC Powis.

On the basis of that report and other information, Ewin and his cohorts were arrested. Everyone was delighted when he was finally charged with the murder, as there was no doubt in any of our minds that he was responsible for this most heinous crime. The Commander was thrilled and called Brian and me up to congratulate us on our work. To put it mildly, we were dead chuffed. Long after his words of praise, we still felt able to dine out on our success.

Ewin was later cleared by a jury of the murder of the security guard, but went on to pursue a long and violent career as an armed robber, burglar and thief. In 1995, aged thirty-eight, while driving a stolen car in Barnes, south-west London, he was shot dead by PC Patrick Hodgson. After three criminal trials as the first police officer to be charged with murder after shooting a suspect while on duty, PC Hodgson was finally cleared of the killing in October 1997.

My mother's deteriorating mental health continued to worry both me and my brother. One day she got lost on a short train journey. Gradually friends and neighbours started to voice their concern. I visited her as often as I could, and Pete and I took turns to do her shopping and household chores, but it was obvious that she was becoming more distant and confused. I remember visiting her one evening after work.

'Hi, Mum, how was your day?'

She seemed amazingly bright as she answered: 'I've had a lovely day shopping, dear. I met Dad in the High Road and he took me for a cup of tea.'

I stopped and looked at her. 'But he's dead, Mum,' I said as gently as I could.

Smiling, she ignored me completely and added: 'And I saw him yesterday on the television. He was on *Crossroads* and he spoke to me.' I shook my head, knowing that challenging her would be a complete waste of time.

One afternoon on a very hot day, I dropped in unexpectedly between shifts and found her indoors wearing two skirts and a heavy coat. In her hand, she held her dressmaking scissors and a five-pound note which she had cut into pieces. Another time I left her peaches and custard in a bowl to eat as part of her Sunday tea, but when I called round again first thing the following morning she was standing at the stove, frying the fruit and custard, telling me she was cooking her breakfast.

She had lost the ability to tell the time and would go to bed when it was dark, but in the winter that meant that she was often in bed by four o'clock and then raring to go at 1 a.m. The neighbours would ring and complain that Mum was fully dressed and playing the radio in the early hours. I bought her a huge clock, measuring nearly fifteen inches across, and told her she shouldn't go to bed until the little hand was on the ten, but it made no difference.

After long, difficult discussions with Pete about what to do, we agreed that I should apply to the Court of Protection to be her legal guardian, acting for her in all her affairs. In other words, we went into role reversal and I became my mother's carer. Pete had a wife and family and a business to run, so to the outsider's untrained eye, I was the one with time on my hands and nothing else to worry about.

Mum's GP later backed my application to Brent Social Services for help. As a result, a wonderful lady called Maud began visiting my mother for about three hours every day to feed and generally care for her. The fact that Maud was able to do this released me from what had become a daily responsibility, visiting my mother on my way to or from work. I was delighted to relinquish the burden, because looking after her was causing me increased distress: as her dementia worsened, so did the manifestation of her dislike for me.

She accused me of stealing her money and reminded me over and over again that she loved me least of all. This was to become one of the most hurtful times of my life and the strain added enormously to the long list of things I was trying to forget through drink. I became resentful of her and of the time and attention I gave her which she abused. I felt full of self-pity that the load had fallen on my shoulders, not Pete's, and the bitterness I harboured enabled me to dig myself into a still deeper hole. But at least I had the Flying Squad, which kept me busy, or so I thought.

The call came out of the blue. My commander told me he had informed DAC Powis of our success in arresting David Ewin and that I had consequently been mentioned by name. I was to go and see him at Scotland Yard. Rarely do officers get the honour of being called up personally by a DAC. It usually means either a pat on the back or the biggest bollocking of your life and, as I had done nothing wrong, I was looking forward to my trip. I had already received eight commendations for outstanding work and there was no harm in having another, I told myself rather cockily as I made my way from Acton Town to St James's tube station and walked across the road to Scotland Yard.

I arrived early in my best bib and tucker and took the lift to the fourth floor. I bought myself a cup of coffee, and settled down to attempt the *Daily Telegraph* crossword before nipping into the ladies' loo to preen myself for the forthcoming occasion.

On the dot of our agreed appointment, I knocked on DAC Powis's door and entered on the command 'Come.' He was sitting in a high-backed swivel chair behind a small conference table. As I walked up to him, stood to attention and announced myself, he looked at me over the top of his spectacles. Half expecting him to invite me to sit down, I began to look around for a suitably vacant seat, but as he began to speak I realized that I should stand exactly where I was.

The bollocking didn't stop until I left ten minutes later and he never even paused to take a breath. I stood to attention, black leather briefcase in hand without a chance to put it down. I've been frightened many times before, but this was a new kind of fear, accompanied by a distinct sinking feeling which told me I was in double trouble.

'Bristow!' he bellowed. 'I understand you passed the inspector's exam ten years ago and yet you have repeatedly avoided promotion for purely selfish reasons. Because – a little bird tells me – you're enjoying yourself too much. But, let me tell you, unless you take yourself off to the earliest available promotions board, I will have you back in uniform patrolling the streets in the next two weeks. This is no idle threat. Do I make myself clear?'

I stood stock-still, unable to move a muscle before managing to open my mouth wide enough to croak: 'Yes, sir.'

'Right then, get out and get to it.'

I knew he meant what he said, and as I shut his door with a sigh I cursed the name of David Ewin for bringing me to the Commissioner's notice.

The promotion boards for sergeant to inspector were no more than a few weeks away. For some years now I had successfully avoided promotion by submitting a report just before the selections were made which always said much the same – that I recognized that the promotion boards were imminent but that I did not wish to be considered for the rank of inspector because 'I did not think it the appropriate time in my career for development or personal advancement'. I always wrote incredible waffle which somehow had the desired effect. But, with hindsight, I should have recognized that it wouldn't wash for ever.

DAC Powis had a reputation for meaning exactly what he said; as twelve of my fifteen years as a police officer had been in the CID, I did not fancy returning to uniform and learning a whole new way of life back on the beat. My choices were limited, so I decided that the most sensible idea was to volunteer for promotion. All I could do then was hope that I would fail the selection procedure.

A few weeks later, I reluctantly found myself being interviewed by three senior officers on the DI's promotion board, with the uncomfortable feeling that whatever I said or did was irrelevant. Surely I could make myself look really stupid, I thought as I answered all their questions. But of course I never did.

I passed and was told that I would be promoted to the rank of detective inspector just as soon as a vacancy arose. I received the news with a heavy heart, not least because it would mean a premature transfer from the Flying Squad, the hardest wrench of my career. What the hell was going to happen to me now? And, more importantly, where would I be sent?

The posting, as ever, would be crucial and I prayed I wouldn't have to sit out the rest of my career doing paperwork in South Mimms or Uxbridge. I waited for the location with bated breath. When it came, it felt like a body blow. West Hendon, of all places. I'd been in the thick of it for so long that I half regarded West Hendon as a remote London outback in the foothills of Cricklewood.

With no choice but to accept, I prepared myself to move. On 11 August 1980 I was transferred from the Flying Squad, kissing goodbye to all that I knew and loved. I hated the idea of relinquishing all the high tension and the drama involved in kicking down doors and chasing real villains only to have it replaced by nothing but middle-class, middle-aged residential crime. There was an urgent vacancy at West Hendon, I was told. I bet there bloody is, I thought.

8

'GOOD-MORNING, MA'AM. CAN I GET YOU A COFFEE?' A VOICE asked from somewhere behind me. I looked over my shoulder, expecting to see the high-ranking woman officer to whom this young man had been directing his comments, when I suddenly realized he was speaking to me.

What a novelty it was to be called 'ma'am' or 'guv' or 'boss'. I wondered how long it would take before I answered first time. For months after my promotion, the junior officers had to accompany the 'ma'am' with a theatrical cough, to make me realize they were addressing me.

I was thirty-seven years old when I walked into West Hendon nick and was shown to my new office, across the corridor and away from the hubbub of the main CID traffic. I suddenly appreciated that I would no longer have to share a desk with anyone, but the isolation of my new position was not going to be something that I relished.

Within five minutes of my settling in, my new commander asked to see me. I expected the usual handshake and welcome, and I was right. But there was more. The Commander asked me for my pink firearms authorization card.

'May I ask why, sir?' I bristled.

'Police policy,' he said, holding out his hand. 'Women officers are not allowed to be shots on division. It is totally unheard of.'

I've never been one to accept nonsensical decisions gracefully, and have always politely but firmly stood my ground and stated the obvious. Not that I had ever wanted to become a shot in the first place, but having been through all the training, it wasn't something I was going to give up easily. This was my first day and our first encounter, yet I felt intimidated. I pulled myself up to my full five feet five inches and let rip.

'I'm sorry, sir, but that doesn't make sense. The police force has just spent thousands of pounds of taxpayers' money teaching me how to use a gun but, because of policy, I cannot carry on as a shot? It's a terrible waste and a stupid decision.'

I could see the commander was a man who was not accustomed to being spoken to in such a way. His face reddened and he told me not to answer back. But I couldn't let it go. I remained in his office for nearly half an hour, arguing the toss. Finally he said in exasperation: 'If you don't like it then I suggest you outline your grievances in a report and send it to the appropriate department at the Yard for them to consider.'

As I turned on my heel to leave, he called after me. 'DI Bristow. Your firearms card, please.' His hand was outstretched. I had no option but to remove it from my warrant-card wallet and hand it in. I was now suspended from carrying a gun.

I went straight to my new office and started typing furiously. Within twenty-four hours my report was on its way, but I knew that any ruling on whether women could be categorized as shots on division was likely to take months.

Still, I had plenty of time on my hands. Compared to other stations in which I had served in the past, West Hendon was not the busiest place on earth. But at least it meant I could familiarize and pace myself, learning the responsibilities of my new rank.

I quickly discovered that my new role as one of two detective inspectors in charge of twenty or so officers was a largely supervisory one. The occasional major crime required my particular attention, but on the whole I got stuck into other people's work in a managerial capacity. The CID office, situated on the first floor, was filled with budding Maigrets and Poirots and many of them must have been thoroughly cheesed off with my persistent enquiries into their investigations. The truth was I was pretty fed up with being a chief when all I desperately wanted to be was an Indian again, playing at being a real detective.

I rarely left the office and my routine became predictably dull as a result. Up at 6.30 a.m., into the office by 8 a.m., where I took my first look at the crime book to see what overnight crimes there were – the bulk of which were burglaries – and to find out if anyone had brought in any prisoners overnight.

The crime book was a large ledger into which an officer who received a complaint of crime would report the vital details. Before the days of computers, this ledger had to be completed painstakingly by hand. For years as a DC and DS I had filled in my crime sheets and clipped them into the crime books of the various police stations, with hardly a second thought.

Now as a DI it was my responsibility to supervise the investigations and read all the reports to make sure that the officers had done their job properly. I would check to make sure they had filled in all the little boxes and would chase them up if I felt there were elements missing, such as house-to-house enquiries. The crime report reads much like a diary – when the call came in, from whom, to whom, where, when, how and why. By the time you reach the bottom of the last page, there should be a pretty detailed picture of what has happened and to whom – unless of course the officer's handwriting is so appalling that you can't read a word, or they are particularly poor at explaining themselves on paper.

When an officer on duty overnight took down details of a burglary or an assault and entered what he knew in the crime book, it was my job to ask one of my day-duty men to go to the scene and do the follow-up work. The jobs were allocated on a rotation basis, or on the basis of experience. I gave the work to whomever I chose, but I had to be very careful not to make enemies and to be as fair as possible. It was also obvious to me that the only way the more junior men would get the experience they lacked was to double up with the practised CID officer who had been assigned the job, but this could upset one or two of the more seasoned detectives, who occasionally took the view that they were a little above teaching some wet-behind-the-ears rookie the right way to do things.

Only when a crime had been fully investigated and followed up would I countersign the report in the crime book, send a copy to G10, the statistics department, and place the original in our filing system. I had to be scrupulous about what I let pass, because if the wheel came off at a later date I would be the one to get the blame.

I had a further supervisory role to play when an officer in charge of a criminal case had to present the facts of his particular investigation in a written report to the solicitors' department at Scotland Yard. Employed by the Commissioner to give us legal support, it was up to these lawyers to decide whether or not they would proceed with a prosecution. That decision could only be reached once the officer on the case had presented good strong evidence, properly written up, making sure the department had all the information at its fingertips. It was my role to ensure that everything that could be done was completed as quickly as possible.

This was long before the Crown Prosecution Service established itself in 1987 and effectively did away with the old solicitors' department. Like most police officers I was no great fan of the CPS, preferring the old ways of the solicitors' department, where the staff at least seemed to be on our side. These were trained lawyers working for the Home Office, who thought like highly trained police officers and appeared to understand how we worked. It always seemed much easier to persuade them to prosecute a case than it was later with the CPS, which comprised legally qualified civil servants brought in to examine each potential case from a mainly fiscal point of view.

The CPS quickly developed a reputation for stopping prosecutions or not going ahead with them without, in my view, giving adequate explanation. It became a 'them and us' situation, and occasionally it seemed as if we were working on opposite sides of the fence. The theory was that unless they considered that there was a 51 per cent chance of a conviction they did not proceed and the case was never brought to trial. Many of us took the view that they actually worked to a 75 per cent chance of winning – no matter how hard that might have been for the victims or the police officers involved to accept. The rapport was just never the same.

I know the CPS had to be seen to be acting independently of the police force, thus showing no prosecution bias, but sometimes their decisions appeared to have been utterly crass and made without any intelligent consultation. To say there were teething problems would be an understatement. There was little or no informal contact encouraged between the police and the CPS, in case it compromised their impartiality. This deliberate stand-off frequently meant that when a prosecution case was rejected it would come back to the officer concerned by way of a short, snappy memo giving the briefest of details by way of explanation.

This often alienated the disappointed officer who had worked hard on a case, because he or she was given no real insight into how that decision was reached. They then had to face the victim or aggrieved member of the public and come up with some tin-pot excuse as to why their complaint would not be pursued. Not surprisingly, this sort of outcome was frequently seen by the public as a failure by the police, who had gone soft on crime.

It cost countless frayed tempers, including mine, to improve the system, and it took a good ten years to change the public's perception of things. Happily, the CPS and the police now work together, and their joint efforts are beginning to deliver the type of criminal justice system the public want and are entitled to expect.

I have always understood the importance of writing an accurate and detailed report because it seemed to me that, if I was sincere with my words, the chances were that I would be listened to. I hoped and believed that even if I hadn't come up with the unwritten 75 per cent, the CPS would have little choice but to opt for a criminal trial because of the genuine portrayal of the evidence. Some of my colleagues clearly thought I was mad, staying in the office for hours, trying to fit all the pieces of the jigsaw together. 'You don't have to do all that, Carol,' they would say. 'Just give them the basics and let them do the rest.' But I knew from experience that my method worked, and I rarely had the CPS reject my opinions or stop court proceedings in a case where I felt it important to go ahead.

Not that I didn't use all my persuasive powers to achieve what I wanted. I made a point of getting to know the lawyers who worked in the CPS and I frequently delivered my report in person, placing it in the hands of the individual designated to examine the case. Nor was I averse to loading the report heavily in favour of the victim if I felt it was needed.

On more than one occasion, different bosses would come to me holding my CPS report and ask: 'Is this the same job you and I went on, Carol? I hardly recognized it. Don't let anyone ever tell you you haven't got the makings of a Jeffrey Archer, cos you certainly have.'

But I was never deterred, viewing it as one of the most enjoyable parts of my job. It was a challenge, answering all the questions I thought they might ask and pulling the whole thing together into a readable story. Only then did I put it all into a brown envelope and deliver it to the CPS.

In time, I came to know and admire many of the advocates and I would sit down opposite them and convince them that this was a case worth pursuing and that the report in front of them wasn't just full of empty promises. If it was appropriate, I would assure them that the victim would make an excellent witness, that the forensic evidence was compelling or that the guilty demeanour of the suspect would work against him. Many of them were bloody good at their job, some cut the mustard, and it was good for me to know that I could pick up the phone to some of the friendlier ones to ask for their advice or have them endorse a decision I had already made.

'Hello, Jean, it's Carol Bristow here. I've got another bad rape. Any chance of you looking at it over the next couple of days, because I'd cherish your opinion on the evidence?'

'Fine, Carol, mark it up for my attention and I'll see what I can do. Maybe we could meet and discuss any problems over a cup of coffee.'

I wasn't the only one who worked that way. Any detective worth his salt would want to do the same, but paperwork wasn't everyone's cup of tea and many of them loathed the prospect.

There were isolated incidents when the system went against me. One such example was the case of a handicapped child in a prominent children's home, whose parents called us in because their child had reportedly been sexually abused by a member of staff. This home had some very high connections with the Establishment, and an extremely hostile headmaster who was determined that nothing should sully the name of his precious organization. Even though I managed partially to corroborate the child's story with evidence from another member of staff (who had been threatened with dismissal by the head for talking to us), and the accused virtually confessed to what he had done, the powers that be rejected the case as being unsuitable for prosecution on the grounds of it 'not being in the public interest', and in any event the evidence was weak. I took the view that the case was stronger than they admitted to but the word 'justice' seemed to elude them. I managed to get a personal interview with the Assistant Crown Prosecutor and told him I believed the case was 65 per cent prosecutable, but the answer was still no. To this day, it infuriates me to think about it.

My enthusiasm for intelligently presented reports to the lawyers never waned, especially when I was a DI at West Hendon. God help any young tec who put some wishy-washy rubbish my way. I did my best to show them how the system worked, and I attempted to inspire them with enthusiasm and literary skills – but not always with much success. Some reports were a joy to read while others left me wondering if dyslexia was contagious.

The paperwork had become such a regular feature of my job that I seemed to do little else. But there were also the meetings, at least one a day. I was totally unfamiliar with these and they took up so much of my time. I would find myself mentally wandering off, looking out of a window or twiddling my pencil, while my colleagues waffled on about police strategy and overtime budgets, issues they rightly saw as important but which held bugger-all interest for me.

'So, we are agreed. Extra officers to patrol Brent Cross in the run-up to Christmas, with back-up from the CID. Am I keeping you awake, DI Bristow?' My chief superintendent's voice would shake me from my daydreams.

'What? Oh, yes, sir. We'll be there,' I chirped as enthusiastically as I could. How much longer could I pretend to be interested? I wondered.

All the meetings, supervision and paperwork only served to remind me why I never wanted the rank in the first place. I didn't join for this, I told myself, and suddenly realized that I was jealous of the troops, the ones out on the streets, the ones whose crime files and reports I seemed destined to get lumbered with. Then I heard the voice of reason saying, 'Just bloody get on with it, Bristow, and stop complaining.' But how I longed for the good old days. Not that there wasn't the odd moment that reminded me of times past.

'Sorry to trouble you, ma'am,' a voice from behind me faltered. 'I can't say as I know what it is we've found but it looks like it could be the remains of a body. I didn't really like to touch it and the truth is that it stinks so much that I found it difficult to get right up close to it, but it's in a black plastic bin liner up the top end of the ground on a grass verge beside a field.'

The young PC couldn't have been more than twenty and he looked terrified of me. Did I really have this effect on people? 'Sit down,' I said, 'and tell me about it.' He explained that a man out walking his dog had come across the bin liner after the animal started sniffing furiously at it. The man had a quick look into the bag, didn't like what he saw and called the police. The PC went to the scene and the smell from the bag had so overwhelmed him that he felt nauseous. He had left a colleague standing guard and driven back to the police station for advice.

'I wondered if you could come and have a look and give us your expert opinion, ma'am,' he enquired, his face as white as a sheet.

'It's that bad, is it?' I asked, wrinkling my nose.

'If you mean the smell, ma'am, I've never smelt anything worse.'

I found the station SOCO (scene of crimes officer), a lovely chap called Alan, and told him what I knew and together we made our way up to the edge of the field. I swear I could smell the contents of the bag as I stepped out of Alan's van, parked some fifty feet away from the offending material. As I got to within twenty feet of it, I instructed him to examine the contents as best he could and give me his verdict. I had reasoned that, as an inspector, I could safely delegate this particular responsibility.

Alan then dived into the back of his van and reappeared wearing a rubberized overall, plastic gloves, plastic shoe covers and a face mask. Under his arms he carried two plastic containers with tightly fitting lids. Calmly he walked up to the bin liner, opened it and scooped the rotting material out.

'Can't be sure of anything,' he told me, 'but it could be human. I think it ought to go straight to the lab. They'll be able to tell us what it is. I'll take it up now if you want.'

'That would be great,' I said, and I thanked him for getting 'stuck in', so to speak, but refused to go anywhere near him until he had disposed of the stinking material and had a good scrub. The smell was absolutely putrid and to avoid it further I was prepared to walk back to the police station.

The Metropolitan Police Laboratory must have loved Alan as he walked through their doors with his two plastic buckets, filled with the most unholy-looking mixture of blood and guts. But within two hours they were on the phone. 'DI Bristow, you'll be happy to know that the material you sent us is bovine. It's the guts of a cow, probably illegally slaughtered for religious purposes, on unauthorized premises.'

'Thank God for that,' I sighed, and suddenly felt able to join my colleagues in the canteen for lunch. Top of the menu was liver and bacon. Next down was steak pie. 'On second thoughts . . .' I said. I got up and left the building, deciding that a brisk walk was the only thing that would clear the stench which still hung round my nostrils.

Despite the odd trip out or funny moment, my time at West

Hendon was not particularly memorable. I was reluctant about my new rank, I hated all the crap that went with it, and I missed the excitement of life at the sharp end. My mother continued to decline, mentally and physically, which required all my spare time and attention, and my drinking was as bad as it had ever been.

Without realizing, I had started to drink more and more, this time not in celebration of jobs well done, or to calm the adrenalin or numb the pain of the Renatas and Janies of this world, but out of self-pity and loneliness. I didn't want to be this serious, lonely woman approaching forty, caring for a decrepit old mother, secretly drinking her life away. Often when someone called me 'ma'am' I felt like snapping at them. The title only served to remind me of my increasing age and responsibilities.

It seemed only a matter of time before my mother would have to go into a home. Maud was wonderful and did all she could, but when she wasn't there I was left to provide the missing cover. Things were often tense and my mother's attitude did nothing to help. She made it very clear that she regarded my constant visits as an interference, an intrusion into her private life. The old accusations about money reared their ugly heads and I always left her house fit to bust, needing a bloody good drink. There wasn't even the excitement of work as an antidote.

How had it come to this? I wondered. For the first time in my career I had lost the enthusiasm to pull myself round and I felt completely alone in the world. Had my drinking diminished my ability in some way? Had it been noticed? Was this all there was? I felt increasingly lost and these days I confessed to not knowing all the answers.

Sympathy and some measure of understanding had always been shown to me by a male friend and former colleague whom I suspected was the tiniest bit in love with me. We had met at Detective Training School some years previously and when I was at my lowest I knew I could rely on him. It felt wonderful to be with someone who really cared about me and, at a time when I had never felt lonelier, I agreed to spend a weekend with him at a beautiful hotel in Suffolk.

It poured with rain the whole weekend and we got as drunk

as skunks. Needless to say, I ended up in bed with this lovely man, knowing full well that the relationship could never go further because I simply had nothing to offer him emotionally. But falling asleep in the arms of someone who made me feel loved and wanted did me the power of good.

I had almost forgotten the issue of whether or not I kept my firearms authorization card when, months after I had written the report complaining of its suspension, the policy makers' official reply landed on my commander's desk. He called me up to see him.

'Seems policy has been changed to suit your ideas about women shots on division,' he said. I was absolutely delighted. Common sense had finally prevailed, I thought, and I was glad I had bothered to send the report. My pleasure was short-lived, however, because the Commander added: 'But as it's months since you held a gun, much less practised with one, you'll have to go on a refresher course before they let you have your authorization card back. If you're successful and they deem you a proper person to be let loose with a gun, then you can indeed be authorized to carry a pistol on division, if and when the need arises.'

I sighed but accepted his verdict – it was fair enough. It had been a little while since I had handled a weapon. Two weeks later, the notice arrived. I was to go to the firearms unit for a day's refresher course the following week. I went off, quietly confident.

They gave me a .38 Smith & Wesson and I fired my first rounds. It seemed only minutes later when one of the instructors tapped me on the shoulder and said: 'Sorry, Miss Bristow, but that's just not good enough. You've failed.' And that was that. I could never work out if I had been well and truly 'had' or if I had genuinely been so bad that I really didn't deserve to pass. I suspected the latter was probably true, but it wasn't in my nature to be that magnanimous and accept failure without question. I left the range feeling a right dork. And to think that I had made such a stand over the whole issue. Needless to say, I never held a gun again.

I had been at West Hendon a little under eighteen months when I heard that the Central Drugs Squad was looking for a detective inspector. More to the point, I received a telephone call from an old boss of mine at New Scotland Yard asking me if I was interested. My record was squeaky clean and he thought I, as an ex-Flying Squad officer, was the perfect candidate for the job.

I didn't need asking twice. Working on the Central Drugs Squad meant that I would be back in the thick of it, while still being the DI in charge of a team. I made my enthusiasm known and waited for an interview. It came and I passed. It was December 1981. Once Christmas was over, with a terrible year behind me, it looked as though I could be on my way again.

The Drugs Squad is unique in that it comprises both CID and uniformed officers and specializes in investigating drug-trafficking on a large scale. Our job was to target the people who imported, made and peddled drugs, and to make as many seizures as we could. A lot of the faces we were looking at I already knew; I had grown up with them. They had started off as small-time crooks and, as they got older and richer, had reinvested their money in the market which gave them the highest return – drugs.

There were three teams of twelve officers and I was one of the three DIs in charge. I shared an office with my two male counterparts at the end of the corridor, and the troops shared a long main office on one of the upper floors at Scotland Yard. Still something of a rarity as a woman DI, I was none the less treated well and with enormous respect. Drugs crime on a large scale was a new field for me, which meant I needed all the help I could get, and by some miracle I had inherited a team with a wealth of experience and common sense.

A huge task lay ahead of me. When I was on division, I thought I knew all there was to know about the local drugs scene, but from the day I joined the Drugs Squad I realized that I had previously only scratched the surface and would now be starting the equivalent of a degree course in mind-altering substances – anything from cannabis to highly sophisticated chemical concoctions. I suddenly had to learn the history, origins and methods of importation of the weird and wonderful drugs that were in vogue at the time, and investigate the complicated network of criminals willing to promote them to innocents.

One of the first networks I looked at involved Sidney Solly Frankel, a man who was responsible for giving me one of the hardest times in court since I had faced the barrister representing Francis Bacon.

Frankel had two unlikely cohorts, Michael Gampbell and Constantine Victor Ludwig von Tucka, whom he met in Ford Open Prison in West Sussex. Frankel was a wealthy man in his fifties, formerly managing director of a chain of chemist's shops with a turnover in excess of £1.25 million. In October 1980 he was convicted at the Old Bailey of illegally producing millions of slimming pills called 'speckled blues' through his own pharmaceutical manufacturing company. Fined £115,000 plus £7,500 costs, he defaulted on his payments and was sentenced to two years nine months for non-payment of fines. He claimed that, after an expensive divorce, he was broke.

Michael Gampbell was a disgraced lawyer, struck off in 1982 after being convicted at the Old Bailey on several counts of theft and deception, and sentenced to three years' imprisonment. Aged fifty, he had embezzled his clients' money to fund his extravagant lifestyle.

Constantine von Tucka, in his sixties, was a Hungarian immigrant and a brilliant chemist. In 1982 at Chelmsford Crown Court, he was sentenced to two and a half years' imprisonment for illegally producing amphetamines. He had previous drugs convictions in West Germany and there was a clear demand for his special expertise.

When they were released from prison the three men set up shop to illegally manufacture an amphetamine-based drug known as 'speed'. Using several separate pharmaceutical companies, they bought the necessary components, which were individually innocuous and included ether, hydrochloric acid and red phosphorous. Mixed together properly, the combination was dynamite.

They might never have been noticed but for the enormous quantities of the chemicals they purchased and then stored at a warehouse near Heathrow Airport. They had ordered sufficient chemicals to produce in excess of five million tablets, valued at £1.5 million. Staff at one of the pharmaceutical companies became concerned and alerted us to the fact that unusually large quantities of red phosphorous had been ordered by a man calling himself Dr Leitzgen (Von Tucka's pseudonym). This chemical is normally used in safety matches, fireworks and fertilizers, and Leitzgen did not appear to be associated with any of these products.

I went to see the sales staff at the British Drug Houses and took down the delivery address, a large warehouse in Southall. I then made contact with the landlords, who knew nothing about what was being stored, and arranged to visit the premises with one of my team. I had taken the advice of the Metropolitan Police chemists about what to look for and, as we slid back the heavy steel doors, the ingredients on my list were all stacked in boxes before me. The place was piled floor-to-ceiling with a frightening array of chemicals and we knew we were on to something. There was little doubt that there was sufficient here to flood the market with methylamphetamine hydrochloride – just the kind of drug the youth of the day were crying out for.

Our next task was to find the factory where the drugs were actually being produced but, despite all our best endeavours, it eluded us. The term 'factory' is used to describe an area where a small laboratory can be quickly erected and fitted up with Bunsen burners and the like, to manufacture drugs. It is designed to be dismantled as speedily as it can be assembled, and is small enough to be set up in a kitchen, garage or garden shed. No matter how much undercover work we did, they always seemed to be one step ahead of us.

After months of fruitless labour, we heard that Frankel was about to take possession of even more supplies and we realized that something had to be done, and fast. But on the day the information came through there was no one around. Nearly everyone, it seemed, was out on other operations. Grabbing whoever I could, I attempted to set up the simultaneous arrests of the three men from various parts of London, personally nicking Frankel myself, but as luck went Gampbell and Von Tucka couldn't be found.

Understaffed and under pressure, I interviewed Frankel myself at Leyton nick to see what he was prepared to tell me. He was an old hand and wasn't particularly co-operative. Still, I went through the motions, noting everything he said verbatim on sheets of foolscap paper.

Faced with the possibility that 'friends' might have pointed a finger at him, he opened up a little and mourned the fact that there was no longer any honour among thieves. When we had finished, I asked him to sign the bottom of each page but he refused. I signed them anyway, as required, and got a colleague, DC Elaine McIntosh, to witness my signature.

Gampbell was arrested eight weeks later and, although we never did find the laboratory, we had enough evidence to charge them with conspiracy to produce the drugs unlawfully. Months later, when Von Tucka was arrested in the Channel Islands, he confessed to his role and stated that he would be willing to give evidence against the others. It was a job well done, mainly because we had prevented at least five million tablets from hitting the streets.

Eighteen months later the case came up for trial at the Old Bailey. I had done my homework and was prepared for the not-guilty pleas from Frankel and Gampbell, accepting that I was likely to come in for some pretty severe grilling in the witness box. Faced with overwhelming evidence against them, defendants like Frankel frequently take the view that their only chance of acquittal is to suggest that the police officers involved have acted dishonourably and manufactured evidence against them. The Drugs Squad was an easy target for these allegations.

Giving evidence at court was always a daunting experience because I knew in advance that whatever I said was going to be in dispute (otherwise the defendant would have pleaded guilty). Trying to anticipate the ferocity of the defence attack was a mug's game – I could be faced with the best, or the worst, counsel but, until I was standing there facing him or her, I simply didn't know. I have been attacked, verbally and psychologically, in the witness box a hundred times or more and I never got used to it. Of course, the more it happened and the older I grew, the better able I was to cope with it, but it still grated – the anticipation of being called a liar, or being accused of planting evidence, or the attempts to make me falter or contradict myself and end up looking like an idiot. It was something I always felt apprehensive about. I was much more comfortable gathering the evidence and presenting it all on paper in the best possible way, which I was confident I had done in this case.

True to form, Frankel adopted exactly this defence and accused me of falsifying the notes on his interviews, which I had faithfully recorded and signed. He claimed that I had asked him to sign a set of blank sheets of paper, which he had refused to do. He said I must then have filled them in with details of a fictional interview, including his mention of there being 'no honour among thieves'. When I argued that the interview transcripts had been signed first by me in his presence and then witnessed by Elaine McIntosh – who countersigned them – his barrister suddenly produced an expert handwriting witness who told the court that on one sheet of paper part of my signature was on top of that of DC McIntosh, instead of underneath as it should have been. I was flabbergasted.

The clear implication was that I had lied about the interview notes. The expert made it look as if Frankel was telling the truth when he suggested that I had presented him with blank sheets of paper, asked Elaine to sign them and then signed them myself, and not the other way round.

I have to say that when I heard the expert give his evidence I suddenly went cold. His testimony that my signature was on top of Elaine's was so convincing, I found myself in the uncomfortable position of wondering whether I might have made a mistake on that one page. It was nearly eighteen months since the interview had taken place. Could there have been some error because we were under pressure?

The judge stopped me from giving any further evidence and, peering over his glasses, suggested that I might like to seek the advice of counsel. My heart almost stopped. The only other time I had ever heard of this type of thing happening was when an officer had been suspended and reported to the Director of Public Prosecutions for corruption. As I left the witness box, nauseous, I was sure I could see a smirk on Frankel's face.

After taking the advice of prosecuting counsel, I took the offending page to the handwriting experts at the Metropolitan Police Laboratory in Lambeth and asked for their help.

'You're in luck, Carol,' one of the scientists there told me. 'We've just installed a new high-tech X-ray machine which should clear the matter up once and for all.' I carefully handed over the page which, I was painfully aware, held the key to my future with the Metropolitan Police. It took them two days to do all their tests before they phoned to say that their report was ready and that their expert was available to give his testimony at the Old Bailey.

Pacing up and down in the corridor outside the court, I waited for the nod from the prosecuting counsel that I was in the clear. It never came and, as I sat in court to hear the expert sworn in, my heart was in my mouth.

The scientist started to explain to the jury the complicated technique by which the piece of paper had been X-rayed from behind to try and ascertain which signature had been written first. 'The simplest way to explain what we found is this. Water and oil do not mix,' he said. 'The Elaine McIntosh signature had been written in felt-tip pen – which is water-based – and the Carol Bristow signature in biro, which is oil-based. As McIntosh's felt-tip pen crossed the oil of the biro signature, the water-based ink ran to the extremities of the biro letters, thus making it appear that the felt-tip pen had been used first. The evidence is clear, however, that this was not the case. Miss Bristow's signature in biro was the first to be written on the page.'

I was elated. All my fears and worries were washed away by the expert's words. Called back into the witness box by the judge to finish my evidence, I sailed through the final points, knowing I had been vindicated. Frankel's face was not such a picture any more, and became even more morose when the judge sentenced him to four and a half years.

Another awkward moment came during a separate Drugs Squad operation in the summer of 1983. Customs & Excise had nicked two Italians for importing a substantial amount of cannabis. The pair went down for lengthy periods, but we were told by an informant that two more Italians were to be sent over to pick up where the others had left off. The grass gave us the address of a house in Wembley, which was vacant but which he said was about to be occupied by the replacement Italian drug dealers.

Sure enough, a few weeks later an Italian called Mario Scaccio moved in to the Wembley house with, we suspected, a large quantity of drugs. I went to the local magistrates' court to apply for a search warrant and, taking my team, backed up by some uniformed officers, went round to the house. It was early morning when we knocked on the door, but no one answered. Knowing our suspect was inside, we smashed a window and forced our way in. Scaccio did a runner out of the back window and legged it down a nearby road, but was apprehended as he tried to board a bus, dressed only in his pyjamas.

The house contained little or no furniture, but was filled with packing cases. We had brought sniffer dogs with us but they didn't find any cannabis inside the house. However, the dogs went wild when we showed them out into the garden. The lawn was littered with piles and piles of empty grape boxes which had been stacked one on top of the other. They were four deep, eight high and ran the length of the garden. There must have been almost four hundred of them and the dogs went absolutely crackers.

We let them off their leads and they dived in, sending the boxes everywhere. It seemed obvious that, although now empty, they had recently contained large quantities of cannabis, probably hidden beneath the fruit.

Then, to my surprise, we found a small rabbit hutch hidden underneath the largest pile of boxes; I lifted it out and carried it back into the house. By this time Scaccio had been escorted back to the house and was sitting in his pyjamas in the living room.

In front of him I emptied the contents of the rabbit hutch on to a coffee table. Out tumbled several filthy rolls of money and a large amount of gold jewellery, heavy link bracelets and thick crucifixes with chains, the sort of thing you'd expect to see the Godfather wearing. Because of what we'd been told, I felt certain that the cash was the proceeds from the sale of cannabis. There was plenty of it, several thousand pounds at least, and I picked up one of the rolls and asked Scaccio who it belonged to.

'It is mine,' he said. 'It came from the sale of the fruit.'

'How much is here?' I asked him.

'Forty-two thousand pounds,' he said, staring at me.

'Why is it in the rabbit hutch?'

'I was afraid that burglars might break in and steal it. You know there are a lot of criminals here in Britain.' He smiled.

'Can you provide evidence that the money came from the sale of the fruit?'

He considered my question for a moment before smiling once again. 'I am so sorry. I have made a mistake. I did not intend to mislead you. The money – it belongs to three Italian friends of mine who asked me to look after it for them. They intend to purchase antiques in Britain with the cash.'

I had heard it all before. 'Why did you just say the money came from the sale of the fruit?' I asked wearily.

'My friends, they have had considerable trouble with the authorities over taxes they owe the Italian government. I wanted to protect them.'

'Can your friends verify your story?' my DS interjected.

'No, sorry. They are still in Italy. They are not due in the UK until next week.' He waved his hands about expressively and shrugged.

'Why did you feel the need to climb out of the back window in your pyjamas and run away when we knocked on the front door?' I enquired.

'I have a lot of parking tickets outstanding against me from earlier this year, when I was last in your country. I thought you were going to arrest me.'

'We are,' I told him as I read him his rights and arranged for him to be taken to Wembley Police Station for further questioning. Arriving with him in the cells, I showed the custody sergeant the rabbit hutch with its bundles of money and jewellery and asked Scaccio again how much was there. 'Forty-two thousand pounds,' he repeated. He was locked in a detention room while we counted the cash to be sure.

The old Drugs Squad staff had been completely cleared out some time before I joined, after several allegations of corruption among officers were found to be true. Some senior detectives had accepted bribes and gifts amounting to several thousand pounds, and had sold seized drugs back to dealers. Those who were caught and convicted were rightly sent to prison for long terms. The reputation of the Drugs Squad had been shattered for ever by their misdemeanours. I didn't want any mud sticking to my name. So I sat in the custody suite with another officer and carefully counted out all the cash. Try as we might, we couldn't make it any less than £52,000.

I went back to see Scaccio. 'How much money do you say is in the rabbit hutch?'

'Forty-two thousand pounds,' came the answer, again accompanied by a meaningful look.

'But we have just counted out fifty-two thousand pounds,' I told him, confused.

He had to spell it out for me. 'All I am saying, officer, is that when I leave here I am only expecting you to give me forty-two thousand pounds. Is that clear? When will you let me go?'

As soon as the penny finally dropped, I blushed at my stupidity. I left the cell quickly and slammed the door shut. 'That bastard just tried to bribe me,' I told a colleague. He laughed and asked me how much I had been offered. 'Ten thousand pounds,' I said breathlessly, and explained what had happened.

'Well at least he hasn't claimed that you fitted him up,' he guffawed. 'It could have been worse.'

On my instructions, he hauled Scaccio out of the detention room and stood him in front of the desk, as I and another officer flanked him. 'I have brought you out here to officially inform you that I have counted this money three times and I make it fifty-two thousand pounds, not forty-two. The money will now be logged on to the custody record sheet as belonging to you, along with seven items of gold jewellery found in a rabbit hutch. Do you understand, Mr Scaccio, and do you agree with the amount of cash shown here?'

Out of the corner of my eye, I could see Scaccio shifting his weight slightly and shrugging his shoulders. He glanced sideways at me but I refused to meet his gaze. 'OK,' he said grudgingly and signed the custody sheet before being returned to his cell.

Sadly, without any clear evidence of cannabis at the Wembley house, and no established link between the money and drugs, I was forced to release Scaccio on police bail, pending further enquiries. We kept the £52,000 and the jewellery, however, and asked for the names and addresses of the three Italian friends he claimed the money belonged to. The Italian police later confirmed that they had been unable to trace any men by those names at any of the addresses Scaccio had given.

Scaccio failed to answer to his bail and it looked like he had fled back to Italy. We forwarded his cash and property to the Prisoners' Property Office at Scotland Yard, where it would be kept until he asked for it back. Strangely, no one appeared in any hurry to claim it and, to the best of my knowledge, more than a decade on, they still have it. Not a bad morning's work, I'd say, and well worth the search warrant.

The offer of a bribe in return for freedom featured on two other occasions while working on the Drugs Squad. On both occasions I entered dwellings owned by prolific drugs importers and found cocaine. The villains asked to speak to me privately and indicated that I could take whatever I wanted from their homes if I would just get out and leave them alone. In one house, I found £15,000 in cash rolled up in a tin box and was offered it on the spot – but I have never been that way inclined, unfortunately for the drugs dealers. I got a much greater kick out of telling each of them: 'Sorry, mate, I don't work that way and you're nicked.' It pissed the hell out of them.

Search techniques were vitally important to the Drugs Squad because so often our task was like trying to find a needle in a haystack. Sometimes I could be looking for something as small as a single pill, a thumbnail-sized piece of dope, or powder weighing no more than a gram. There was no specific training apart from being told time and again of the importance of being thorough.

The success of a search could be due to either luck or a hunch. My policy had always been that if you couldn't find it, at least give your colleagues the opportunity of going over the same ground because they might find something that you had missed. Never give up, in other words, and never be too proud to admit that a fresh pair of eyes might find what you have overlooked.

That policy paid off in full several times, including once when, following the arrest of a suspect, our fastidious colleague Ted – who was brilliant at sifting through seemingly unimportant correspondence and coming up trumps – found a telephone bill which gave us the suspect's second address. There, at an otherwise unremarkable flat in Notting Hill, we found what we were looking for.

Not that it was immediately obvious. Six of us working in pairs went over this apartment with a fine-tooth comb. We took a room each and started the laborious process of opening drawers, lifting carpets, feeling the seams of curtains, emptying cereal packets and bags of sugar, yet finding nothing. We didn't have drugs dogs trained for anything but cannabis in those days – they couldn't therefore have found the amphetamines we were searching for – so it was down to us. Having scoured our respective rooms and found nothing, we agreed to swap and repeat the process all over again.

It took hours, and was very frustrating because we were certain that somewhere right under our very noses the drugs were waiting to jump out and bite us. We swapped rooms again, so that by the time I got to the kitchen it had already been searched twice. Like my colleagues before me, I found nothing and was left, hands on my hips, wondering what else we could do. The only thing we hadn't done was take the fitted cabinets off the walls. Surely nobody would go to that trouble, but then – of course – I should have known better.

My colleague and I found a screwdriver and started to dismantle the cabinet beside the sink. Once all the screws were loosened, we managed to lift the cabinet up and off the fascia board which remained screwed to the floor.

'Bingo!' I shouted as I looked down at what lay at my feet. Between the fascia board and the bottom of the door was a cavity big enough to conceal a substantial amount of drugs and we had nearly missed it. A fat roll of white powder, a foot long and three inches thick, wrapped in plastic, lay on the kitchen floor. The man in custody was not a happy chappie when we returned, triumphant, his chief source of income in our hands.

The first experience I had of search procedures was at West End Central when, as a uniformed officer, I had to search women, many of whom had been arrested on suspicion of possessing drugs. We were not allowed to search private orifices, but we could make them strip in the hope that anything suspect would become obvious. Not surprisingly, perhaps, it was usual for such women to hide their drugs in the most personal of places, and one of the best ways of getting the offending material out was asking them to jump up and down without their knickers on. Only those with excellent muscle control could keep their hidden parcels *in situ*.

On one such occasion, early in my career, I was called to a hotel room to search a prostitute called Tamara who had been accused of stealing a roll of money from a punter after sexual intercourse, a sum which amounted to about £250. The sergeant who had interviewed the punter, a foreign businessman, spoke to him in the bedroom while the tom was detained in the bathroom by me and another female officer.

'Matey here says it was a single roll of cash, rolled tightly and held together with an elastic band. He found it was missing just as she was about to leave. Should be easy to find,' the sergeant told me. 'It's probably under that wig she's wearing. But make sure it's all there, this bloke's a big cheese and we don't want him upset!'

Tamara was extremely hostile and didn't want to be searched at all. It took me an age to get her to take her clothes off and then her wig. But the money was nowhere to be seen. As she stood stark naked in front of me, I encouraged her: 'Come on now, be a pal and give me the money.' She hung her head and told me she didn't know what I was talking about.

'Right then,' I told her. 'Up on the side of the bath.' She did as she was told. 'Now jump off.'

'What are you trying to do? Make me break a bleedin' leg?' she asked.

'Just do as you're told,' I scolded, 'or I'll call a doctor and he'll soon get it out.' I was in no mood for her sulkiness. Off she jumped, but to no effect, so I made her get up on the bath again and jump once more. Again nothing happened. It took five jumps before the roll of money finally started to work its way loose. Her face was a picture of concentration as she tried to hold it in, and she cursed me when, on the sixth jump, the wad dropped out onto the bathmat.

Triumphant, I donned my plastic gloves, carefully picked it up and dropped it into a plastic bag. Opening the door, I handed it to the sergeant standing waiting outside.

'Brilliant,' he said, as his eyes lit on the money roll. 'It was under the wig, right?' he asked.

'Just be careful how you handle it,' I joked.

'Yeah, right,' he answered, closing the door while I stayed with Tamara as she got dressed.

When she was finished, I took her by the arm and opened the door. 'All finished here, sarge,' I said. 'I'll take her down to the car.'

He nodded but was too busy to speak. As I watched in horror, he licked his fingers and carefully counted out the individual notes from the roll of money I had just retrieved. Seeing him, Tamara cackled and I marched her from the room as quickly as I could before she spilt the beans. I couldn't pluck up the courage to tell him the truth.

My days at the Drugs Squad were enormously happy ones, even if the long hours and intensive nature of the work ensured that I was still seeking solace in a bottle. Satisfying in every way, I felt back on track, although I knew that the new anti-corruption rules meant that my term could only be a maximum of three years. As the deadline of 1985 loomed I realized that there was nothing for it but to bite my lip and sit tight. I hadn't a clue what lay around the corner and could never have guessed what the next ten years would hold.

9

THE CALL CAME AT 6 A.M. ON 7 SEPTEMBER 1985. I WAS HOME
in bed, out for the alcoholic count, when the telephone rang. It
was Lizzie Quaile, one of the detective constables at Acton
Police Station, a sub-division of Ealing in west London, to
where I had been transferred immediately after the Drugs
Squad.

'He's struck again, guv,' I heard her say through the pea-
souper in my head. 'It's Acton again, a flat by a railway line,
only this time the victim is eighty-six.'

'Jesus,' I muttered as I pulled myself out of bed, my head
pounding. I got dressed and drove to the Central Middlesex
Hospital to see her.

On that journey into town in the early hours, it seemed I had
been here a hundred times before, feeling like death, trying to
shake myself awake, the window open to clear my head, my
brain trying to focus on the unappetizing task ahead. The early-
morning rush hour was just starting and all around me business
folk were heading for their offices, some with nothing more
pressing than a few meetings and perhaps a pub lunch to break
up their day.

These were the people that made up juries. People who had
no idea what a stinking rotten lot some members of the human
race could be. Some of them were the type of blinkered people

who couldn't bring themselves to watch the more provocative and challenging programmes on television in case their senses were offended; many of them would acquit rapists because they simply refused to believe that the nice smiling young man sitting in the dock in a suit could have done the unspeakable things of which he was being accused. Who could accept that a young man would rape and humiliate an eighty-six-year-old woman, or that another would try to saw off the hand of a young woman he had just brutalized? There were plenty of people out there who would decide that the allegations must be the product of some overactive feminine imagination.

Nothing in their safe little worlds had prepared them for man's inhumanity to woman. And when in court they were presented with what seemed like a perfectly respectable young defendant and a woman who claimed to have been his victim but who was not, as they expected, a mass of emotions and nerves, they would favour the defendant. Little did they know that we had just spent the previous six months building that rape victim up from the mess we found her in so that she could recover her self-respect sufficiently well to cope with the unforgiving cross-examination she would face in court without suffering a complete breakdown.

I looked at the people around me now and couldn't help but feel some envy as they sang along to the radio and ducked and wove through the traffic in the great race to work. What could they possibly know about the rape of an old lady? I asked myself. More to the point, would they want to know? I wished I had a little of their naïvety. I knew I had long ago lost their ability to take life less seriously.

And what was I about to face? Good God. The oldest and the youngest were always the worst. I would never be able to walk away from this one and not leave a little piece of myself behind. It was what I had to give away each time that sapped me, and, without having the chance to recharge my batteries, the small fragments of the jigsaw that went to make up who I was were diminishing. After all these years, how many little pieces did I have left to give? I was an incomplete puzzle, with large parts lost for ever. This latest woman was eighty-six years old, for

Christ's sake. How much of her suffering would I take home with me and stare at in the bottom of a glass?

Ivy Watts was the sweetest of little old ladies. A widow who lived alone, she reminded me of the grandma I once had. All of us who dealt with her felt she was special.

She lived in a first-floor flat by the railway line, her home for thirty-three years, and her attacker had broken in at 4 a.m. through an insecure sash window, via some ladders.

The first she knew that something was wrong was when she awoke and noticed the hall light was on. She thought she must have inadvertently left it on when she went to bed at nine o'clock, so she got out of bed to turn it off, wearing pyjamas and a bedjacket. As she walked to the door, a masked man wearing large industrial gloves suddenly appeared in the doorway.

'Oh God, oh no,' she cried. She was petrified and froze to the spot.

He moved forwards, forcing her back towards the bed.

'Take them off!' he shouted and pointed to her pyjama bottoms. She was understandably terrified and knew she would never have the strength to fight him off, so she did as she was told. He pushed her back down on to the bed and, as she started to scream, he clamped his gloved hand over her mouth.

'Scream and I'll kill you,' he threatened, before raping her. Ivy had been widowed for thirty-five years and had not had sexual intercourse with anyone since the death of her husband Derek. The act of rape was both extremely painful and very distressing.

He now demanded to know where she kept her money. She directed him to her handbag and, still sobbing, told him: 'That's all the money I've got.' He took a ten-pound note and scattered the loose change from her purse all over her bed.

There were three rings on her dressing table, including her precious opal engagement ring, which he grabbed and put in his pocket. When he wandered into the kitchen to look for more money, she locked herself in her bedroom. He tried to get in but couldn't. Ivy ran to the window, threw it open and screamed the place down. Using her walking stick to hammer on the drainpipe, she woke her neighbours who rushed round to discover her alone.

As soon as I got to her bedside in hospital I realized that her extreme distress would delay or prevent her giving me the fine detail. I also sensed that I would never manage to restore her confidence to such a degree that she could face a judge and jury in a court of law. Within minutes of my arrival she was already beginning to pull the shutters down on the whole incident and found it extremely difficult to fill in the gaps in her statement.

'I kicked him in the balls, you know,' she told me conspiratorially, through her tears. 'I gave him a right seeing-to and told him where to go. I wasn't having none of it. Dirty little bastard.' Her bottom lip trembled.

I pressed her bony little hand gently and nodded, knowing full well that she was exaggerating or even lying but understanding her completely. So many vulnerable old people seem to think it is wrong or weak for them to have been frightened into submission, and make up stories of heroics, and at times like this what is to be gained in challenging them? Wasn't it far kinder to congratulate them for being so brave and go along with it?

'Did you see what he was wearing, when you kicked him?' I asked. Her eyes flickered but she chose to ignore my question.

'I told him, if my Derek'd still been alive, he'd have seen him off.'

'Well done, Ivy. Can you remember, did he have a knife?'

'These kids today, they think they can take what they want without a by-your-leave. They think they can frighten people like me, but I lived through two world wars, you know. He didn't frighten me.' I nodded and smiled and continued trying to coax information from her. She turned to look at me, her face suddenly wet with tears. 'He took my engagement ring,' she wept. 'Derek bought me that in 1924. He saved up all his money and bought it from Wilkinson's on Stirling Corner.'

I stroked her hand. 'I know, Ivy, I know. I'm so sorry. We'll do all we can to get it back for you, I promise, but can you try and help me some more? Did he say anything to you when he attacked you?'

But the shutters had well and truly come down. She lay back on her pillows, crying silently and wringing her hands. I knew there was no point in labouring my questions so I squeezed her arm and left, my own eyes smarting.

Why did the television programmes make it all look so damned easy? I wondered as I drove out of the hospital car park. I was supposed to walk away now and come up with a name or a face or a flash of inspiration that would lead me straight to the door of the man who had just attacked Ivy Watts. 'You're nicked, sunshine,' I was supposed to say as I kicked in his door and twisted his arm up his back. The reality was that I didn't have a clue and the lady who should have been my best witness wasn't going to be much help at all.

I spoke to Ivy's neighbours and discovered that she had no living relatives and few other people who cared a damn about her. The initial stages of the investigation were taken up as much with trying to trace distant friends, neighbours, social services and support agencies as they were with the hunt for the rapist.

She looked so sad and alone each time I went to see her in hospital. She was tiny and quite frail, swamped by the bed and her hospital gown, her walking stick at her side. Her lovely face was framed with short white hair and I felt utterly helpless as I sat at her bedside, holding her hand, trying to reassure her and yet desperate to find out more about what had happened.

She never did reveal everything. The scant details Lizzie and I managed to extract took days, but each day there was less and less to tell. One of the last times I went to see her, I arrived with some chrysanthemums which I put in a vase on her bedside table.

'Hello, dear,' she said, reaching for my hand. 'I've got something to tell you.' I sat on the edge of the bed, looking at her little-girl eyes lit with anticipation.

'What is it, Ivy? What have you got to tell me?'

She looked around her as if wary of anyone else hearing what she had to say. Pulling me towards her, she said: 'I'm afraid I've been rather silly, dear. I've been wasting your time.'

I pulled back and looked at her. 'How's that, Ivy?' I asked.

'That young man I told you about,' she went on, 'he didn't attack me at all.' As I waited for the next sentence, I recalled the forensic examiner's evidence of forced sexual intercourse. A particularly cruel attack, he had reported. Semen was found inside her and she had sustained injuries that could only have resulted from a rape. 'I woke up this morning and suddenly realized', Ivy continued, 'that it was all just a bad dream. I have them all the time, you see, only this one was so very vivid. I'm so sorry to have wasted your time. But, you see, it didn't really happen at all.'

It was obvious that this dear little old lady could no longer cope with the awful truth or the thought that she might have to give evidence about it in public one day. But it wasn't for me to tell her that. I nodded and smiled, pretending to believe everything she was telling me. When she was finished, I told her not to worry and kissed her goodbye. I had already spoken to the social services to get her the help she needed and they promised to take care of her. I hoped they would be as good as their word.

Aware that my continuing contact with her as a police officer would only add to her distress, and having decided that a prosecution in her case was impossible, I gradually withdrew. Much as I would have liked to remain Ivy's friend, I was acutely aware that I would remind her for ever of something she was desperately trying to forget. I was also doubtful that I was in any fit shape, mentally, at this stage to take Ivy's suffering on board.

I heard later that she had died and I cried.

The Ealing position had come in my twentieth year as a serving police officer when, in January 1985, my senior officers asked me if I would like what they called a home posting, one relatively near to where I lived, meaning an end to the 4 a.m. starts and midnight finishes. Ealing was an interesting area, just ten miles from my home, and I accepted it with thanks.

In all the years I had been working I had, for the most part, been getting up at dawn to go to work, be it in east London, south London or somewhere more central. I could hardly imagine the luxury of a regular lie-in, the chance for an extra hour to overcome my hangovers, and a more civilized opportunity to prepare myself for the arduous day ahead. It would also allow me more time to cope with the problems I was having on the home front.

My mother was by now in a very fragile mental condition and I knew the time had come when I was going to have to arrange for more outside help. Every time I saw her I felt she had slipped away that little bit more and it cut me to the quick. Now she was distracted and wizened, unable to take care of her most basic needs, and I simply couldn't handle it any more.

When I went to see her GP and told her I was at my wits' end, she arranged for my mother to be admitted to the Shenley mental hospital in Hertfordshire for a twenty-eight-day psychiatric assessment, knowing it would give me a break. Mum was, by this time, in another world. I packed her suitcase and told her she was going on a journey but she was so far out of it that Shenley meant absolutely nothing to her.

However much I tried to reject the inevitable, I knew that once the psychiatric assessment was over I would have to plan for her to have permanent care in a nursing home. There was simply no other way to look after her. I would have had to give up my job to cope with her full-time, and even if I did I was far from qualified for the task of looking after someone in the advanced stages of senile dementia. Feeling incredibly guilty, I made enquiries and found what seemed like suitable accommodation quite nearby, keeping her close to both my new office and my house. Pete and I agreed that, in the absence of any funding from the local authority, we would sell Mum's place and use that money to pay for her care.

Once the cash had run out – and we estimated that, properly invested, it would take about five years – we could apply for local-authority help. The house we had grown up in, the one my parents saved so hard to buy before the war and which a German bomb had nearly finished off, was put on the market. I still had a key and kept an eye on the old place, popping in once or twice a week to check that all was well. It felt so strange, wandering through the rooms one by one, caressing the furnishings and remembering my childhood years there.

I wished there could have been some other way, that my mother would miraculously return to us and tell us that everything was all right, but I knew that it was hopeless. She had left us the day Dad died and I knew it was now only a matter of attending to her physical needs. When the matron at the nearby nursing home I had seen met her at Shenley and agreed to take her on full-time, I was hugely relieved.

On arrival at Ealing nick that January, I was quickly introduced to the new responsibilities associated with being a DI in suburbia. Acton had its own CID and a DI in overall charge with direct responsibility to Ealing's Detective Chief Inspector. The two stations operated as a team, albeit split. Acton had its own detective sergeants and detective constables, plus the luxury of Lizzie, an experienced woman DC, and Ealing had theirs.

Needless to say, if sex reared its ugly head anywhere between the two stations, it was as sure as eggs were eggs that I would be asked to help in due course. That is exactly what had happened when Lizzie Quaile rang me early that morning in September to attend to Ivy Watts.

Soon after settling in, and following the rape of three women in Chiswick and Acton, I was asked whether or not I thought these, and Ivy's rape, were the work of a single man. Good preliminary enquiries had already been done on the separate investigations and some links had been made. What stood out was that the attacker's *modus operandi* was virtually identical in each assault.

The attacker had gone to considerable lengths to evade detection. He was always hooded or masked, he dressed in dark or black clothing and carried a knife. He wore gloves, cut telephone wires to prevent his victims from raising the alarm, removed light bulbs and tied his victims up before sexually assaulting them. My DCI asked me if, with a small squad, I thought I could catch the bastard. It was too good an offer to turn down.

I was given an excellent team in the form of three seasoned male detectives, and a uniformed constable with good local knowledge. Later I was to add a friendly face in the form of Christine Douglas, a brilliant young officer who was particularly good with sexual assault victims.

I knew that it would be a hard case to solve. Many of the attacker's victims couldn't even be positive about the colour of his skin, because he always made sure that he was covered up. He had tried to be shrewd by stopping himself from ejaculating, so as to leave no semen for Forensics to find, but he wasn't always successful. He spoke with a London accent, but there was little else we knew about him.

Prior to my arrival, the investigation had been necessarily fragmented. I ordered a further sweep of all the unsolved rapes in the area to establish which ones we could reasonably say one man was guilty of, and asked the surrounding divisions to search their crime books for unsolved sexual assaults, requesting that they forward the details to me. I ended up with a mass of cases, selecting those which I believed my suspect was responsible for, including one or two which were off my patch.

Using witness statements, we tried to analyse the character of the individual we were looking for. In those days professional criminal profiling was not generally available – it was rarely used and was too costly – so the only picture we could paint of the rapist had to be done by me and my team. We knew, because we had all seen it a hundred times before, that a rapist often has a distorted view of the opposite sex, uneasy relations with his family, particularly his mother, and a string of failed relationships with women. We felt sure he lived locally and we knew that he was fit because of the height of some of the walls he scaled. Otherwise, we knew sod-all about him.

We plotted the area of all the attacks on a map and tried to figure out where our perpetrator lived. We suspected that he lived near a railway line because most of the attacks happened near one of the main British Rail routes through west London. Some of the houses he entered even backed directly on to the railway, and we wondered if he might be an employee of British Rail, which would have given him easy access.

We assumed he was black because one witness had seen a flash of skin where his glove met his sleeve, and that he was primarily a burglar owing to his agility and his expertise at getting into houses. He always stole property from the women he raped but left no fingerprints. DNA profiling wasn't readily available, although the science was just becoming known. We knew from body fluids left at the scene that his blood grouping was B, but on its own that didn't take us very far.

I drew up a huge wallchart with all the cases listed on it, along with the identifying features and similarities in terms of *modus operandi*. In each case I listed the attacker's general description, evidence left at the scene and MO. He always followed a similar pattern: breaking into a flat or house somewhere near the railway line, nicking a few valuables, checking to see if there was a woman alone on the premises, stashing his stolen goods and returning to break in again. Sometimes he stole after the act of rape, but he always took something at some stage.

He often talked to his victims while he raped them, adding to their humiliation by asking them if they were enjoying it. The way he spoke and the things he said were added to my wallchart. He favoured tying his victims' hands and preferred to rape from the rear. We assumed this was so that his victims would have less chance of studying him, and the mask or hood he wore was often an item of clothing adapted from the woman's own wardrobe.

There was another unusual feature that I initially thought might provide the lead we needed. We discovered that whoever was raping these women was dropping his trousers and defecating in the garden just outside the property before going in to commit the attack, presumably as the adrenalin rush got to him, and being scared shitless – literally – by the thought of what he was about to do.

I always had to second-guess the criminal I was chasing, so that I could try and anticipate what his next move might be. As I gradually got to know this one, mulling over his style and characteristics, I realized that as bad bastards go he was not the worst, although that didn't mean to say that he didn't scare the hell out of his victims. But after all that had happened to Janie and Renata, I couldn't help but compare each new rapist to Lashley and his psychopathic traits. This boy, fortunately, wasn't in the same league. Never particularly violent, although he always carried a knife, he often showed remorse and, with one victim, he even sat at the end of the bed afterwards and apologized. Lashley had never shown such humanity.

Wading through the mass of information we had received from neighbouring stations and looking at sex offenders known to us in the area, I religiously worked through the indices of all the men who might reasonably fit the bill, but no one showed up immediately. Still, we had thirty or so possible suspects and over the next few weeks my team did a terrific job knocking on their front doors, checking their alibis for the nights of the attacks. It was a laborious process of elimination and, despite exhaustive enquiries, no one suspect seemed the likely candidate.

The next phase was to start checking through the indices of all those in the area who had a history of burglary only. This was a much broader sweep and involved hundreds of young men in and around Acton alone. Quite often all my detectives got was a brusque 'Piss off' from their enquiries, which made life very difficult. It took us weeks of research, working long hours, and with no leads I realized we weren't going to get very far until we got lucky, or until the attacker struck again.

Christmas and the new year came and went and still we hadn't caught the man who had attacked Ivy and the other women. I was consumed with frustration that we weren't getting anywhere and that this man had been able to do what he liked, when he liked, and we were always way behind him. It made my blood boil to think of him out there somewhere, smugly contemplating his next attack, while we seemed powerless to stop him.

By mid-January, and with no new leads, I decided to go back over all the information we had, to try and see if there was something we had missed. Telling the team was hard. I knew they were as frustrated as I was and wanted to catch this bastard, but I also knew they were as tired as I was and felt they had given it their all.

'Sorry, guys,' I said, anticipating their disappointment after I had gathered them together in the incident room. 'But we're going to have to go back to square one and check this lot again.' There was a collective sigh but, whatever they felt, I never heard a moan from any one of them as they put their heads down and got on with the job.

On 23 January 1986 our man struck again. Juliet Davies, a twenty-year-old single woman who lived in a ground-floor flat in Churchfield Road, Acton, was burgled and raped in her bed at 4.15 a.m.

I liked Juliet from the minute I saw her at her flat at six that morning. Pretty, slim, with shoulder-length brown hair and large green eyes, she had a smile for everyone. She struck me as one of God's lovely people as she fumbled to find the words to tell me that she was sorry for having to get me out of bed so early. She was obviously extremely distressed but, like so many women I had seen, she struggled desperately to keep herself together and maintain her dignity as we wrapped her in blankets to take her to the special rape suite at Brentford Police Station. How far we had come from the spartan matron's office at West End Central, I thought, as I led her into the softly lit suite of rooms that we would put to regular use over the next couple of days.

I knew that all Juliet really wanted at that time was a hot bath and the scrubbing brush so that she could remove every last trace of her attacker's filthy contamination from her body. But I explained that before she washed our police doctor would give her a full medical examination in the hope of finding body fluids which might eventually identify her attacker. Juliet seemed to understand and without more ado went with me to the examination room, where she put up with all the prodding and poking admirably.

I have never been able to cope well with somebody else's tears because it shows me they are hurting. Instinctively I want to put my arms around them and promise that I will make it better, whether I am able to or not, in the hope that they will stop crying and the pain will disappear. And I've always hated the emotions that their tears generate in me. Why do I always feel so bloody angry? Between trying to console my victim, I also have to deal with the offender and although I always want to scream obscenities at the individual who had the audacity to intrude, humiliate and injure these women so, I bite my lip instead.

Nobody but nobody will ever understand the destruction rapists do by committing these appalling acts and anyone who dares utter the words 'I know exactly how you feel' deserves a smack in the mouth, unless, God forbid, they have suffered likewise. We will never know their pain and they will never forget it. No matter how well they recover, most aspects of their lives will be touched for ever by the experience and, for many, nothing will ever be the same again.

But for the moment, I had Juliet to deal with and I could see the effort she put into not crying and, as for so many of the others, I suddenly had this overwhelming respect and admiration for her. So I put on the front that I thought she would expect to see and I hid the anger and suppressed the emotions that might have shown me in a less professional light. They would emerge later and be dealt with in the privacy of my home.

Juliet's personality was a credit to her. By nature a bubbly and energetic individual, she worked for a large company as a marketing manager and had a super boyfriend called Simon. From the outset, Juliet appeared determined to help us in every possible way and, as she sat curled up with a mug of tea in one of the soft armchairs of the rape suite, she gave me a very clear picture of what had happened a few hours earlier in her flat.

Designed to make victims of sexual abuse feel more at home, the rape suite was decorated like a living room, with table lamps, peach wallpaper, a coffee table strewn with magazines and the all-important kettle. A relatively new concept in the Met at that time, similar rape suites were springing up all over London as their effectiveness at making the victims feel more comfortable became known.

Simon was a wonderful man and truly one of the most understanding partners I had ever come across. Patient, kind, sympathetic and never overtly angry, he put no pressure on Juliet to tell him what had happened, but said that if ever she wanted to confide in him she could do so in her own time.

It is the close friends and family members of those who have been raped who are the 'hidden victims'. In trying to come to terms with what has happened to their loved ones they invariably react in an absurd and uncharacteristic manner. It is like a cancer, eating away at them, as many of those close to the victim often feel unable to touch or comfort her because their own feelings of guilt and shame get in the way.

Rape is a taboo subject. Victims are never named, to protect them from publicity, but that same anonymity compounds their own feelings of guilt and shame. There is no one they can talk to about what happened to them; there is the sense that the neighbours mustn't know and fathers, brothers and boyfriends, in particular, often avoid talking about it altogether, believing it will suppress the horror of the act. Some spouses reject their wives physically because they feel that such intimacy may be intrusive. Others respond angrily and feel terribly hurt because their partners have been contaminated by another, all of which only serves to heighten the victim's trauma. I have witnessed these responses many times and occasionally try to intervene to ease the healing processes where I can.

Out of Juliet's view, I could see Simon's anguish and I asked her permission to sit with him while he read her statement two days after the attack just in case I could help him come to terms with her terrible predicament. She agreed and, although I could tell he was full of emotion at reading what some stranger had done to the woman he loved, he controlled it beautifully. When he had finished, he thanked me for showing him the report, left the room and went for a long walk. About an hour later, he returned and gave Juliet the biggest hug. He wanted to be strong for her and was determined never to let her see his pain. Not surprisingly, my initial impression of him proved right and they ended up happily married, putting the past well and truly behind them.

Finding strength from within to tell me everything she remembered, Juliet started to tell me the details of her attack. On the fateful night she went to bed about eleven-thirty, with her flatmate asleep in the room next door. In the middle of the night she awoke to find the room in darkness, which was unusual because she normally left the bedroom door ajar and the landing light on. Leaning across to the bedside table to turn the lamp on, she realized that the bulb had been removed. Sud- denly aware of the presence of someone else in the room, she began to fear for her life.

Leaping up to pull the curtain back from the window and call for help, she was grabbed by a man, who put his gloved hand over her mouth and held her tightly by the wrist. He pulled the curtains closed and told her: 'Shut up, be quiet, I'm not going to hurt you.'

Pushing her down on to the bed, he tied her wrists tightly behind her back with her dressing-gown cord. She started to plead with him but he stuffed a scarf into her mouth to keep her quiet. 'I'm not going to hurt you,' he told her again, as he moved around the room, rummaging through drawers and cupboards. She prayed he was just a burglar and would leave when he had got what he came for. He moved back towards her and she froze, unable to scream or move. 'Give me your rings,' he said, and started to prise them from her fingers. Reluctant to part with one which her grandmother had given her, she resisted when he came to that finger. 'All right, I won't take it. I'm human, you know.' He replaced the light bulb in the bed-side lamp and turned it on. She still couldn't see him because the duvet was half over her face as she lay face-down on the bed. He pulled the duvet off. 'You're trying to escape, aren't you?'

She shook her head, but he checked her bonds, tightening them. He turned the light out again and told her: 'Get out of bed.' When she sat up, he grabbed her shoulders and made her kneel on the floor.

'I'm going to tie your legs together, don't move,' he said. Changing his mind, he suddenly forced her ankles apart and said: 'I'm going to make love to you.' Spitting the scarf from her mouth, she started to plead with him. He pressed a hand over her face and demanded: 'Who's in the next room?' When she told him it was her flatmate, he replied: 'I've got a gun in the other room and if you make one sound I'm going to blow her brains out.' He put the scarf back in her mouth, grabbed a pair of Juliet's tights and tied them around her head, knotting them at the back.

Repeating the words 'I'm going to make love to you,' he lifted her T-shirt and yanked off her pyjama bottoms while kneeling behind her. He then raped her from behind, interrogating her as he did so. 'Do you like this? Do you hate black people?' He also asked her if she loved him and when she shook her head he withdrew quickly without ejaculating.

He pulled her up on to the bed so that she was lying on her back and raped her a second time, trying to kiss her when her gag slipped. When he had finished and dressed himself, he untied her wrists and turned the light on. Sitting up, she saw him for the first time. He was dressed in a black tracksuit with grey shorts on top. Pulled down over his head and face was a green knitted bobble hat, which she recognized as hers. He had turned it inside-out and cut out eyeholes. She could tell from the glimpses of his skin that he was black. Her six-inch bladed kitchen knife was sticking out of his pocket.

'Have you got any money?' he asked.

Sobbing, she told him: 'No, none, neither of us have got anything valuable. If I had I'd give it to you.'

She told him to take the television and video, but he said he already had them. He told her he wanted cash.

'I haven't got any,' Juliet cried. 'I didn't go to the bank yesterday.' He then rifled carelessly through a jewellery box on her dressing table, taking rings and a lighter. 'What are you doing this for?' she asked him.

'I can't get a job,' he said, before sitting on the edge of the bed. He added: 'I didn't rape you, I made love to you.' Appearing to show some remorse, he then asked her what he could do to make her forgive him.

'The best thing you can do is leave,' she said. He was silent. Hoping to keep him friendly, she added: 'Or make me a cup of tea.' He laughed. He took two cigarettes from a packet and held one to her lips, offering her a light from a plastic lighter he was carrying. Shivering and wishing he'd go, Juliet half lay, half sat on the bed, her hands still tied tightly behind her back and as he moved towards her she jumped nervously.

'I'm going now, I'm sorry,' he told her. He left the room, closing the door behind him, and she heard him walking towards the sitting room. As she sat holding her breath, waiting for him to go, the door opened again and he said once more: 'I'm sorry.' She heard him leave through the kitchen door. This time he didn't return. When she realized he had gone, she ran into her flatmate's room crying. The police were called at 5 a.m.

At my request, Juliet made up a list of all the things he had stolen. She was a cracking witness and did all she could to detail what had been taken but, not surprisingly in the circumstances, she couldn't remember every single item and we agreed to come back to those points later.

I had Forensics go over Juliet's flat with a fine-tooth comb. The SOCO found a single white animal hair in the middle of her green bedroom carpet that we speculated had been brought in by her attacker, so we kept it. We discovered that he had entered the flat by hooking his hand up through the cat flap in the kitchen door, but prior to that he had jumped over her back garden wall, landing in soft earth and leaving a footprint. Outside the back door was a plastic bucket full of human faeces. I had someone pack it up carefully with a view to carting it over to the Metropolitan Police Forensic Science Laboratory. I'm not sure what evidence I thought it might yield, but before it ever reached the reception desk I got a terse message back from the lab which read: 'Thanks but no thanks, Carol, we can't do testing on faeces, it is simply waste.' So much for that.

After taking a plaster cast of the footprint in the garden soil, DC Dick South with whom I was working, told me he had recently nicked a young man for burglary. Back at the police station, he had taken the bloke's old trainers off his feet and tried to match the unusual sole pattern, which featured a special design, with some imprints left at the scenes of other crimes. None of them matched but he now thought the sole pattern on the trainers very similar to the one found in Juliet's garden. The burglar's name was Winston Messam.

Winston Messam. Where had I heard that name before? Going back through all the papers for the umpteenth time, I came across a seemingly unimportant piece of information which we had been given by a young constable just before Christmas. Out on his beat at 2 a.m., he happened upon a young black man jogging near Churchfield Road, Acton. He stopped to question him because he was suspicious about what he was doing out so late. The man was called Winston Messam and he told the officer he couldn't sleep. Knowing that we had not yet identified the rapist, the young PC had informed us about Messam all those weeks earlier and we had logged it with the information on other possible suspicious sightings of men in the previous months.

Looking at his file now, I asked the local officers about him and what they told me made the hairs rise on the back of my neck: nineteen years old, a tall, clean-shaven, athletic young man with no previous convictions for sexual offences although several for burglary. They described him as an arrogant youth pretending to be a man but with no adult communications skills. He came from a big family where the father was a strict disciplinarian and the mother a devout Christian, who always wore a big grey floppy hat with JESUS SAVES on it.

I hadn't got one shred of evidence to say that Winston Messam had raped Juliet Davies or any of the others, but I suddenly found him a very interesting prospect. He fitted the description, he had form for burglary, he lived near the railway line and he came from an unusual family background. A gut feeling deep inside told me that he might know something. I could at least bring him in for a chat.

Expecting Messam to be unco-operative, I decided that Dick should first return his old trainers in the hope of striking up a conversation, before tackling the thorny question of his whereabouts on the night of Juliet's rape. We agreed to start looking for him at his mother's house. Dick South and DS Derek Cairns, who had also dealt with Messam in the past, agreed that he could be a right handful if the mood took him. So we grabbed a further four members of the crime squad and decided that we would all congregate on the pavement outside his mother's house in Uxbridge Road, Acton, but that only Cairns and South would go to the front door to see if he was in. The rest of us would try to blend in with pedestrians and shoppers, while keeping an eye out for trouble if Messam did a runner.

The distance between the front door and the street was about twelve yards. I stood nonchalantly near the bottom step at pavement level, while the four crime squad lads sauntered slowly along the road, pretending to window-shop. Derek and Dick knocked on the front door, expecting his mother to answer, but before we knew it Winston Messam himself was standing there blinking at us. He was taller than I imagined, and as fit as a fiddle.

Suddenly, all hell broke loose. Messam took one look at the two coppers on his doorstep, brought his fist back and punched Dick South in the face, knocking him for six. As Derek stepped backwards, Messam side-stepped him and decided to try and leg it. As planned, the four lads from the crime squad sprang into action and rugby-tackled him to the ground.

Messam then went absolutely bonkers, lashing out at everyone in sight. None of us had the chance to tell him the purpose of our visit and it didn't take a genius to work out why he didn't want to speak to us. Within a few minutes the mêlée of arms and legs had rolled into the centre of the busy main thoroughfare. I stood in the middle of the road, both arms in the air, looking like a demented duck, screaming at the driver of the bus to my right to stop, while trying to convince the traffic to my left that it was not appropriate to proceed. With Messam still fighting like some crazed madman, I called for 'urgent assistance' on my radio.

'It's all gone boss-eyed!' I shouted into my handset. 'Get the van down here.'

By this time the rest of the Messam family had poured out of the house and appeared to be chanting in unison for us to leave young Winston alone. Not content to shriek abuse at us, Mrs Messam decided it was time to get personally involved and, complete with JESUS SAVES hat, she joined the throng and started to drag the officers off her son.

'Where's the bloody cavalry when you need them!' I cursed as I watched a sprightly young bunch of hooligans from the local probation hostel suddenly sprint out and hurl abuse. Within a short space of time, the whole event had turned into one enormous dog fight, and was fast getting out of hand. I was genuinely concerned for the safety of my colleagues and myself, and was more than fearful of the outcome. By now the traffic was stationary back to Shepherd's Bush Green and the Bayswater Road, not helped by the fact that the struggling Messam was in the middle of the road, being sat on by four men who were themselves being attacked from behind.

My radio eventually crackled into life above the commotion. 'The van bringing assistance can't get through,' the controller radioed. 'It's stuck in some almighty traffic jam in the Uxbridge Road.'

'We *are* the bloody traffic jam!' I shrieked. 'Tell them to get their finger out.' I knew that if the reinforcements didn't arrive soon someone was going to get hurt.

The tension was at its height when Mrs Messam broke free from her relatives, ran up to me and screeched: 'Judas, you Judas!' in my face, before retreating back to the steps of her house. It was a terrifying spectacle.

Eventually the van appeared, weaving its way through, driving down the pavement, lights and siren blaring. Five officers jumped out and restrained the hecklers, while others helped lift the angry, frenzied Messam into the back of the van.

'What a soddin' mess,' I told a dishevelled Dick South as the traffic finally began to flow again. I stayed for a while in an attempt to placate the Messam family but had difficulty making myself understood above the cacophony. 'Let's get you out of here, guv, before you get lynched,' one of the crime squad lads advised, and he was right. There is a time to stay and a time to go, and this was definitely a time to leave.

Back at Acton Police Station, Messam was shown into a cell to cool down. Once we had slammed the door shut on this berserk young man, we all but collapsed.

'Well, ma'am, I'm buggered if I know what that was all about, but we've got him,' said Dick, nursing his bruised jawbone. 'Even if we don't know what the fuck for.'

I called my team together and asked for their help. I made it clear that in the absence of nothing more than suspicion we had precious little else to hold Messam on. The weekend was coming up but everyone knew that there would be no early nights or sliding off. We would all stay until it got sorted. If Messam hadn't done the rape then what the hell had he done? Because he had not exactly hung around to explain himself.

Taking our lives into our own hands, we returned to the Messam house, with a warrant to search Winston's bedroom. We found his new trainers, almost identical to the old ones, with a sole pattern that exactly matched the indentations found in the soft soil in Juliet's back garden. But the Puma shoes were by no means unique and the company told us that they made several thousand, so it could only go towards circumstantial evidence.

Stuck to the sole of one of the trainers, however, was an Asda supermarket price label with about three white animal hairs stuck to it, very similar to the ones found on Juliet's carpet; and beside his bed was a white goatskin rug which was moulting fast. We rolled it up and sent the lot to the lab for comparison.

But it still wasn't enough. We had to have more, and we knew there wasn't a hope in hell's chance of getting it voluntarily from Messam. Needless to say, when I sat opposite him in the interview room he didn't admit to a thing. Most of us would have considered it an occupational hazard, but the public rarely saw how difficult it was to deal with an individual who loathed authority with a vengeance. When his solicitor arrived on the scene, Messam was asked to account for his movements on the night of Juliet Davies's rape and he claimed he had been in bed asleep at his mother's house. He denied all knowledge of the attack.

I knew I needed more time, so I went to the magistrates' court the following day, a Saturday, and told the justices the background to the serial rapes and my suspicions concerning

Messam. I told them I needed extra time to gather the evidence. Under the Police and Criminal Evidence Act, known as PACE, I had to give very sound reasons to a court to extend a period in custody for a suspect. Claiming that I had *prima facie* evidence implicating Messam, I asked for two more days. Granting my request, the magistrates said that if I didn't have what I needed to charge him by ten o'clock on Monday morning I would have to let him go. It was all very different from times past when I used to hold on to suspects for days without access to a solicitor on grounds not dissimilar to these.

I felt sure I had the right man in this case but I just didn't have enough evidence to charge him. On Saturday evening, I placed a large bottle of Scotch in the centre of the incident-room table and invited the team to join me. 'Go and get the glasses, Dick,' I said. 'We're going to check and recheck these bloody statements until we can safely say we've missed nothing.'

Dick South, Derek, another detective called Ossie Svard and I each took a bundle of statements and documents relating to the different attacks and we worked our way through the whole lot. We racked our brains for inspiration and when it eventually came, at 2 a.m., it was Dick who provided it. 'I see Juliet had a lighter stolen from her flat,' he said suddenly, looking at a statement in front of him.

'Yes, she came in this morning, said she was sorry that she'd not mentioned it before, but that she'd only just missed it,' said Derek.

'But haven't we got that lighter?' Dick asked, his face lit up.

'No, we haven't,' I interrupted. 'I showed her the lighter we found but it didn't belong to her.' I thought he was referring to a black plastic lighter I had found in Messam's bedroom when we searched it.

'Are you sure, guv?' Dick asked as I poured us all another Scotch.

'Of course I'm bloody sure,' I snapped, tired and angry at him for asking. We sipped from our glass and carried on reading through the typewritten statements.

'Ma'am,' Dick piped up. 'Are you absolutely positive about that lighter?'

'Dick South,' I said, impatiently. 'It was a bloody black plastic lighter that we found. Now will you shut up and let me concentrate.'

'No, no,' Dick said excitedly, pointing to a statement I had never seen. 'Not that lighter. I'm talking about the long gilt-plated one I found in his pocket when I arrested him. Maybe you haven't seen it, but it was broken, it didn't work and the custody officer was in two minds whether to allow him to keep it or not, because it was useless. I think it was just like the lighter that Juliet describes here in this statement, the one she has only recently realized was stolen.'

We all stared at each other for a second until I broke the silence. It was like God had just turned the lights on. 'Bugger me, Dick,' I said. 'Get down there and find the bloody thing!'

Dick and Derek both leapt up and flew down the stairs to the cells as I sat waiting in the incident room, praying. It was the early hours, the nick was quiet, and I could hear their hurried steps echoing down the stairwell and the door to the custody suite slamming shut. He must have flushed it down the toilet by now, I thought. The bastard has surely got rid of it. I even thought through the pros and cons of opening up the police-station drains to see if we could find it, if he had.

Then I heard the shout. A cry of victory came from Dick South a floor below in the cells. The door of the custody suite crashed open downstairs and I could hear the two men running up the stairs towards me. As they got to the landing, they yelled: 'Guv, we've found the lighter. We've fucking got it!'

The office door burst open and Dick slung a slim gilt pencil lighter across the table at me. I grabbed it and picked it up in my hand, but I still couldn't believe it. I turned it over carefully in my hand and grinned. The initials JD were only just visible, faintly engraved on the side. How on earth could I have missed that? I shuddered.

As dawn broke and the sun started to rise in the sky outside the smoke-stained window, I sent a car round to Juliet's flat to bring her back to the nick. I made a pot of black coffee and we waited like expectant parents until she arrived.

At just after eight-thirty that Sunday morning, with only twenty-four hours to go before we would have to release Messam, Juliet picked up the gilt lighter in her hand, turned it over and said: 'This is my lighter. The man who raped me took it from my jewellery box.'

I looked into her face, smiled broadly and said: 'Got him!'

10

I FELL OUT OF BED AND FUMBLED FOR MY DRESSING GOWN. MY head pounding, I staggered into the bathroom and leant heavily over the white china sink. Forty-two years old and at the bottom of the heap, I couldn't bear to look at my reflection in the mirror any more. I reached for the toothpaste and clumsily squirted some on to the brush. Opening my mouth, I suddenly retched violently. I could no longer remember a morning that had been any different. Dry heaves and the shakes were part of my daily routine.

When there was nothing left to bring up, and my stomach had gone into spasm, I staggered back to bed, my head in my hands. I closed my eyes and ears against the drumming noises in my brain and wished I was dead.

I had imagined my own funeral a hundred times and I did so now once again. 'Ashes to ashes, dust to dust,' the vicar solemnly read out as my coffin was lowered into the freshly dug grave on canvas straps. I could see my brother Pete and his wife standing dry-eyed at the grave, but there was no one else. The undertakers looked more upset than the mourners. I imagined that Pete hadn't gone for the expensive option.

It was only a matter of time before my fantasy would become reality. How much longer could I carry on drinking myself into a stupor and passing out? I would either choke on my own vomit in the night or commit suicide in the despair of the early hours. I knew exactly how I would do it when the time came: Valium, paracetamol and booze, a cocktail to instant oblivion. The doctor had already prescribed the sleeping pills and I could easily get hold of some more.

I would try to arrange it at a time when I would be missed and discovered soon afterwards. I had a morbid fear that otherwise some poor sod would find me decomposing in my bed weeks later. I probably wouldn't even leave a note. So far as my family was concerned, there was only Pete, and I hoped he would understand.

I was up at six-thirty on the morning of Thursday 6 March 1986 and I had never been lower. Messam was in custody awaiting trial and I had several loose ends to tie up and complete for the Crown Prosecution Service. I was still running the team at Acton nick, with all that it involved, and for the first time in my career I felt I was losing it. I'd had enough. I wanted a rest. I wanted out.

When the worst of my hangover was past, I pulled myself up again, showered and got dressed. It was to be another hectic day, much of it spent at the Metropolitan Police Laboratory in Lambeth discussing Messam's body secretions and other forensic evidence with the scientists.

I had eventually charged Messam with four counts of rape, after establishing that they were virtually identical in method. I had also looked at several other rapes and serious sexual assaults in the area, seven of which were similar in style to those I had charged him with. However, I took the view, for one reason or another, that it would be better not to muddy the waters by charging Messam with them all. The evidence I had on the four was absolutely clear-cut, and common sense – coupled with my experience of the judicial system – dictated that if I could succeed on these he was very unlikely to receive a less severe sentence than if he had been convicted for all eleven.

The evidence I had gathered went to prove something called 'similar facts', a legal term used to show that one individual was likely to have committed all of the offences because of the obvious similarities in style. It would have been very unusual, for example, for another rapist to be operating in the same area at the same time, looking and speaking much the same and using the same techniques.

Following the positive identification of Juliet's lighter, I had taken Messam to Acton Magistrates' Court and asked that he be remanded back into police custody for a couple of days. My request was granted and I took a very subdued and sullen young man back to the police station with me.

I knew an identification parade would be a waste of time because none of the victims had ever seen her attacker's face; but all of them had heard him speak in his soft London accent, and Juliet in particular was convinced that she would never forget his dulcet tones.

So at Acton Police Station on 28 January 1986, I set up what I believe to have been the first ever voice-identification parade in the country, something that has been done many times since and with great effect. Messam and seven other Afro-Caribbean youths, all dressed in masks and gloves borrowed by me from the BBC, were asked to stand in a line. As the victims passed each of the men, they were asked to read aloud extracts from a front-page story in the *Sun* which had suggestive words in it, similar to the ones used at the time of the attacks. 'I want to make love to you,' each man was asked to repeat.

When it was Juliet's turn, she walked up and down the parade, listening intently before picking Messam out. 'That's him!' she told me excitedly after the parade, before bursting into tears.

So far as Messam's alibi was concerned, he had always claimed that he had been tucked up in bed at his mother's house on the night of Juliet's rape. But when I questioned one of his closest friends, he told me quite innocently that Messam had turned up at his house at 5.30 a.m. (shortly after the attack on Juliet) and had slept there until 1.30 p.m. before going to his mother's house, where we found him at 3.20. His alibi had been smashed.

This was very positive stuff and was to prove evidentially crucial to the prosecution case. But we had a few more nails to hammer into his coffin. We found a watch case with the innards missing among junk in Messam's bedroom and showed it to all the women in the hope that one of them would recognize it. One of Messam's first victims, Linda Stoughton, identified it as hers. It had obvious scratches on the back of the case where she had inadvertently damaged it, but had been working on the night it was stolen and she was raped.

The white hair from Juliet's bedroom was positively identified as coming from the rug beside Messam's own bed and we concluded that it had become detached from the sticky label which had originally held it to the bottom of his trainers, before depositing itself on her green carpet.

A few weeks after I had submitted this same rug to the laboratory the scientist rang me to say that deep in the pile he had found a tiny stud earring. We showed it initially to Juliet, who went immediately to her jewellery box and produced the matching stud. She hadn't even realized it was missing. We believed that Messam must have dropped the earring on to his bedroom rug while he was sitting on his bed, gloating over his booty, shortly before we arrived to arrest him.

More evidence came from the lab. Although there was not enough semen left at the scene to be of any use, saliva was found on the breasts of one of the victims that matched his blood type – B secretor. Fragments of pubic hair matching Messam's were also found on the bedsheets of another victim.

We still needed further evidence and I wondered where to look next. Because so many of the women's homes were overlooked by the same railway line that backed on to Messam's family home, I decided to search the area that ran alongside the track. It would have been very easy, I thought as I studied the embankment, for Messam to have left his parents' home via the back gate, climbed up to the railway and jogged in either direction along the tracks.

By this time it was January and freezing cold, with snow on the ground. The distance between Willesden Junction and South Acton Stations was seven miles. I walked the track myself and realized that my team and I simply couldn't search it on our own, so I rang the Cadet Training School at Hendon and asked if I could borrow some budding cadets to help me. The following day about thirty of them arrived at my office.

British Rail had approved the search and given us bright orange jackets to wear, so, suitably dressed, I took my little team and the cadets up to the railway line to start the search. Each cadet had a pole or heavy stick which they used to prod and poke into the thick brambles.

I actually did bugger-all, except supervise, which was just as well in the circumstances because I was so cold my body ached. Within an hour we had reached a section of the steep slope which overlooked the side of the Messam house. There was a lot of deep brush and bracken on the embankments which proved very difficult to search and as we dropped down, near Messam's back gate, it was extremely hard going. We were having to examine thick undergrowth which had formed over a steep incline and everything appeared frozen solid. I would have found it virtually impossible to complete the search single-handedly, but the cadets were brilliant in their keenness not to let me down, even though some of them must have wished they were back doing theory in a warm classroom.

Frozen to the bone, trying to break up the bracken, slipping and sliding down the prickly slope, they struggled on until one of them suddenly shouted: 'Ma'am, I've found a handbag. Over here.'

I rushed over and was disappointed to find the brown leather bag empty. But we had the scent by then and the chase had become much more exciting. The cadets could sense it and see it on my face. 'Good boy!' I told the rosy-cheeked cadet. 'Now see what else you can find.'

After that, it was almost like a lucky dip. One of the cadets found a purse frozen into a solid block of ice, others found scattered documents and then someone fished another handbag out of the undergrowth, its leather stiff with cold.

'I think I can force the catch,' one of the lads told me, as he took a penknife out of his pocket.

'Just be careful,' I said wryly: 'that could be vital evidence you're holding.' As if the good-fortune fairy had been listening to me, the catch of the bag sprang open and a driving licence with the name 'Caroline Broadbent' fell to my feet. Caroline was another young woman who had fallen foul of Messam when he broke into her home and robbed her a year earlier. He had, it appeared, slung the bag into the brambles behind his mother's house before slinking through the back gate to the safety of his bed.

With the light fading and the temperatures plummeting, we decided to call it a day and return to the station for a hot drink and to warm up. I told the SOCO to take the frozen purse back and thaw it out on a radiator. When it looked like most of the water had dripped on to the floor, I picked it up and prised open the rusty catch. Inside, staring me in the face, were a lipstick, mirror and other feminine effects listed as stolen by another of Messam's victims.

I knew that months of intensive preparation and planning lay ahead of me, when every piece of evidence would be scrutinized and recorded, for it was up to me to make sure that nothing went wrong at his trial. How many more pieces of the puzzle could I fit together before then? I wondered.

Poring over a microscope that March morning with senior scientist Ann Priston at the lab, I heard my name called out. 'Is there a DI Bristow here?' someone yelled.

'That's me,' I said.

'Phone call for you, ma'am,' a junior research assistant told me.

It was Dick South. 'They're looking for you, guv,' he said. 'There's been a bloody awful rape down at Ealing Vicarage, next to St Mary's. Three nasty bastards broke in, beat the vicar and the boyfriend senseless with a cricket bat, dragged the daughter into the bedroom and did the business. They're all down the hospital and the boss is expecting you to get your arse down there to deal with it.'

My heart sank. 'For fuck's sake, give me a break. Let's open another box of policemen,' I said, more to myself than Dick, who was still on the phone.

'What'd you say, guv?' he said anxiously.

'Nothing. I'll be there in an hour,' I said.

When I walked into casualty at Ealing Hospital, all hell seemed to have broken loose. There were people everywhere, policemen, doctors and nurses, and a group of press photographers standing around in the doorway, cameras in hand. I spotted some of my team who were talking to the medics.

Sitting wrapped in blankets in a wheelchair at the back of casualty was a young dark-haired girl with a pale face. I immediately recognized the look in her wide eyes and grabbed Dick South's arm. 'Is that the victim?' I asked. Dick nodded. 'Well, for pity's sake, Dick, don't leave the poor girl sitting there on her own. Let's move her into a cubicle, away from the vultures, eh?'

Jill Saward, the victim of the Ealing Vicarage rape, was just twenty-one and a virgin when she was raped and buggered by two of the three men who had burst into her family home at 12.45 p.m. that day. The attack made headline news from the start, shocking the nation and causing a public outcry that there was no longer any sanctuary from violence, even in an English vicarage. I, too, felt outraged but was no longer surprised by anything.

Once I had moved Jill into a side ward and gently explained to her the need for a medical examination, I realized almost immediately that she was a Christian in the true sense of the word. Despite what she had been through, her only concern seemed to be for her boyfriend, David, who had been rushed to Charing Cross Hospital's neurological unit for the serious head injuries he had received, and for her father, Michael Saward, vicar of St Mary's, who was being X-rayed for broken bones.

Sadly, we didn't have any women forensic doctors available that day and the medical examination had to be carried out by one of our on-call (male) police doctors. By the 1990s many female GPs had been recruited specifically to deal with women who had been sexually assaulted. Each underwent special 'rape training', enabling them to deal with the victims as sensitively as possible. Many of them were already skilled in gynaecological work or in the field of sexually transmitted diseases and all of them understood the need for meticulous, accurate work, including the collection and preservation of forensic medical evidence.

The job of forensic medical examiner is an entirely voluntary posting and one which can be extremely lucrative. For example, a prisoner may complain of a headache and ask for an aspirin, but the custody officer is not allowed to give it to him, in case the headache is a symptom of something more sinister and the prisoner dies in police custody. So the FME is called out, examines the prisoner, prescribes two aspirin and leaves the station. For that one call, he can expect a handsome fee. If he is called to an adjacent police station on his way home for the same problem, he can charge a similar fee. So in less than an hour he can earn good money. Many do it for the supposed kudos of working for the police, but at the time of the vicarage rape there were very few women who had taken it up for either reason.

I explained this to Jill but she didn't bat an eyelid. 'I don't care who does it or why,' she told me. 'I just want it over and done with as quickly as possible.'

My heart went out to that young woman. Here she was, having just gone through the worst experience of her life, receiving treatment from a doctor who, to my mind, prodded and poked, plucked and clipped as if he was carrying out nothing more than a routine examination. He asked her a lot of personal questions about the details of the attack, and at that stage I felt obliged to intervene. Taking him to one side, I said: 'For God's sake, go easy on her, doctor. You can surely see her distress.' I wished he would hurry up and leave her alone, despite knowing that any evidence he found would be invaluable to the police investigation.

When he had taken all the necessary swabs and samples, I helped Jill into fresh clothes which had been brought from the vicarage and drove her to the Brentford rape suite. Well away from the hustle and bustle of the main building, it was the ideal place to sit quietly for a few hours and talk.

Detective Chief Superintendent David Lamper met us there and introduced himself to Jill. 'Carol will be in charge of you, while I concentrate on the main inquiry,' he told her.

'How are David and my dad?' she asked.

'Your dad's going to be fine,' he reassured her. 'He has a fractured skull and a black eye but they'll be sending him home tomorrow.'

'And David?' Her bottom lip trembled as she said his name.

DCS Lamper told her: 'Not so good at the moment, I'm afraid. He has a fractured skull, a perforated eardrum and a blood clot on the brain. They're doing all they can and we'll keep you informed.'

I thought Jill might faint at that point, she looked so pale. I held her arm and steadied her as Lamper added: 'We're lucky it's not worse. God knows, you've all been through it today.'

He left us alone for me to take her statement, which I knew would occupy most of the evening and much of the next day. I still felt terrible after my own dreadful start to the day and I asked Jill if she would care to join me in a fish-and-chip supper before we started. Neither of us had the greatest of appetites, but we ate what we could in an atmosphere which helped to break the ice before we began.

Sipping from a mug of hot chocolate, she recounted everything that had happened to her in a calm and deliberate way. All I could do was sit, listen and write, trying desperately to focus on what she was saying. Rushing from the lab to the hospital had exacerbated my headache; my head was now pounding. The paracetamol I had already taken weren't helping and I felt decidedly queasy. How many times had I sat here before, doing exactly the same thing? Were the victims getting stronger or was I just getting weaker? Only a few months earlier it had been Juliet Davies in that armchair, Rachel somebody before that and a dozen girls whose names I could not for that minute recall. Now it was Jill's turn. How many more could I, or would I, have to face?

I marvelled at her strength of spirit and her photographic memory as I scribbled details on to sheets of foolscap, getting as full a description as possible of the three men we called Man 1, Man 2 and Man 3, who were all white and relatively young with London accents.

Unemployed at the time, she and her boyfriend David had

been in the lounge watching a video that lunchtime while her father wrote a sermon in his study. The doorbell rang at 12.45 and her father opened the door. Two men walked into the lounge; Jill initially assumed them to be workmen, but she quickly realized that one of them was carrying a large kitchen knife and both appeared to be high on drink or drugs.

'Move yourself!' he shouted, and punched David hard in the face with his fist. He continued to beat David as Jill ran into the hallway to find a third man threatening her father. 'Give us your fucking money,' he was shouting, and her father replied: 'We don't have any money here. This is a vicarage.'

Man 2 grabbed Jill away from her father, held a knife across her chin and threatened to slit her throat unless they were given some money. He stank of stale cigarettes and alcohol. In desperation, her father and boyfriend turned out their pockets, but they had no cash, which seemed to infuriate the men even more. Man 1 took Jill's arm and dragged her upstairs. 'We're going to look for jewellery,' he said.

They went from bedroom to bedroom, the man rummaging through jewellery boxes for anything of value. He rejected a couple of things she offered him as if he was somehow being magnanimous. 'Remember, I was kind to you. Don't tell the others,' he told her mysteriously, before taking her back downstairs. Jill found her father and David in the study with the other two men. Her father wasn't wearing any trousers and David's were around his ankles. Man 1 told the others that there was nothing upstairs, but before Jill could do anything Man 2 grabbed her by the arm and dragged her up the stairs again, claiming he was going for a second look.

Pulling her into the spare bedroom, he faced her with the knife and smiled. 'Take your clothes off,' he ordered. 'Everything.' She hesitated, trembling, but he threatened her again and she stripped. Once undressed, he forced her to engage in oral sex. She retched and he pushed her on to the bed, making her sit on top of him before forcing her again into oral sex.

As Jill was recounting this part, she looked close to collapse, the only time she floundered throughout the entire ordeal. 'I'm sorry, Carol. Emotionally I had cut off by this stage and was just going through the motions.' As she got up and walked around, taking a breather for a minute, I smoked two cigarettes, lighting one from the other, and waited until she felt able to carry on.

While she was being so abused, the other two men herded her father and David past the bedroom that Jill was in. David was distraught at the sight and shouted: 'Leave her alone!' Man 2 then pushed her out of the bedroom and into her own room, throwing her a towel with which to cover herself.

In her bedroom he tried unsuccessfully to rape her, calling her a 'slag', a 'bitch' and a 'cow'. He forced her to engage in oral sex once again as Men 1 and 3 wandered in and out of the bedroom. Man 1 – he who had been 'kind' to her earlier – told Man 2: 'I want nothing to do with this. This is a totally different ballgame. We didn't come here for this. We came here for the money.'

Man 3 stood and watched while Man 2 turned Jill over on her stomach and told her: 'I'm going up the back as well.' He then buggered her, causing her excruciating pain. Man 3 joined in, forcing Jill to suck his penis while Man 2 raped her. She was also penetrated with the large handle of the kitchen knife he was carrying. While this was happening, she could hear David crying out in pain in an adjacent room. Jill shouted, 'Leave him alone!' David and her father were both being beaten senseless with a cricket bat by Man 1.

Suddenly it was all over. Satisfied, the men dressed themselves and offered her a swig from a half-empty bottle of vodka they were drinking, which she declined. They covered her with a duvet and tied her wrists and ankles with a skipping rope. A few minutes later, she heard them go downstairs and slam the front door behind them.

She managed to free herself of her bonds and walk along the corridor to the spare room, desperately afraid of what she would find. Her father and boyfriend seemed scarcely alive, having been badly beaten and tied hand and foot with electric flex and a belt. She freed David who started sobbing uncontrollably before lapsing into semi-consciousness.

Jill's father asked if she was all right. 'Did they?' he asked.

She nodded.

'I'm sorry,' was all he could say as his daughter telephoned the police.

When I was sure that Jill could add nothing more to her remarkably detailed description of the attack, I knew it was time to stop and make arrangements for her to return home. She was exhausted, it was getting late and to go on would have been cruel. I arranged for her to be taken home and agreed to collect her the following morning, to bring her back to the rape suite and continue where we left off.

The rest of that night passed in a blur. I went straight home and reached for the Scotch. I fell asleep some time after 2 a.m. and spent another restless night dealing with the relentless turmoil of my emotions. I awoke four hours later with a stiff neck and a throbbing head.

At ten o'clock that Friday morning I pulled up outside the Ealing Vicarage to collect Jill and was appalled by the sight that greeted me. The gates of the vicarage were besieged with reporters and photographers, television crews and passers-by, all wanting their pound of flesh. I ran the gauntlet, pushing past their lenses and their questions, and found sanctuary inside the house.

Jill had had a worse night than me and was by now in shock. I told her that I would get her to Brentford as soon as possible, but suggested that she leave under a blanket so that the press couldn't photograph her. The law states clearly that victims of rape must not be identified, but this case had attracted such massive publicity that it seemed the rules were being broken.

I got her out and away to Brentford where, after a cup of coffee and a chat, we continued with her statement. By the time we had finished, I had twenty-three handwritten foolscap pages and we were both shattered. 'Well done, and thanks for making my job so easy,' I told her. 'Come on, let's get you home.' I drove her back to Ealing and once more through the pack of wolves at the gates.

Back at the nick, I had Jill's statement typed up and circulated to all the investigating officers so that everyone knew exactly what we were dealing with. Later I discovered that David was still on the critical list and that Mr Saward was more comfortable and recovering in hospital. None of us under-estimated the task ahead and I had a funny feeling that this one just wasn't going to come easy.

On the Saturday morning I woke up in a cold sweat, remember-ing Winston Messam. I had been down at the lab piecing together the forensic evidence when the call had come through about the vicarage rape. I still had to persuade the CPS that the Messam case was entirely sound and proceeding in the right direction, which was no mean feat. I phoned the lab and arranged to spend the following Monday there after popping in to see Jill in case she had remembered anything else.

Putting together a prosecution case the size of Messam's was no picnic. We had taken more than six hundred foolscap pages of written evidence and had to tie up all the loose ends. Slipping up could cost us dear. If I left any holes in the case, the defence lawyers would prise them wide open. Give them an inch and they take a mile. I couldn't afford to lose Messam – not for my sake, but for Ivy, Juliet and all the others – but nor could I duck out of my responsibilities to Jill and her investigation.

This was all happening at a time when my drinking and its consequences were becoming much more than even I could handle. Returning to my office that Saturday evening, I sur-rounded myself with the Messam papers and poured myself a drink. I knew I'd had enough; it was obvious to me that some-thing was going to give and I felt sure it would be my sanity. Glancing upwards, I caught sight of the sign I had bought years ago to hang over my desk that read: OF ALL THE THINGS I'VE LOST, I MISS MY MIND THE MOST. It didn't seem quite so funny any more. I felt a pathetic mess and deeply ashamed of myself.

I awoke on Sunday morning to hear the telephone ringing loudly in my ear. 'Shit!' I screamed as I reached out for it, accidentally knocking the cradle and handset to the floor.

'Hello, Carol? Carol, are you there?' I heard a voice down the line. The receiver lay on the carpet next to the phone. I rolled over, groaning at my thumping head, and picked it up.

'Hello?' I said, hoarsely. It was Marion, my sister-in-law. She wanted to know if I would like to join them for dinner that night. 'Fine,' I said. 'See you at six.' Pete had chosen well when he asked Marion to be his wife. I had always wanted a sister and she was certainly the next best thing.

I spent the day nursing my head and trying to pull myself together to face them. They hadn't seen me for a while and I knew I wasn't looking my best. By the time we sat down to dinner, I had already sunk two large Scotches while I told them the background to the vicarage rape, which remained at the forefront of the news. As I picked up my napkin Pete placed a half-full bottle of malt on the table in front of me. 'Help yourself, Carol,' he told me, matter-of-factly. 'If I leave the bottle with you, it saves me from having to get up.' His words compounded the shame I already felt about being hooked on the bloody stuff and I felt disgusting. Peter and his wife had never judged me for my drinking habits and I loved them all the more for it.

The evening progressed much as it normally did, with one exception. After dinner I stopped drinking and opted for a cup of black coffee before leaving at half-past nine to drive the four miles home. When I got in, there was a message on my answering machine from Angie, an old friend who was always great fun to be with, and the only person I knew who could match me drink for drink. We had been good drinking buddies and, in one unguarded moment, we had both confided to each other that we might have a problem. Nothing more had been said and she was the only person to whom I had ever made this confession.

I made another cup of coffee, poured myself a neat Scotch and dialled her number. She answered the phone almost immediately and sounded great. It was good to hear her voice. We chatted for about ten minutes and I told her all my news. She chatted back and, in the briefest of moments, I instinctively realized that she was stone-cold sober.

'You sound pissed,' she said.

'I guess I am,' I answered. 'I've just come back from my brother's place. So what's new?'

'I've been trying to pluck up the courage to ring you a few times because I've got something to tell you,' she said. I gulped from my glass hungrily. 'I haven't had a drink since the first of January.'

I was silent.

'Carol? You still there?' she asked.

'Yes, yes, I'm here,' I said, my mind spinning with a mixture of anger and jealousy. 'How come? New year's resolution?' I asked.

'God, no. I'd have been drinking on the second of January if that's all it was. No, I finally took the plunge and asked for help and someone introduced me to Alcoholics Anonymous. They're a smashing bunch of people, and there's nothing you can tell them about booze. Most of them have been pissed for the better part of their lives and are trying to stay sober. They've helped me to stay away from drink one day at a time and so far it's worked. I've never felt better. I'm telling you,' she added cautiously, 'because I think they could help you, if you wanted to give up.'

I swallowed hard.

'I mean, if I can do it then anyone can,' she laughed. 'Nobody is saying it's easy but, if you want a different way of life bad enough, you can have it. Why not give them a ring some time?'

I made my excuses and ended the conversation as quickly as I could without being impolite. 'Thanks, Angie, you're a good sort, I'll be in touch.'

I replaced the receiver carefully and leant back in my chair. Was it possible? Angie seriously on the wagon? But she was a drunk, like me, and up to this point I had always assumed she would die with a Scotch in her hand or end up in the nuthouse. I had even considered how we might be forced into keeping each other company. How the hell had she managed it? I was gobsmacked. Who were these AA people? They sounded like a bunch of born-again goody-goodies. Could they help me? How would I cope with a boring, and even more miserable, existence without alcohol? Surely it hadn't come to this?

While I was mulling it all over in my head, I found myself drinking the coffee and ignoring the Scotch. Sitting in front of the electric fire, the concept of staying 'dry' swam round and round in my head. Of all the times to contemplate it! I was up to my eyes in muck and bullets as usual. There was Jill to look after, Messam's case papers to get to the Crown Prosecution Service, the office to run and other serious matters to deal with. How the hell could I manage all that without a drink? I must be bloody mad even to think about it, I decided.

But then I knew I didn't want to die just yet either, and I loved my job which I didn't want to lose. What would it really be like without the booze? Could I manage? Or would I go nuts without the release valve that a drink gave me? How would an addict like me ever survive without the cushion of alcohol?

Two coffees later, I realized that there was only one way to find out. I stood up as if on automatic pilot, picked up the whisky bottle and poured the contents down the sink. I made myself another cup of coffee, headed for bed and lay there thinking of all the possibilities of long-term sobriety.

Feeling full of pessimism, I decided the simple truth was this. It was obvious to any fool that it would be nigh-on impossible for someone like me to stay off the booze. I was, after all, a hard-working detective inspector with too much on her plate to even contemplate the idea. How the heck would I manage without the only form of relaxation I knew? But something was going to have to give, and I knew that, so what did I have to lose? Why not try to give booze a miss for a while? I was deep in such thoughts when I suddenly fell into an undisturbed sleep.

Day one of my sobriety started the following morning, Monday 10 March 1986, and I won't pretend it was easy. I had tried twice before but failed, after five days of white-knuckled mental agony, and I knew that the slightest problem could send me straight back to the bottle. Over the next few days I went through all the awesome miseries of having to adjust to abstinence and I suffered the worst of my anxiety attacks. It was, without doubt, the single most difficult thing I have ever had to do in my entire life.

But, in a strange way, the pressures that had previously overwhelmed me were to become my saviours. I actively embraced them, happy for the space and time they occupied in my mind. I put as much heart and soul as I could muster into my work, relieved that I had no time to dwell on matters alcoholic. I was glad for the pain of exhaustion and the anguish I felt for the latest victim of crime. It dulled my own anxieties and eventually made me realize where my priorities lay.

By the middle of that first week, I was dry and feeling amazingly calm. I was smoking like a trooper and chewing gum as if my very life depended on it, but for now I was off the booze.

I saw Jill quite a lot that week and I spoke to her on the telephone at least once a day. Fortunately for me, the powers that be had looked at my caseload and decided that I should cease actively to investigate the vicarage rape, although I would continue to support Jill whenever possible and make myself available to my colleagues still working on the case. I took her to see a friend of mine, Dr Joan Nabarro, the consultant in genito-urinary medicine at the Central Middlesex Hospital, who examined Jill for any sexually transmitted diseases she may have caught from her attackers. As far as I was concerned, Dr Nabarro was nothing short of an angel in disguise because she made special, out-of-hours appointments for all my victims and could not have been kinder. The alternative would have been for these women to attend special clinics in their own time.

Looking at Jill, I could see that the strain of it all was beginning to tell. She had gone from being calm and responsive to being almost permanently silent. It was my opinion that this courageous young woman was on the brink of the serious depression that so often savages a victim's mind, destroying what is left of her sanity.

As I spoke the words of encouragement that she needed to hear, I realized for the first time that I needed to hear them too. 'You have two choices, Jill,' I told her. 'You can bury this thing dead once and for all, by working through this pain and leaving it all behind. Or you can bury it alive by shutting down and closing your mind to the hurt you're feeling. You might be able to pretend it isn't there now but, unless you deal with it, it will be buried alive inside you and you will always have to live with the consequences.'

235

Telling her to pick up the pieces of her life was the same message I had to keep repeating to myself, and for once I felt that I was beginning to heed my own advice.

Later, when the men who attacked her were arrested and charged, I hoped Jill would be able to see the light at the end of the tunnel. But there was a lot to go through yet, for us both, and the trial, set for February 1987, seemed a million years away.

Angie's words returned to me again and again in those first few days of abstinence. 'Why not give AA a ring?' she had said. But surely someone like me couldn't call? I was a detective inspector, for God's sake, not some old bag-lady in the dirty mac brigade, who slept on park benches. But by Thursday of that week, I had somehow found the courage I needed to pick up the phone. Sitting in my armchair at home, I hesitantly dialled the number.

'Hello. How can I help you?' a man's voice answered.

'I – I don't know if you can,' I said. 'A friend suggested I call.'

The man's name was David and before I knew it he had started to tell me about himself. He had been a successful businessman, married with children, living in a big house. Success had been too much for him. Initially, he drank to relax. Within two to three years he had become a daily drinker. After five years, his business began to suffer and his wife threatened to leave him because of his unpredictable behaviour. 'When drink costs you more than money, you know you've got a problem,' he said. 'I knew that I had to stop or risk losing everything. Let me give you the address of your next local meeting.'

I scribbled down the details and wondered if I would ever go. The following night, my fifth away from booze, I thought I would go mad if I didn't have a drink. Either that or I could try the sodding AA meeting.

When I walked into the room at my local hospital and looked around at all the happy smiling faces, I thought I must have got the wrong night. I had expected a man resembling Billy Graham to be ranting at a bunch of old drunks about the evils of alcohol – but I couldn't have been more wrong. Sitting around the room, chatting over plastic cups of coffee, were ordinary people, men and women, just like me, from all walks of life.

I nodded to them and stood there, wondering what to do. A woman I later discovered was a schoolteacher and mother came up to me, shook my hand and led me to the kettle. Within a few minutes I was chatting happily to her and it felt great. Anonymity is the spiritual foundation of AA, so nobody asked who I was (other than my first name) or what my background was, and I quickly felt at ease.

I had walked into that first meeting carrying some pretty heavy baggage on my back, labelled SELF-PITY, FEAR, ANGER and 'LONELINESS'. That night I dumped the sack marked LONELINESS in the middle of the floor and I've never carried it since. All I had to do, my new friends were telling me, was to be willing to keep an open mind and to be honest with myself. They knew how I was feeling because they had been there, and suddenly I no longer felt alone.

I would be a liar if I pretended that it was easy, particularly with the workload I was facing, but I felt lifted and positive for the first time in my life because I began to rediscover my self-respect. Whatever the job threw at me, I knew that – working through it 'one day at a time' – I could control it. That was progress.

As expected, the case against Messam took months to prepare and I thought about booze a hundred times. The trial lasted several days and was very complicated but, on Monday 24 November 1986, he was found guilty at the Old Bailey of all four specimen charges of rape, including the attack on Juliet Davies. I was triumphant.

Messam never took the witness stand and his main defence, argued through a very clever defence advocate, suggested that my team and I had planted just about all the evidence. In such instances police officers, along with their rape victims, find themselves virtually on trial, but fortunately, having heard it all before, I felt confident enough to handle it.

For the victims, sitting a few feet away from the man who

had devastated their lives, it adds insult to injury to be called a liar again and again in cross-examination. Many of them, having been challenged for the umpteenth time, must seriously have thought that they should have declined the offer to prosecute their attacker. And who would have blamed them?

Messam's victims, as ever, were the heroines of the day. The court heard that the ordeal had been so distressing for some of them that three had never returned to their homes. Two sold up at a loss and left, and one moved abroad. Another victim, a twenty-five-year-old estate agent, changed her job because she now felt afraid of being alone with strangers.

These women gave the most determined evidence in court and I never ceased to be amazed by their courage. I had taken each one to the Old Bailey a few days before the trial to familiarize them with the inside of the court and without exception all had been extremely nervous at the prospect of taking the witness box opposite the oak-panelled dock and facing the man who had raped them.

Thanks to the damning evidence of Juliet and the other women, the jury saw fit to throw out Messam's scurrilous allegations that he had been 'fitted up', and returned verdicts of guilty. Sentencing him, Judge Richard Lowry told Messam: 'Anyone who watched those women reliving their ordeals in the witness box realized there must be grave emotional scars inflicted on them. Each of their lives has been gravely affected by what you did. My main concern must be to the public and in particular to women. There has been no sign of remorse and anyone who knows of this case is fearful of crimes you might commit in the future because you are a confident, strong young man.'

As the judge's words were spoken I looked up at Messam, who had clearly turned a deaf ear to the proceedings. But when the judge sentenced him to four terms of eighteen years' youth custody, both Messam and I paid equal attention. I couldn't quite take in what the judge had said and clearly neither could Messam. I wrote on my notepad in front of me: 'Eighteen months,' thinking that is what the judge had said, and it was only when he repeated the sentence on each charge, saying,

'Eighteen years,' that I felt a rush as good as anything the bottle had ever given me. Messam looked far from happy as he was taken down to the cells.

I was overjoyed at the sentences and took my team to the pub to celebrate. I had now been teetotal for eight months and I was getting used to 'wetting the baby's head' with Coke. At the bar we bumped into some members of our jury and a couple of the women came over to acknowledge me. I thanked them on behalf of the victims for returning guilty verdicts and praised their ability and reasoning for rejecting the allegations of 'planting'.

One of the women put down her gin and tonic and said: 'Well, there was just too much for you to have planted everything.' I was relieved, but before I could answer she added: 'We thought you'd probably slipped the stud earring into the rug, though. Nice touch.' I wished I'd never raised the bloody subject.

In February 1987, it was Jill Saward's turn. The three men who took part in the vicarage rape appeared at the Old Bailey and pleaded guilty to the charges. Of the three men who attacked her, Martin McCall and Christopher Byrne (Man 2 and Man 3) were said to have been out of their minds on a cocktail of drink and drugs at the time of the attack.

Between them they admitted rape, buggery and aggravated burglary, all of which carried a maximum possible sentence of life imprisonment. Furthermore the Attorney General had recently recommended that, in the case of an individual attacked in her own home where aggravating features included repeated rape, the use of weapons, two or more men acting together and other acts of violence, the sentence should be more like ten years to life.

But after stating that the trauma that Jill had suffered was 'not so very great', Mr Justice Leonard gave the two rapists three and five years respectively for the rape and buggery, rounded up to a total of eight and ten years with the additional sentencing for aggravated burglary.

Robert Horscroft (Man 1), the gang leader who had recruited

the others for the robbery but who had shown 'kindness' to Jill and taken no part in the sexual assault, was given fourteen years.

The judge's sentencing of the men who had viciously raped and terrorized Jill was considerably less harsh than his sentencing of Robert Horscroft for aggravated burglary. The powers had been there, but they had been ignored. I, for one, thought that the judge must have slept through the whole trial. I simply couldn't believe it.

There was widespread public outrage over the sentences. Jill, who was withdrawing more and more into herself, said she felt as if she had been raped again, this time by the judge. In modern times, police can appeal against the leniency of such sentences, but that privilege wasn't available to us then. As politicians, the media and women's groups bayed for the judge's blood, Jill, David and the Saward family were left bewildered at the injustice they had suffered at the hands of the court.

My anger at some of the judges' sentences had never waned. But this outraged me more than most. Could I be blamed for sometimes thinking that the world had gone completely mad? I was so furious with Mr Justice Leonard that in a fit of pique I broke an unwritten rule and spoke on the record to the local newspapers, stating that I thought the judge could not have been listening. I meant every word but was shocked to see it plastered over two of the national newspapers the following day. It made the bollocking I got afterwards worthwhile.

Many years later I was invited by George Carey, the Archbishop of Canterbury, to participate as a trustee in a charitable trust called HURT (an acronym for Help Untwist Rape Trauma) which had Jill as its director. Its three highly laudable aims were to advise victims of rape, educate the public and reform the law. It hoped to set up a twenty-four-hour telephone counselling service for victims, offer speakers for educational talks and lobby MPs for change. It urged increased sentences for rapists, reducing the trauma of giving evidence and shifting the 'guilty until proven innocent' emphasis away from victims.

Sir Richard O'Brien, former chairman of the Manpower Services Commission, was to be chairman, and Helena Kennedy

240

QC, the Bishop of Leicester and Frank Field MP were to be among the fellow-trustees. I felt very proud and privileged to be asked. I wholeheartedly supported all that the charity was trying to achieve and, for the first time in my police career, agreed to stick my head above the parapet and officially offer my help where it could be of most use.

The charity was launched from Lambeth Palace on 7 March 1994 and I attended the first few trustee meetings with high hopes. But very sadly, despite all the public support there had been for Jill at the time of her trial, when it came to the crunch the support dropped away. The necessary funds to set up the charity could not be raised and HURT folded within months of its launch.

I stayed in touch with Jill for several years and was delighted when she overcame her depression and wrote a book about her experiences, courageously identifying herself as the victim of the Ealing Vicarage Rape. Her father was promoted to Canon of St Paul's Cathedral and her former boyfriend David moved away. Jill's own story eventually had a happy ending. After a brief marriage that failed, she married again and had children. It seemed that, although her experience had exacted its price and left her emotionally scarred, she was strong enough to create a new beginning for herself and her new family.

11

'WHAT DO YOU MEAN, YOU DON'T DRINK? I SUPPOSE NEXT you're going to tell me that the moon's made of cheese. Of course you drink, woman. You've drunk most of us under the table before now.'

I smiled as I held the flat of my hand over a glass that Chief Superintendent John Purnell was about to fill with wine. It was six o'clock on a Friday evening in early summer 1986 and I had been summoned to his office, where my detective chief inspector, Graham Searle, had already made himself comfortable in one of the easy chairs.

'That's right, sir, she's been on the wagon for a couple of months now,' chortled the DCI.

'So what's all that about, Carol,' enquired John Purnell, 'because I can hardly believe what I'm hearing.'

'Doctor's advice, sir,' I lied. 'I've been told I have a blood condition that won't get better until I lay off the drink.' I had known John Purnell all my service. We had joined training school together in 1965 and, despite never having previously served at the same nick, we had always somehow managed to remain in contact.

In February 1977 John Purnell, then Acting Chief Inspector at Paddington Police Station with responsibilities for St John's Wood, had ordered that the first extensive searches be made for

Janie Shepherd. Years later, here we were, finally working together at the same nick, and it felt good to know that John, with his credentials, was the man in charge.

Having offered me some tonic water, he sat back in his chair and smiled. 'We have a proposal to put to you and we think it's one you'll like. Graham here mentioned the idea some weeks back, and I'm all for it.'

They then explained that following the success of the Messam investigation it had occurred to them both that it would be a good idea to have a dedicated team, dealing with all sexual crime matters, under one senior officer. Ealing and Acton had, it seemed, been dealing with more than their fair share of sexually motivated attacks and the newly formed team could be tasked to deal with the lot, thus freeing up other CID officers to deal with the rest of the crime.

'We thought', said my DCI, 'that the team could deal with everything from flashers to rapists and take on the added responsibility of dealing with crime allegations made by children, anything from beatings to rape and incest.'

'Which brings us to you,' said John Purnell, grinning. 'The Messam case was handled very well and cleared up quite a number of outstanding crimes. We wondered if you would consider heading up the new squad to dig out the other unsolved matters and give them a second look.'

My mind was racing. I knew this was a wonderful opportunity, but I didn't want to overplay my hand. Speaking as calmly as possible, I asked: 'And what about staff, sir?'

'Within reason, you can have whoever you need. We thought a mixture of uniform and CID might work, and we didn't reckon on you needing more than about three to start with. What do you say?'

Not really giving myself time to consider the implications of what I was being asked, I agreed. I had – still have – a tremendous sense of wanting to give the public a good service. I know it sounds corny, but I really do think that way. I had never lost sight of the fact that the public paid my wages, so the least I could do in return was a good job.

'Thank you, sir. Yes, I'll do it,' I told them.

The repeated investigation of sexual crime is not everyone's cup of tea because it can drive you nuts in a very short time, so the selection of staff becomes very important. I would only ever take volunteers and, for one reason or another, I had no shortage of officers who apparently felt they could learn a lot from this particular posting or had a genuine desire to contribute.

It took quite a few weeks to set up, and I knew I would be taking on a lot, but I had no idea just how much until I really got stuck in. On the first sweep of the division's unsolved cases, I discovered that I had more than sixty unsolved sexual assaults, spanning a four-year period. This would certainly keep my mind off booze, I thought, although with just a few months' abstinence behind me I had already begun to learn the benefits of staying away from alcohol.

I had begun to take a good look at myself and, with a growing acceptance of who I was, often felt supremely happy. Sometimes I found myself giggling at silly things and, on the few occasions that I got to bed early with a cup of cocoa and the crossword, I felt near to heaven. I also had a gut feeling that this contentment could survive, so long as I accepted that drink was my enemy and that I should avoid it at all costs. I was happy in my new job and looked forward to the challenges it would bring, challenges I could now face sober.

The first few cases I dealt with were certainly challenging; they were as difficult and harrowing as anything I had come across before (Renata excluded), and I soon found myself going over the details of their sad stories in my now unforgivingly temperate mind.

During this time I was contacted by a solicitor about a client of hers, a woman in her twenties called May, who had been referred to her by an incest counsellor. May's father had been some kind of monster, it seemed, a man who had constantly abused her until, aged sixteen, she ran away from home. She went on to tell me that, at the age of fifteen, she had been made pregnant by him and he had tried unsuccessfully to abort the baby with a coat hanger. As the pregnancy continued, he had kept her off school, telling the authorities that she was ill. At nine months, she had given birth alone in the garden shed to a baby boy. Her father discovered her and ordered her to kill the child.

After remonstrating with him, he threatened to chop off her right hand unless she completed the deed. Totally unable to cope, the fearful, distraught and weeping teenager smothered the infant and gave its body to her father, who burnt it the following morning on a bonfire.

I listened to her horrific story aghast. It was so awful, so harrowing to watch her relive the dreadful events of her childhood, that I had to leave the room three times, once to wipe away a tear, and twice to try and shake off the blinding headache her story was giving me.

I believed May completely. All those years later, and long after she had managed to escape from the clutches of her father, the girl who was now a woman was still grieving for the loss of her child. After finally being persuaded by friends to seek help, she had gone to a counsellor, then to a solicitor and finally to me. I grieved for her; her life was in shreds and she had no idea how to pick up the pieces. But, despite my own wish to help her and see justice done for her dead baby, I knew that the case didn't stand a hope in hell. In the absence of corroborative evidence, witnesses and obvious signs of sexual abuse, May's courage at finally breaking her silence was never going to be enough to mount a prosecution. The CPS gave their assurance that she would never be prosecuted for anything that had happened during that period, but I felt that was the least of her worries. She wanted the father she hated with a vengeance punished for what he had done, and if that meant her going to prison too, then so be it.

I asked one of my officers to interview the father and it came as no surprise to anyone, except the daughter, that he denied everything. I watched her face crumple at my pronouncement that in the absence of further evidence he could not be prosecuted. I hung my head as she was led away, a little ashamed that I couldn't help any more.

My little unit was never without work. No sooner had we put the lid on one case than three more popped up needing urgent attention and, despite some of them being fairly straightforward, many of them were anything but. Some, like the investigation into a religious cult who set themselves up in west London and who were accused of sodomizing and raping many of the young women recruits, took months to conclude but came to nothing when the alleged perpetrators fled back to the Far East.

The cases were unrelenting and included the mother who punished her baby son for crying by dipping him into a bath of scalding water which was so hot it took the skin clean off his little feet. There was the headteacher who fell in love with one of his underage but extremely well-developed pupils, and she with him. They had a passionate affair which was discovered by the girl's parents, and this charming, gentle man – going through not much more than a mid-life crisis – ended up in prison. I felt very sorry for him as he was led from the dock, his lovely wife, who had stood by him throughout, weeping openly in the public gallery.

I reckoned that for every twenty of the serious sexual crimes that we investigated, a little over 50 per cent had the evidence required to prosecute. However, by the time these had been through the CPS and the 51 per cent conviction theory had been applied, probably no more than six of the original twenty actually made it to the Crown Court. And then, subject to whichever way the wind was blowing, I expected no more than three convictions. Three out of twenty. What a disappointment. I always tried to persuade myself that the ones we had successes with made the failures just about bearable – but they never did.

How difficult it was to look into the eyes of women like the young Swedish *au pair*, raped as she got home late one night, and tell her there was nothing I could do for her. She saw nothing that would identify her attacker, who grabbed her from behind wearing a balaclava, and since no one else saw or heard anything and we had no forensic evidence to go on, the investigation hit a brick wall. She had undoubtedly been raped, but the attacker was clever and knew what not to leave behind. The poor girl returned home to Sweden with a very jaundiced view of Britain and, I think, of me.

Even when I possessed something tantamount to a confession

from the alleged rapist, there were no guarantees. Take the case of Sandra, a young woman who shared a house with several fellow-students, male and female, and became friendly with a young Rastafarian called Stephen. He made his fondness for her obvious when he bought her gifts of CDs and chocolates, and would occasionally go to her room where they would study together while listening to music, sometimes sharing a joint.

One night, while she was sitting writing at her desk, he locked the door without her realizing. He came up behind her gently, picked her up and dropped her on to the bed. She thought he was playing about until he started fondling her breasts. She fought him off as hard as she could but he pulled down her pants. She bashed him with her fists and screamed but the music was too loud. He unzipped his flies and raped her as he held her down on the bed. When it was over, she screamed at him and he left the room. She ran to a girlfriend's room and the matter was reported to me twenty-four hours later.

I believed her completely and brought Stephen in for questioning. During the police interview and in the presence of his solicitor, he sat smiling at me as he said: 'She has fancied me for months. It was her body language, I knew she wanted me. Up to that night when we had sex, we had never kissed, held hands or done anything to show our love for each other, but it was always there.

'When I picked her up and put her on the bed when the music was playing so sweet, I knew that she wanted me. Yes, we had sex and yes, she did pretend to fight with me, but that's natural – most women play hard to get, it just means they want you all the more. Yes, she did bang me with her fists, but I knew it was just a come-on. Yes, she did push me away with her legs, but that was just the thrusting of her hips as I entered her. Yes, she did scream but they were screams of delight. It was wonderful, just wonderful.'

I took him to the Old Bailey and Sandra gave her evidence resolutely. We must have got him, I thought to myself as the largely female members of the jury retired to consider their verdict. It seemed little more than five minutes before they were back. The jury foreman delivered the verdict: 'Not guilty,' he said, and Stephen, sitting in his large knitted Rastafarian beret, threw back his head and laughed.

I'm not daft enough to suggest that there should always be a conviction in a sexual assault case, especially when there is little or no good corroborative evidence, but having been privy to so much inside information which is never admitted to a jury, I have come to believe that the balance of justice has, for too long, been tilted in favour of the accused. In the majority of cases, juries will never be told about the past criminal history of the man in the dock because of the very prejudicial nature of that information – the argument goes that, if the jury knows he has raped before, they will automatically assume he is guilty a second time. But none of us can surely deny that, if the defendant comes from a background of repeated sexual offending, it is extremely relevant and crucial to the issue of his denial in the situation which now places him on trial.

And while he sits there, supposedly without a blemish to his name, the victim of the assault, who now has to give evidence about it in court, is likely, in cross-examination, to undergo nothing short of a character assassination. It would not be unusual for her to be asked how many lovers she had had, how long she had to know a man before she slept with him or how old she was when she lost her virginity. All these questions, it will be argued, must be asked to assist the accused with his defence that she consented to the act. In effect it is her character, not the defendant's, that is put on trial and a victim could be forgiven for thinking that she will have to pass the Persil 'whiter than white' test before anything she says is believed.

It is not only the cross-examination that stacks the odds against her. After years of haggling by police and other agencies acting on behalf of the victims, screens have been made available to the courts to protect the victims from having to see the men they are giving evidence against because it is accepted that this sudden visual confrontation can so traumatize a witness that it can severely affect her presentation in court. Permission to use the screens, however, is up to the judge of the day.

Clever legal argument by defence barristers that their use can be prejudicial to fair justice has meant that some women still have to recount their dreadful experiences directly across the court-room from the man they accuse.

In such instances, the victim's emotional state is rarely considered by the court. Post-traumatic stress disorder is a specific form of anxiety which follows a very stressful or frightening event. The psychological effects of rape are often severe and will include significant depression, nightmares, panic attacks and flashbacks. In my opinion it is crucial that, if a victim has suffered or is still suffering from this disorder, then the judge and jury should be told. It is an aspect they may wish to consider when judging her credibility in the witness box, or when assessing how much harm the attack has caused her. Would a liar with a wild imagination have suffered such trauma? Shouldn't they be told if the effect of the attack has been so devastating to her life that she has attempted suicide, or been forced to sell her home? The system by which rape victims are dealt with is much improved from the dark old days when I started out, but it still has a very long way to go.

Dealing with victims of sexual assault was no picnic, but we did have a few light-hearted moments even in the face of such sadness. I suppose we were much like undertakers and coroner's officers, or anyone who deals with grim and gruesome subjects as a matter of course: we had to find what laughs we could, where we could. No less sensitive to the needs of the victims and their families, we revelled in some of the more humorous stories that became antidotes to the sickness we dealt with daily. Sometimes we shared some of the most legendary tales with the victims themselves – God knows they needed a laugh – and usually they enjoyed them as much as we did and were relieved to change the subject.

Many of the stories originated in court, where judges and juries never failed to provide us with new material for our coffee-break chats or bar-time soirées. Some of them have been told for so long that no one can now remember which particular case they referred to or which officer was involved. But, no matter. They each did the job required, which was to make us throw our heads back and laugh until it hurt.

One of my favourites involved the case of a rape victim who was finding it difficult telling the jury what had happened to her. She whispered most of her evidence and, peering at her over his half-spectacles, the judge asked her if it would help if she could write down on a piece of paper what it was that the defendant was alleged to have said to her.

'Yes, my Lord, it would,' she replied, and duly wrote down the words 'I want to fuck you' on a scrap of paper handed to her by the court clerk.

Inspecting it first himself, the judge instructed that the piece of paper be handed around the members of the jury, so that they might know what was said. One by one, the jurors opened the folded piece of paper, read it and handed it on to the juror sitting next to them. Sitting in the back row, right at the end, was a man who had been asleep during much of the afternoon's proceedings. Awoken with a nudge by the woman juror sitting next to him, he took the piece of paper she now handed him and unfolded it. Reading the words quietly to himself, he smiled, winked at the woman, refolded the piece of paper and placed it in his top pocket, unaware that the entire court was watching him.

'Young man,' the judge called out. The man looked horrified when he realized the judge was addressing him. 'Kindly pass that piece of paper you were just handed to the usher.'

The man reddened and got to his feet. 'I'm afraid I can't do that,' he replied, after clearing his throat. 'It's personal, it's between me and the lady sitting next to me.'

It took the judge several minutes and some heavy banging on his gavel to silence the squeals of laughter in the court.

Because the odds so often seem stacked against us, it took time and a hell of a lot of effort to check each allegation of sexual assault. It is particularly difficult when, on rare occasions, even the victims themselves turn out to be not all that they appear. I was at Ealing when we had a report of a young Asian woman who claimed she had been raped early one evening walking through a local park with her three-year-old son. She was beside herself during my interview and when she became reluctant to give precise details of her attack and refused the medical examination, I assumed it was because of the strict rules surrounding her ethnic background.

We started all the usual routines – interviewing passers-by and carrying out house-to-house enquiries, and I went through that park with a fine-tooth comb. Along with several others, I even crawled around on my hands and knees in the undergrowth, looking for clues. I talked to people and searched for witnesses who had been in the vicinity at the time of the attack, which was said to have taken place in broad daylight. I spent hours with the woman, coaxing her to give me the precise details, before asking her to accompany me back to the park to show me exactly where she said she had been attacked. Something wasn't right but I was damned if I knew what it was.

Walking in the park where she said the assault had taken place, she pointed out the perimeter path, which meant that she had taken the most indirect route with a small child, when she had earlier indicated that she was in a hurry to get home to cook her husband's tea.

'Why was that?' I asked.

Still sobbing, but being comforted by my able assistant Christine Douglas, she muttered: 'Sorry,' and claimed that I had misunderstood her; the man had run off round the perimeter path. She had, she said, walked along the straight path running directly across the park, as it was the obvious and quickest route. But it still didn't make sense. Why would her attacker run that way and not head straight for one of the gates?

Back at the police station and four days into the inquiry, I confronted the poor woman with my doubts. I asked her why her husband hadn't been at her side throughout her ordeal and she immediately burst into floods of tears. He was having an affair with another woman, she said and, it appeared, he was the reason she had made up the whole story, in the hope that he would sympathize and rush back into her arms. He hadn't, and she knew she could not go on telling lie after lie.

Fuming, I told myself that we had only spent four days of on the inquiry and that it could have been much worse. I sent a report to the CPS about her wasting police time but that spelt out the poor woman's marital heartache; 'No further action' was the outcome. Her case papers were filed.

When I first joined the police force, I had been horrified to learn that perfectly genuine allegations of rape had the habit of being challenged in order to test the victim's integrity. An alarming number of men seemed to believe that the majority of allegations were entirely fabricated or had only been raised by the 'victim' once she had been let down or fallen out with the man to whom she later sought to teach a lesson.

Fortunately, by the eighties that practice had ceased and all allegations of rape were dealt with as though each were genuinely truthful. Only when there was an obvious discrepancy or inconsistency would the officer challenge what he or she was being told, but that didn't mean the detective could then rest on his laurels and assume the rest of the allegation to be untruthful also. The investigation would continue and, whatever our thoughts on the matter were, we kept them to ourselves. The victim would be believed at almost all costs, rather than us risk assuming the bad old habits of years gone by.

Personally, I would have preferred to have adopted the middle road to a more open-minded, common-sense approach, but was forced to admit that in the majority of cases, these new, somewhat extreme measures worked perfectly well because over 95 per cent of rape allegations are genuinely truthful and the victims' need to be believed is paramount.

Having said that, there were always going to be those incidents which fell into the five per cent and tested my patience to the limit. One of them started when I was rung at home at two o'clock one July morning by a young WPC who was at the end of her tether.

'Sorry to trouble you, ma'am, but I don't know what to do with this woman who has come in and alleged that she was raped. She's as pissed as a puddin' and can't remember where she has been for the last three hours. She walked into the station claiming that she'd lost her knickers, so, according to her, she must have been raped. I've found her a seat in the front office and we're feeding her black coffee in the hope that she'll sober up and remember what happened.'

I told the WPC I would be there in an hour, and instructed her to give the woman a bucket of coffee if necessary.

'I haven't called out a doctor yet, shall I leave that to you?' the WPC asked.

'Yes,' I said. 'Let's hope she'll sober up, remember where she left her knickers and withdraw her allegation.'

At 3 a.m., I walked into the front office at Acton nick and was met by the WPC. 'Her name's Bridie O'Malley,' she said. 'She lives in a bed-sit round the corner and spent the evening in a local Irish drinking club called O'Shaughnessy's. She's a lot more lucid than when I rang you, but I still can't get much sense out of her.'

'Where is she now?' I asked.

'Being sick in the ladies' loo. She's not been out of there since I started pouring black coffee down her throat.'

Pushing open the door of the ladies', I almost tripped over the reason for my visit, for there on the floor was Bridie, her arms across her stomach, hiccupping. About twenty-five years old, with dark, untidy, shoulder-length hair, she was bird-like in stature and probably weighed no more than seven stone. I slid past her and deposited myself on a bench beside the washbasin before introducing myself.

'Hello, Bridie. My colleague tells me you've lost your knickers.'

'That's right,' she said, her voice still heavily slurred.

'And you think you've been raped.'

'Yes, by the person who took my knickers off, because I wouldn't have taken them off willingly . . . I'm not that sort of a girl,' she hiccupped angrily.

'But you can't remember anything about it?' I asked, softly. She shook her head and screwed her face up. God, she looks awful, I thought.

It took me several minutes to establish that, after leaving the club at 11 p.m., Bridie couldn't remember anything until she woke up in a flowerbed in the park, minus her knickers. 'Do you think you might have taken them off yourself to have a pee?' I enquired.

She grimaced. 'I'm a good Catholic girl. I wouldn't do a thing like that, now would I?'

'Most of us remove our knickers when we want to use the lavatory, Bridie,' I offered. 'Maybe you were just caught short.' As Bridie scuttled across the floor to the toilet bowl to be sick once more, I realized that I wasn't going to get much more sense out of her that night, so I sent my WPC round to O'Shaughnessy's with a colleague, to see what they could find.

Twenty minutes later she returned and joined Bridie and me in the ladies' loo. In her gloved hand she held a pair of red lace panties. 'Found these in the ladies' loo at the club, ma'am,' she said. 'The landlord said she arrived alone and left alone and appeared to be a little the worse for wear.'

I pointed to the knickers. 'Are they yours, Bridie?' I asked gently.

'Yes,' said a sad little voice.

'Do you now think you might have taken them off when you used the lavatory?'

'Yes,' she answered.

'And do you think that you may have taken a short cut across the park, tripped or fallen over, stayed there for a little snooze and woken up feeling confused, only to realize that your knickers were missing?'

'Yes, yes, yes,' she answered defensively, her face red.

'Do you still think you might have been raped?' I asked.

Shaking her head as she pulled herself to her feet, all four feet eleven inches of her trembled. 'I'm sorry to have caused you so much trouble,' she said, close to tears.

'Don't worry, Bridie. Stay there and I'll run you home.' I grabbed my coat and, five minutes later, dropped a very subdued young woman at her front door. It was nearly 5 a.m., just enough time to get home for a couple of hours' sleep before coming back to work. Thank God I no longer drank.

Every case of rape is sad, but perhaps one of the saddest was that of Veronica, a nineteen-year-old ballet dancer who popped down to her local shop in Fulham on a Sunday evening to buy a pint of milk. As she approached the shop a youth in a black Ford Capri pulled up and wound down the window to ask her for directions. Pretending he didn't understand her, he got out of the car and stood beside her with his map. Pushing a knife into her ribs, he ordered her into the car. Believing her life to be in danger, she did as she was told and was driven to a vast area of open ground, which we later thought must have been somewhere in Epping Forest.

Terrified, Veronica was then ordered out of the vehicle and forced to walk beside the youth, who jabbed at her ribs with the blade of his knife. In shaded undergrowth, he stripped her naked, raped and buggered her, then calmly walked off.

Veronica somehow managed to find her way back to the road and flagged down a passing motorist, who wrapped her in a blanket and, at her request, dropped her at a local minicab office. She was then driven home where, in the safety of her own surroundings, she suffered a complete mental breakdown. Days later she was found by friends and, despite their best efforts, she would not speak. Suspecting the worst, they eventually called the local police.

Fulham CID asked for my help in interviewing Veronica because she was in such a terrible state. It took days before I could even get her to lift her head and start to tell me what had happened. I eventually established some sort of story from her, but it was only ever going to be half the truth because the poor woman could not bring herself to speak about the unspeakable. We all did our best, but never stood a cat in hell's chance of identifying the bastard who had treated her so despicably.

Her life was devastated by the attack. Unable to leave her flat and completely incapable of working, she was off sick for a relatively short time before her wages were stopped. What little she got from the state was not enough to pay her mortgage, so within a few months she lost her flat and became homeless. Friends attempted to accommodate her, but when the trauma began to affect her ability to dance and she realized she could no longer achieve her ambition to become a ballet star she fled to friends in Canada and was never heard of again.

I have never forgotten poor Veronica and often wondered if she ever came to terms with her shocking ordeal, because if anyone was a candidate for suicide, that poor woman was. Once vibrant and ambitious, she had become a broken waif, her life utterly in ruins.

My mother's move into the nursing home had been unavoidably delayed for several weeks but before too long we had moved her into the comparative luxury of private residential care near where I lived. Within two days of her arrival, however, the situation suddenly took a turn for the worse when I received a phone call from the home, telling me things had gone pear-shaped.

'I'm sorry, Miss Bristow,' the matron told me, 'but your mother is far too disruptive to be cared for here, so we have returned her to Shenley Hospital.'

'You've hardly given her a chance,' I argued.

'Oh, yes we have,' came the reply. 'But after she emptied the fourth potplant on to the floor and threw the empty bowl at one of our residents, we felt there was nothing we could do, short of tying her down, and since that was out of the question we returned her to the friends and the place where she feels most comfortable.'

Of all people, I knew that my mother could be difficult, but I could not help but grin as I pictured my little old mum, who weighed no more than eight and a half stone, holding the entire nursing home at bay with her antics. Good on yer, Mum, I thought. You never let anyone push you around when you lived at home, so why start now? But then I realized the seriousness of what had been said, because in essence it meant that, unless Pete or I could accommodate her, Mum would have to stay in Shenley, probably for the rest of her life.

When I went to see her there, she appeared quite calm. She didn't seem very sure about who I was, but she looked happy enough sitting in her armchair, relaxing in the now familiar surroundings. Pete and I talked it over and sought the advice of her GP. Mum was certainly no longer able to live alone and neither of us was qualified to take care of her physical and mental needs. In the long term, we agreed, Mum's best interests would be served at Shenley, where we knew she would receive the skilled nursing that she deserved.

We continued to visit her regularly and sometimes, just sometimes, she would astonish us with her clarity of mind. 'Hello, dear,' she said to me on one visit. 'How's the job going? Are you still enjoying it?' I was so amazed by what she had said that it took me a second or two to collect my thoughts but then, as I was about to respond, I could see she had brought the shutters down again and she was away in her other world.

One day, when she had been at Shenley for a few years, I received a phone call telling me that she had been involved in an accident on the ward. She had been standing behind one of the heavy doors when it had swung back and knocked her to the floor and she'd broken her hip. She had been rushed to Barnet Hospital, where Pete and I visited her shortly after she had undergone major hip surgery, which had involved replacing the joint. She looked awful, her wizened features and grey hair ageing her dreadfully. There was no trace of the young beauty my father had fallen in love with.

'She'll never learn to walk again,' said Pete, miserably. 'Her mind's too far gone for her to understand what she's got to do to recover.'

'Don't be daft,' I said. 'No one's ever been able to hold our mum back, she'll be on her feet in no time.' But Pete shook his head. And he was absolutely right. After a week she was returned to Shenley, where she caught pneumonia. The hospital rang me at work to give me the news. 'She's fading fast,' I was told by the staff nurse.

I drove like a bat out of hell straight to Shenley Hospital, but Mum died as I arrived at her bedside. For the first time since the death of my father twelve years earlier, she looked to be resting in total peace.

Just as my sobriety had reintroduced me to joyful emotions that had eluded me for years, it now ushered in feelings of sorrow and desolation in crisis proportions. My mother's death triggered feelings of grief for my father that I had never allowed myself to feel before. I was a forty-something orphan who suddenly felt the absence of her parents as acutely as a ten-year-old might have done.

Those next few months were undoubtedly the toughest test of my teetotalism. I could have drowned my sorrows in a bottle at a second's notice, but I didn't. Someone had told me that if I could live through this awful grief then the chances were that I would look back with joy on my parents' lives. 'Live life a day at a time,' a wise friend had said, 'and, when looking back, never stare.'

When I conjured up memories of my father, I had always seen a very sick man at death's door and that sight had haunted me for years. Now, as if by some miracle, that vision was gradually replaced by a picture of him standing in the garden on a summer's day with his head thrown back, laughing, my mother at his side. As I got better, so the picture got better and today, when I think no one's watching, I talk to them both.

In the grief I felt for my mother, I became racked with guilt for not loving her in her dementia. How could any decent daughter stop loving her mother? I chided myself for entertaining the notion, but then it dawned on me, just as plainly as if someone had switched the light on, that I had always loved her – she was, after all, my mother – I just didn't like her that much any more.

In my recovery, I learnt to focus on the happier times. I also started to appreciate how much of my job I brought home with me and how that pressure had given me fuel with which to feed my alcoholism. I was not about to manufacture excuses for myself, but I would never again underestimate the power that tiredness held for me, nor its continuing effect on my physical and mental well-being. I was beginning to learn to pace myself and I quickly identified where my priorities lay.

Up to that point, I had never realized how much of a beating my psyche had taken from years, with no respite, of sex and violence. Increasingly, I was becoming aware of my revulsion for explicit love scenes which marred my enjoyment of television and feature films. It concerned me that I was fast becoming an old prude who must be past her prime in investigating matters sexual.

Given the chance, I could still be haunted by the faces of all the rape victims I knew – Juliet Davies; dear old Ivy Watts; the young woman who killed her own child; Jill Saward; Veronica; Renata; Janie. The last two never left my thoughts for very long. Janie in particular had lived inside my head since February 1977 when she was first reported missing, and since then I had been inwardly tormented by the fact that her killer had never been brought to book. More recently, she had occupied my thoughts daily and I worried that I might be bordering on the obsessive.

Inevitably, thoughts of Janie prompted images of David Lashley and an entirely different set of emotions. I felt rage at his crimes and frustratingly helpless to do anything about it. It was my father who had instilled me with a strong sense of justice and it was the injustice of Lashley's escape from judgement for murder, as I saw it, which so infuriated me. He was the man whose handiwork I would never forget and as I recalled his last appearance in court, eleven years previously, I became filled with horror at the possibility of his parole. Had it really been eleven years? He had been sentenced to a total of eighteen years' imprisonment and, unless he had really blotted his copybook, he would surely be out soon to reoffend.

I realized that when he was freed he would almost certainly return to west London to live with his aunt and uncle in Southall. From that time on, every woman in the area would be up for grabs from his point of view. None of them would ever be safe, solely by virtue of their gender, and because I now policed an area of west London he was bound to use again, the chances were that I would be one of the officers who would have to deal with him.

As I entertained that thought I once again saw Janie and Renata's faces. As clearly as if they were standing in front of me. I shivered. I was angry, very angry. Surely there was something I could do? It was mid-September 1988 and with Lashley in mind I suddenly picked up the telephone and called the Home Office, asking to be put through to the department known as the Prison Index.

'I'm Detective Inspector Carol Bristow,' I said. 'Wonder if

you could do me a favour.' Within minutes, I found out that Lashley was serving out his time at Frankland high-security prison in Durham. Another telephone call established that he was due to be released on parole in February 1989. He had not, it appeared, blotted his copybook and would serve only twelve years of his original eighteen-year sentence. February. Just five short months away and that bad bastard would be free to kill once more. I felt sick to my guts just thinking about it.

I picked up the telephone again but this time dialled the number of my detective chief superintendent, Guy Mills, a police officer I respected, who worked at Area HQ at Notting Dale. Guy and I had been detective sergeants together and he had always been a smashing bloke and a very good copper.

'Can I pop over and have a word, guv?' I asked. 'I've got a bit of a story to tell you and I need about an hour of your time.' He was obviously puzzled, but told me he was too busy to see me immediately. Checking his diary, he booked me in for two o'clock the following day.

'Come in, Carol, sit down,' he said, showing me a chair. I pulled it up and sat rather nervously in front of him.

'What's the problem?' he cajoled. 'You look really worried about something.'

I took a deep breath and started. 'It's about a man called David Lashley.'

Guy's forehead furrowed as he tried to place the name. He hadn't been in west London at the time of Renata and Janie Shepherd and would have had no reason to know Lashley. Before he could say anything, I gave him a potted history of who Lashley was and what he had done.

'Anyway, he's out on parole in five months, sir,' I concluded, 'and that means he'll be back on our patch and I'll be one of the officers dealing with the victims of his crimes.'

The penny still hadn't dropped. Guy looked perplexed. 'I don't understand,' he said. 'What do you want me to do about it?'

I took a deep breath and blurted out: 'I want Janie's murder reinvestigated. I'm sure Lashley killed her, and maybe there was something we missed eleven years back which needs looking at again. If we don't then God knows what'll happen once Lashley's out.'

The force of my suggestion made him jump to his feet, almost knocking his cup of coffee across his desk. 'You must be raving mad!' he said. 'What are you on about? How can we reopen the case? It's nearly twelve years old and it wasn't even our inquiry, it all got passed over to Hertfordshire. I can't tell them to re-investigate, I don't have the authority.' He slammed his fist on the desk in frustration and indignation.

I've never been one to accept rejection gracefully and I, too, jumped to my feet. 'All right,' I said. 'But what are we going to do when Lashley starts murdering women on our patch? Aren't we going to regret we didn't try to stop him?' My face was red with anger and so was his.

'All right, you've made your point,' he said, scowling. He studied my face for a second as he thought about what he should do. 'I'll ring Hertfordshire. How does that suit you?'

That was all I wanted to hear. I could have jumped up and kissed him on the cheek. Instead, I said: 'Thank you, guv. That'll do me fine.'

As I drove back to the office, I couldn't help feeling a little excited. Guy Mills was not the type to break a promise and if he said he would help then you could rest assured he would.

Within forty-eight hours he phoned me. 'I've spoken to Herts,' he said. 'Detective Chief Superintendent Hill is the head of CID there and he referred me to a Detective Superintendent Ian Whinnett, who now has charge of the inquiry. It's been arranged that we'll all meet up at St Albans Police Station to discuss the way forward and I've said that you'll try to locate Henry Mooney to encourage him to come up too.'

I was thrilled. 'Yes, sir,' I said, 'I'll do that. I'm sure he'll help if he can.'

'By the way,' Guy added, 'it seems that Janie's mother has written to Herts recently asking them much the same and Whinnett has already started some enquiries of his own to see what can be done. I've said we'll help all we can with whatever he decides to do next.'

As soon as I put the phone down, I grabbed my address

book, found the home telephone number of Henry Mooney, the DCS who took early retirement when Herts claimed the Janie Shepherd case from him, and dialled the number. Despite eleven years away from police work, I was confident that nobody knew more about Janie's unsolved murder than he. He was now a solicitor, living and working not far from my own home, and I made an appointment to go and see him with the hope that I could persuade him to come to Herts with me. I knew his presence would add enormously to our appeal.

Henry had not changed one bit. When I sat down and started to try and plead my case, I suddenly realized he was already nodding his agreement. 'I haven't stopped thinking about Lashley either,' he interrupted. 'Of course I'll help.'

On a night in early October 1988 I drove Henry Mooney to St Albans Police Station to be met by DCS Mills. The three of us entered the concrete and glass building and were shown to the conference room, where Detective Superintendent Whinnett was already seated next to Detective Constable Mick Farenden, the only officer left at St Albans who had worked on the original inquiry. Coffee and biscuits arrived and the atmosphere felt good.

As Whinnett opened the proceedings, I felt myself relaxing. I had been quite nervous about the meeting but now realized that we were all there for a common purpose, to discuss the past, present and a possible future of the Janie Shepherd murder inquiry. I knew that, having instigated the meeting, it was up to me to state my point of view and hoped I was up to the task.

I outlined my concerns, then Henry Mooney recounted his memories of the inquiry and the evidence that he believed pointed to Lashley being Janie's killer. Guy Mills then made the point that when Lashley was released he would doubtless go and live with his aunt and uncle in Southall and, since there was more than a slight probability that he would start reoffending on our patch, he would willingly loan some of his officers to assist Ian Whinnett with any further enquiries he had in mind.

To his great credit, Ian Whinnett made notes and listened intently to every word that was said before indicating that he was already in the process of reviewing the murder

262

investigation. When it was time to leave, I shook his hand and felt confident that here was a senior detective who not only had the full measure of Lashley, but who was doing his very best to get justice for Janie.

Henry Mooney and I drove home in silence. My thoughts had drifted back to the hospital; in my mind's eye I was sitting at Renata's bedside staring at her heavily bandaged hand, consumed with anger once again. Janie's face appeared, as it so often did of late, as if she were willing me to do something about her death. Whether Henry was thinking the same thing or not, I don't know, but he seemed peaceful sitting next to me, lost in his own thoughts. As I dropped him at his door and he stepped from the car, I said softly: 'Thank you for coming.'

He turned to me and smiled. 'It was my pleasure.'

I could hardly sleep that night as I pictured Detective Superintendent Whinnett, sitting at a table by the light of a lamp, examining the papers for the umpteenth time. He appeared to be a man of few words who probably played his cards very close to his chest, and I wondered what was going through his mind.

I needn't have worried. Within a few days I received a call from Guy Mills at Area HQ. 'It's been agreed that we will loan Hertfordshire some troops to assist with their enquiries. Ian Whinnett has already started the ball rolling and now, with our help, he might get lucky somewhere along the way.' I felt excited by the news because all that I hoped for had already begun to happen. In over eleven years, no suspect apart from Lashley had been identified for the murder of Janie Shepherd. If a new inquiry secured the evidence that Ian Whinnett would need to prosecute him, then in a convoluted way some sense might be made of Janie's otherwise senseless death. If Lashley had been convicted of her murder at the same time that he was dealt with for Renata's attempted murder and rape, he would almost certainly have got a life sentence and been paroled about now anyway.

* * *

263

The work at Acton went on, but it didn't get any easier. In early 1989, I was introduced to a twenty-two-year-old woman with whom I have remained in contact ever since, largely because of her courage in the face of devastating long-term complications brought about by rape.

I first met Sue after receiving a telephone call from a psychotherapist who asked my advice about a patient she had. 'If I told you I was counselling a young woman who was raped eighteen months ago and was now willing to tell the police what happened, what could she expect from you?'

I couldn't make any promises because the eighteen-month time lapse would undoubtedly cause problems, but I said that I would gladly listen if that was what the young woman wanted. From what the psychotherapist was telling me, her patient's need to be believed was paramount to her continuing psychological recovery. She brought her in to see me the following day.

Sue was a pretty young woman from Cornwall, the daughter of a vicar, who had come to London to study. On the course, she met a suave fellow-student called Alan Jones, with whom she had fallen in love and to whom she had lost her virginity. A year after they started going out, she discovered a Valentine card addressed to him from another woman and challenged him about it. He confessed there and then that he had a common-law wife to whom he was engaged, and a child, back home in the Midlands.

Sue was broken-hearted, and made it clear to Jones that she wanted nothing more to do with him. He panicked and offered to break off his engagement, but she no longer trusted him and told him exactly how she felt. Jones was not the type to give up so easily. Over the next few days he bombarded her with flowers and letters, and promised that he had split up with his former girlfriend. Sue remained fast and refused to see him or give in to his sexual advances.

One evening in May 1987, Jones tricked his way into her flat and tried to kiss her. She asked him to leave and pushed him away, at which point he completely flipped. Throwing her across the room and on to her bed, he removed her tights and knickers and sat across her, trying to force her to engage in oral sex. The more she resisted and fought him, the angrier he became, slapping her hard around the face. He took hold of her by her hair and slammed her head against the wall several times until she could fight him no longer.

Turning her over, he made her kneel on all fours while he tried to force his clenched fist up her rectum. She said it felt as if she was being split in two. Then, after buggering her, he turned her over and ejaculated over her face. Spitting on her breasts, he lit several matches and dipped the hot flames into the pools of saliva, laughing as she screamed.

After raping her once more, he took hold of a bottle with a candle in it and, removing the candle, inserted the bottle into her vagina. He told her that if she moved an inch he would break its neck off inside her. Taking a ruler from a cabinet, he then forced it into her rectum. At the same time, he picked up a hockey stick and, believing he would ultimately kill her, Sue begged him: 'Stop this. Kill me and get it over with.'

We will never know if those words had any impact on this low-life piece of dirt, but Jones did suddenly stop. He put on his clothes and left her room.

Sue spent the next twenty-four hours in a trance, rocking herself backwards and forwards in her quilt until she was discovered by a girlfriend. 'What's the matter?' the girlfriend asked. 'He raped me,' was all Sue could say. Her friend tried very hard to find out more but Sue couldn't speak. Her mind had simply put a block on the subject. She could not express the horror she felt, or the pain she was suffering. She couldn't even look at her own body, she felt so disgusted. She begged her friend not to say anything to anyone.

What followed is about par for the course in circumstances as horrendous as these. Sue's personality underwent an enormous change. Previously a bright, bubbly, happy-go-lucky individual, she withdrew into a shell. She became quiet, depressed and ultimately suicidal. Her friends became increasingly worried about her mental well-being.

To make matters worse, Jones made it known that he too was worried about Sue's apparent mental decline and he wrote to her on a couple of occasions, begging her forgiveness, although never actually spelling out what it was he wanted forgiveness for. Sue did all she could to ignore Jones and, with supreme effort, she attempted to pick up her life again and focus on her studies – amazingly passing her diploma at the end of the year with flying colours.

Recognizing that she was, however, at the end of her mental tether, a friend suggested that she seek help for her acute depression from a psychotherapist, the woman who contacted me.

When Sue and I first met she was unable to look me in the eye. She spoke down at her knees the whole time. I knew that she would never have sufficient confidence to talk unless I broke the ice a little, so I told her something about myself and introduced her to WPC Sarah Triggs, who was about the same age as Sue and one of the sweetest girls I knew. We chatted about the type of work we did, I told her all about the unit and I started to try to win her confidence gradually.

'I promise I will never be untruthful to you or pretend that things are any better or worse than they really are,' I said. 'You hold all the balls in your court and I really cannot move forward without your specific consent, particularly with regard to prosecuting anyone – if indeed that is something that becomes possible.'

Slowly, and almost imperceptibly, her head started to come up. After a couple of cups of coffee and a long chat, she began to tell us her dreadful story. When she had relaxed a little, I left her with WPC Triggs, who spent the next three days with her, taking her evidence down in the form of a statement.

Back at the nick, I examined all the letters that Jones had sent to Sue. They contained whole sections which, to my mind, referred directly to the rape, but which were cleverly worded so as not to spell it out. He wrote: 'I constantly pray to God to ask him to release you of the pain, anguish and suffering I have brought upon you and to punish me, for it is me who has sinned, me who has committed the crime and it is me who should justly suffer.' In another letter he wrote: 'Some idiot, like

266

myself, in a rash, irresponsible moment of lust on my part, destroyed everything.' He added: 'The Bible says an eye for an eye, a tooth for a tooth. I shall definitely, quite gladly take my own life if I know it will solve your problems and restore the happiness we both once shared together.'

With Sue's consent, I arranged for her to be seen by my friend Dr Nabarro, who referred her to a senior surgical registrar in colo-rectal surgery. He confirmed that she had such severe rectal injuries that they were still bleeding eighteen months after the attack. He also said that the injuries were consistent with the allegations she had made.

That was good enough for me. Armed with this corroboration of her story, I had enough evidence to arrest Jones and speak to him about rape and buggery. But I somehow knew that this charismatic, good-looking, no-good son of a bitch would probably balk at the word 'arrest' and exercise his right to say absolutely nothing to me after the police caution telling him of his right to remain silent.

So instead I 'invited' Jones to attend Acton Police Station and speak to me, which was far less formal, and when he arrived I was in full grovelling mode. 'So sorry you've been troubled like this, Mr Jones. Would you like a tea or coffee? I know this must be very inconvenient for you and I want you to know how grateful I am that you were able to attend so promptly, but I did wonder if you would be so kind as to help me with a few answers to some questions?'

In the presence of his brief, he told me: 'I want to tell you the truth, but I really can't remember much about that night. In my twenty-five years I have never forced anyone to have sex. I can remember we had a tiff but that's about it.'

He repeated: 'I cannot remember what I did that night. "Rape" is an awful word. Sex was already part of our relationship, Carol. Is that your name?' I nodded and gripped the table edge.

I asked him about the letters he had written to Sue and the references to 'pain' and 'suffering'. He was as cool as a cucumber. He said: 'When I made reference to the pain I inflicted, it was aimed around my relationship with other women and did not refer to any one instance in particular,' he said. 'When I said I had committed a crime, I meant it was a crime to have more than one relationship. When I wrote about a "rash irresponsible moment of lust" on my part, I was referring to my previous acquaintance.'

The interview went on and on in this vein and became utterly tedious. The only highlight was the look on his face when I turned off the charm and charged him with the rape and buggery of Sue Stewart and told him he was to be kept in custody overnight.

In due course, Jones was committed for trial at the Old Bailey, while WPC Triggs, the psychotherapist and I set about the task of preparing Sue for the next phase of her ordeal – facing Jones in the witness box. My own twelve-step recovery programme, learnt the hard way through Alcoholics Anonymous, enabled me to help Sue. I had always been a great one for looking back and thinking, If only I had not done this or not done that, then things might be different. What my programme taught me was that if I did my personal best the first time around then that was enough – I need not look back with any regrets. If, on the other hand, I cut corners (and, of course, I had that choice) then I must be prepared to settle for any adverse consequences that might arise.

The programme has become a way of life for me; that's not to say I always get it right – far from it – but generally I know when I'm going wrong because I feel so uncomfortable. Whereas before I would have gone blindly forward, blaming everything in sight without ever looking at my own inadequacies.

I've also learnt, and have tried to teach people like Sue, that the past is the past. We can't go back and change a bloody thing, we can only go forward with what we have left.

Life is for the living and, in sobriety, I've tried to live it with optimism and self-respect, two precious words which had earlier escaped my understanding. I keep telling myself that this is no rehearsal, this is it, so get on and live it a day at a time. Whatever I've been able to impart to the likes of Sue is stuff I've learnt from others which has helped me immeasurably. I take no credit for it, because it is there for us all – the trick is understanding it and incorporating it into one's life.

We spent literally hours sitting with Sue, encouraging her to keep her head held high and to give her evidence clearly and precisely. We were always worried what it might do to her if Jones was found not guilty, so we drummed it into her that, regardless of the verdict, if she gave it her best shot she need have no regrets.

The case was listed for hearing in June 1989, and Sue was so pent-up in the days leading up to the trial that she collapsed and was taken to hospital. The doctors blamed the stress she was facing for her wildly variant blood-sugar levels and she was sent home.

It became clear we had done a fantastic job when Sue took the oath. She was a different woman as she gave her evidence dry-eyed and without batting an eyelid. If the jury expected tears, they got none. For the purpose of the trial, Sue had recovered her self-respect, which for those of us who knew her a few months earlier was nothing short of a miracle. It was at times like this that I wished I had had a video camera running when she first came into the police station. How I wished the jury could have seen her, head drooped, stumbling tearfully over her words as she tried to get her story out. They would hardly have recognized her as the smartly dressed young woman in the box before them now.

The medical evidence came next. The consultant who examined Sue gave his evidence about her injuries and explained himself in a very easy manner. But in cross-examination, when asked the hypothetical question 'Is it possible that years of untreated chronic constipation could have caused the same rectal damage?' he answered: 'Yes.'

Anticipating where the defence might be going with that particular line, we called Sue's GP, who gave evidence to the effect that she had never, ever complained of constipation or indeed suffered any problems in that area prior to her attack.

When it was Jones's turn to give evidence, my heart sank. He was dressed immaculately and looked extremely handsome.

He smiled at the women members of the jury and told them that he had volunteered the information to Sue about his relationship with his common-law wife. Sue, he said, had turned nasty and become very bitter about his deceit, culminating in her accusation of rape eighteen months later. Almost as an aside, he mentioned that Sue had suffered from chronic constipation for the whole time he had known her.

Watching someone present a distorted account of the truth, just to save his own neck, has always been difficult. Jones's performance reminded me of the countless other occasions I had played mental judge and jury while sitting in court. My special relationship with Sue and my insight into the case led me to believe that her evidence, as presented, was true.

As I listened to Jones's scurrilous attempt to challenge Sue's integrity and to destroy her for a second time, it was almost impossible to remain dispassionate. But, wearing my well-worn mask of indifference, I had to look unmoved and, to some, I must have appeared heartless.

Two weeks later, when the jury returned their verdict, I knew in my heart of hearts what it would be. 'Not guilty': the words rang out across the courtroom as Jones punched the air with his fist. Sue sat stock-still, staring straight ahead of her, while the rest of us fought back the tears on her behalf. Our success in grooming her for the trial had worked against us. Faced with a cool, apparently unemotional young woman and the sophisticated young man who charmed all the women jurors, they acquitted him. He even walked over to the jurors afterwards to thank them personally.

Sue remained as strong as she could, and returned to her new job at Marks & Spencer after the trial. The company knew about her past and had been very supportive. But not long afterwards she started to suffer black-outs, and when she went for tests doctors discovered that she had developed epilepsy associated with severe trauma. During the course of those tests, a scan discovered severe scarring of her brain consistent, they said, with her head having been repeatedly banged against a wall.

M&S couldn't have been kinder and offered her a new managerial post near her home town in Cornwall so that she could be close to her family. I went to her farewell dinner in London and wished her all the best. It was my plan to withdraw gradually from regular contact with her, conforming to my personal rule not to give too much to any one victim so that I would be able to help the next. I was also aware that my very presence in a victim's life could only serve to remind her of events she would really rather put to one side.

It was Sue's choice to keep in touch with me through letters and postcards. She said time and again that, because of our special bond, I was the only one who really understood what had happened to her. Months later, she wrote and told me that she was now having up to four epileptic fits a day and had been forced to give up her job. The doctors had increased her medication, only to discover that an adverse reaction to the pills had badly affected her liver. The drugs had been stopped, but the damage was done. Without medication, her fits became more frequent and she had to be constantly supervised.

Placed on new drugs and requiring daily nursing care, she none the less embarked on a course to learn counselling. Finally, her mobility became so badly affected that she was forced to use a wheelchair. Further brain scans showed that fragments of dead tissue and bone were floating about inside her skull as a direct result of the trauma to her head.

At the age of thirty, she suffered a stroke which left her severely disabled, hardly able to write or co-ordinate her movements and confined to a wheelchair. Barely able to feed or dress herself, she is unable to move her legs, lives on high doses of medication and still suffers regular fits. She now has cancer of the liver.

Sue's last scans indicated that one side of her brain had withered to a third of its original size. With the help of full-time nursing care, loving parents and friends, she leads as full a life as possible. It is frustrating to think that with the new evidence about Sue's head injuries we cannot reopen the investigation and put Jones on trial again, because the law states that a defendant once acquitted can never be retried for the same crime. So, while he got off scot-free, she endures a life sentence of ill-health.

All of her problems were caused by the man who raped and beat her and yet – like so many of the other members of the Victims' Club she unwittingly joined – I never once heard her complain.

12

FRANKLAND PRISON IN DURHAM IS ONE OF BRITAIN'S FIVE
maximum-security 'dispersal' prisons, holding four hundred
Category A and Category B prisoners, the most serious
offenders in the system. Purpose-built in 1977 with every
modern facility, it opened its doors six years later and David
Lashley – a Category A prisoner five years into his sentence –
became one of its inmates, along with the IRA terrorists who
bombed Brighton, some psychopathic murderers and other
assorted unsavoury characters.

As Detective Constable Mick Farenden from St Albans Police
Station arrived at its heavy steel gates, accompanied by Detective Inspector Dave Sandlin from the Metropolitan Police, he
must have wondered what, if anything, he would discover about
Lashley on the other side. Weeks earlier, and following on from
the meeting between the two forces, a senior member of the
prison staff contacted the incident room with information
that had raised the hopes of the St Albans team. Lashley, it
appeared, had spoken to a fellow-inmate called Daniel Reece
about Janie's murder. Reece, however, had made it abundantly
clear that he did not want to speak to the police about what he
had been told.

Undaunted, Detective Superintendent Whinnett thought long
and hard about the right way to approach the matter and

accepted that Reece would have to be handled with extreme caution. He knew that if he went blundering in he could lose him as a potential witness altogether.

A thirty-two-year-old east London burglar who had progressed to armed robbery, and a man with more than twenty previous convictions, Reece was not even his real name. In 1983, after being arrested for a robbery, he had shown a willingness to turn Queen's evidence and become a supergrass, shopping several of his criminal colleagues in return for a new identity and a reduced prison sentence. His liaison officer at the time was a young DS on the Flying Squad called Dave Sandlin. It was a twist of fate that nothing ever came of the robber's willingness to testify but 'Reece', as he was now known, was branded a grass for ever.

Reece duly served three years in Norwich for his crimes but when he came out of prison he quickly broke the law again; only this time it was a crime which was completely out of character. He discovered that while he was inside his former business partner had been having an affair with his wife. Exacting a terrible revenge, Reece imprisoned his partner, the man's wife and his teenage son in his house and handcuffed them together before carrying out a campaign of sexual violence against them.

After beating up his former colleague, he made him watch while he raped his wife at gunpoint and sodomized his fifteen-year-old son. Reece was arrested for the crimes and jailed for thirteen years and nine months in February 1986. He admitted later to being disgusted by what he had done, and tried to slash his wrists in prison because he felt so ashamed.

In view of his background and his past good relationship with Dave Sandlin, now a DI on divisional duties, it was agreed that Sandlin should be the only police officer to approach him now. If Reece gave evidence against Lashley, it would mean considerable future hardship for him in prison: a removal of privileges and a return to being locked up twenty-three hours a day, for his own protection. If anyone could persuade Reece to do the right thing, it would be Dave Sandlin. His involvement would also mean that there could be no suggestion of

Hertfordshire Police tainting the evidence. Sandlin was a Met officer who had nothing to do with Herts and he would be approaching Reece 'blind', having been told absolutely nothing about the circumstances surrounding Janie's murder.

Sandlin hadn't seen Reece for years, but was happy to take on the challenge and help out if he could. He was told only that Reece might have some information about a fellow-prisoner that could be useful to Herts Police. He took a train to Durham with Mick Farenden in November 1988, but the pair hardly spoke. Arriving at the prison, Farenden talked to prison officers while Sandlin took on Reece. Shown into a visiting room, the DI listened to the clanking doors and jangling keys along the corridor as the prisoner was brought from his cell.

Reece wasn't pleased to see him. A handsome, charismatic man with tattooed arms and a friendly, open face, he nodded cautiously at Dave Sandlin and sat his huge bulk down opposite him. After an exchange of niceties, Reece offered to outline what he claimed Lashley had told him but refused to put anything in writing. Sandlin agreed and asked him to tell him what he knew.

Reece said he first met David Lashley in the prison wood mill, where they were both sent to work, and quickly discovered that they shared a common interest in weight-lifting. Ten times a week they were allowed to go to the prison gym, and would 'spot' for each other – supervise each other's body-building and be there in case the enormous weights they were lifting collapsed on them.

'Lashley is immensely strong,' Reece said, 'the strongest person I have ever met. Him and me are the strongest blokes in here. Some Russian recently broke the world record for weight-lifting but I've seen Lashley lifting exactly the same weights and more.'

He said the pair struck up a friendship, partly through their shared interest and partly because they were both inside for rape, albeit in very different circumstances. Lashley was a loner who often complained to Reece about the length of time men had to serve in prison for rape. He promised that if he ever got out he would conduct a campaign of sexual violence against white women. He said he would start by abducting a woman prison officer on their wing, killing her, severing her head and throwing it out of the prison gates.

'He was bitter about sentences being imposed on rapists generally, and on himself in particular. He also had a deep hatred for a policeman called Detective Mooney. He regularly said he wanted to kill him and his family, by chopping them to pieces with a machete, Mooney's wife first so that he would see her body before it was his turn.'

Reece claimed he had never heard of Janie Shepherd in his life until he met Lashley, who told him that Mooney had questioned him about her murder. It was May 1988 and they were in the workshop of the wood mill when Lashley read a story from a newspaper about a black man sentenced to imprisonment for life for rape. 'He was in a rage and he pointed to the story and said the man should have killed the woman he raped, because he wouldn't have gone to prison for any longer. He said that if he had murdered the woman he was serving a sentence for raping, like he did Janie Shepherd, he didn't think he would be in prison now.'

Reece told DI Sandlin that he was shocked by what Lashley had said. 'I said to him: "So you did murder Janie Shepherd then?" and he said, "Yes." He then described to me what he had done. He was in a sort of trance. His eyes were very staring, as if he was reliving what he had done. It was sick.'

Lashley told Reece that when he first saw Janie she was getting out of her Mini and walking into a shop in Queensway. Seeing a FOR SALE sign in the Mini window, he pretended to be looking the vehicle over as a potential buyer when she came out of the supermarket. He engaged her in conversation and when she was completely off her guard, he suddenly produced a butcher's knife and drove her to Ladbroke Grove, where he attacked her. He gloated as he told Reece how he had torn her clothes off, 'ripped them to shreds', while she tried to fight him off.

Tying her hands, he demonstrated how sharp his knife was by slashing the roof of the Mini. He then raped her, forcing her to tell him she was enjoying what he was doing. 'He said he was choking Janie Shepherd as he was doing it,' Reece told the silent Dave Sandlin.

'Did he say how?' the detective asked quietly.

'Yes, to demonstrate he put his arm around the back of my head to hold my neck; and he put his right fist against my windpipe. He said she was choking. He said he crushed her throat and killed her.'

Sandlin suddenly saw the importance of what Reece was saying. With detail like this, the Herts detectives would surely be able to compare Reece's description with any post-mortem report on Janie Shepherd. Little did he know that the pathologist's description of her injuries was exactly consistent with what Lashley had said had happened.

'Lashley said he redressed her body but because her original clothing was ripped, he used some other clothes,' Reece continued. 'Then he strapped her body into the passenger seat of his car and drove down the motorway to Hertfordshire. He said it was funny because when he went round a corner or a bend, the body would sway from side to side, and he was laughing. He took her to a lovers' lane type of place and carried her body into some bushes.'

Lashley finished his story by telling Reece that the Mini got stuck in the mud in Hertfordshire and he had to push it out. He then drove it back to Ladbroke Grove, eating the food that Janie had bought at the Queensway store. He dumped the car and went home to bed.

'It's the vivid details which stuck in my mind,' Reece told the police officer sitting opposite him. 'The details of the killing have stayed with me. I kept quiet, I tried not to think about it. But I was having trouble sleeping. It destroyed the relationship between Lashley and me. We couldn't work in the gym together any more. I changed my job in the wood mill because I couldn't work there no more. I couldn't be with Lashley no more. I got a job on the wing as a cleaner.

'In the end it just got too much. I couldn't hold it in any longer, it was giving me nightmares. I told a friend of mine, a fellow-prisoner, and then I told one of the screws [prison officers].'

DI Sandlin took in every word and asked Reece once again if he would be prepared to put what he had been told in writing, but he adamantly refused.

The detective returned to London with Mick Farenden and reported the outcome of his interview to the St Albans team. Superintendent Whinnett was astonished and delighted by what he heard and felt sure that this was the evidence they needed to get the case re-examined by the Crown Prosecution Service. Reece had told Sandlin things that could only have been known to Janie's killer or to the police. The only problem was that Whinnett could not possibly proceed against Lashley without a written statement from Reece, stating his willingness to become a witness.

Sandlin went back to Durham and spent several more hours with Reece, trying to persuade him to put the details of the confession in writing. He promised him 'protection' and assured him that his statement would not be released until he had been made 'safe'. It took all Sandlin's powers of persuasion, but he finally persuaded Reece to tell the truth in court about what Lashley had said.

Without warning, a few weeks later the *Mail on Sunday* published a front-page article claiming a suspect was being reinvestigated for the murder of Janie Shepherd. Reece had not yet been moved from Frankland and when he was shown the article by a friend he became terrified of reprisals. The story was followed up in the *Daily Mail* with the added information that a man nearing the end of his prison sentence was about to be rearrested.

Later that day, in the exercise yard, Lashley summoned Reece over to him. He asked him if he had seen the newspaper articles and when he said he had, Lashley told Reece: 'That's you. Talking to the police.' Reece told him not to be stupid, but Lashley replied: 'That's you because in twelve years I've never told anyone any details they couldn't find out from a newspaper.' Reece denied it as emphatically as he could, but Lashley sneered at him and said, 'We'll see,' before walking off.

Reece was transferred to Reading Prison in February 1989, where Sandlin visited him on at least two more occasions.

Throughout their interviews, Sandlin was at pains to make it clear that Reece would not be receiving any favours from the Home Office for testifying, and that the only concession would be the promise of safety. Accepting the terms, Reece prepared himself to give testimony against Lashley for murder.

Even with such a witness, however, diligent work was needed to bring Lashley to trial. Hundreds of original statements were reanalysed, witnesses reinterviewed and new statements taken from people who were being asked to recall the events of eleven years earlier. The boys who had found the body were now men, the girl who had served Janie at the Queensway foodstore was married with children – it took Mick Farenden three months to track her down – and the newly married young couple who had seen the dead Janie swaying in the car were divorced. Only Janie remained fixed in time, her youthful, exuberant face once again beaming at detectives from photographs pinned up in the third incident room to investigate her untimely death.

Once every stone had been overturned, every angle re-examined, every factor considered, a bulging new case file was dispatched to the CPS. It would be up to the lawyers to make the final decision.

Call it intuition, or whatever you like, but I could sense that something was about to happen. I had heard through the grapevine that counsel had been sent the new evidence and had initially responded favourably. It seemed like for ever since I had sat in St Albans Police Station pleading Janie's case, and here we were, already in February – the month when Lashley was due to be released – and there was still no news. Surely I would hear something soon, I thought.

I was sitting in my office at Acton Police Station on the morning of 21 February 1989 when I opened the inner pages of the *Daily Telegraph*. My eyes fell upon a small story of just three paragraphs which made me catch my breath.

I read and re-read the few lines which told me all I needed to know – that twelve years after the murder of Australian heiress Rosemary Jane Shepherd a man had been 'gate arrested' on suspicion of the crime, just as he was about to be released from

Frankland Prison, Durham, from a previous sentence. His name was David Ronald Lashley.

I felt as if I could fly. My breathing resumed and with it my heartbeat. 'Yesss!' I cried aloud. 'Bloody fantastic!' I knew that in reality someone who is 'gate arrested' is taken from their cell by warders to the prison's disciplinary room, where local officers inform them that they are being rearrested for another crime. But in my mind's eye I lived and relived the most delicious scenario of Lashley, suitcase in hand, gasping for his first breath of freedom, keen to feel the sun on his face, standing at the heavy prison gates as they slid open for him, only to be grabbed by the lapels from either side by Detective Superintendent Whinnett and DC Mick Farenden and told: 'You're nicked, sunshine.'

I could see the crestfallen look on his face, I could taste his disappointment and anger. I envisaged a big black meatwagon from St Albans nick, its back doors wide open and four burly coppers sitting inside, grinning and beckoning Lashley. It was a fantasy, but it was the best I could do in the absence of any first-hand experience of his arrest.

For the next three days Lashley was interviewed by Herts detectives, interviews which were all tape-recorded and conducted in the presence of his solicitor. The prisoner was garrulous and repetitive and said a good deal which was totally irrelevant. It was as if he thought that by chattering on he could somehow win the game.

He claimed he had been hounded by the press and the police for years and was not even guilty of the attack on Renata. He repeatedly asked the detectives why, if the police had evidence about his involvement in Janie's death, he had not been interviewed or charged before.

Janie had thoroughly cleaned her car the evening before her disappearance and was not known to eat peanuts or chewing gum, although peanut shells and skins were found in her abandoned Mini, along with some Wrigley's spearmint gum wrappers. Similar items were also found in Lashley's car and in the van he used. When asked specifically if he liked peanuts, he admitted buying them in their shells in one-pound bags from a shop in Edmonton, north London. He also admitted to being an occasional user of chewing gum, but claimed that DCS Mooney had planted his particular brand of chewing gum bearing his secretor type of saliva in Janie's car, along with a negroid hair which matched one taken from his comb. He insisted that Mooney was 'bent'.

He claimed he had a watertight alibi for the night of Janie's disappearance. He said: 'I can't see no jury or judge breaking this alibi, no way.' He claimed his car had broken down and that he had gone to bed early at his aunt's home in Southall, after chatting to his cousin Merton. The following morning, he said, he got up early and went to work by bus.

He was shown the sharp white-handled kitchen knife which had been found stuck in the flower border of a communal garden near to where Janie's Mini was discovered. He denied ever having seen it or used it, despite it having been positively identified by the canteen manageress at his place of work as being the knife she used to peel potatoes.

When challenged on Reece's evidence, Lashley denied having confessed. The interviewing detective asked him: 'Do you remember saying that? ("I'm in here for rape but if I had killed her like Janie Shepherd I would not be in here.")'

'No,' said Lashley, 'but anyway it doesn't make sense.'

'Why is that then?'

'Because I never killed Janie Shepherd.'

'So what you're saying is "I'm in here for rape, but if I had killed her", meaning the one you were sentenced for?'

Lashley smiled and said: 'I was only trying to be jovial.'

Three days after his arrest, Lashley was charged with Janie's murder. Guy Mills rang to tell me and expressed his delight at the news. It was reassuring to know that, for the time being at least, women in west London were safe from this monster.

There was more good news too for Mick Farenden and the new team of seven detectives who had set themselves up in an incident room overlooking St Albans town centre. Following on from Lashley's arrest and initial appearance at St Albans Magistrates' Court, two more prisoners who had served time with him came forward to admit that Lashley had confessed or partially confessed to them.

One was Robert Hodgson, serving life for murder in Parkhurst on the Isle of Wight, who had spent time in Wakefield Prison with Lashley in 1981. He said that Lashley admitted killing Janie after Hodgson confessed his own crime of murder.

'That's fuck-all,' Lashley was said to have retorted. 'I killed a girl in a Mini. You should have took the car and dumped the body like I did.' He went on to give a similar account to the one he had given Reece. This time, he mentioned that he had tied Janie's arms with the strap of her shoulder bag. He said she had clawed his face and bitten him and he had punched her.

A second man, Michael McDonagh, who served time in Wandsworth Prison with Lashley between 1977 and 1978, asked him outright one morning during slopping-out: 'Is it correct that you've killed a girl?' Lashley smiled and replied: 'That's right and they'll never prove it.' Ten years later, after hearing that Lashley had been arrested for the murder, he came forward with the information, claiming to have done so because he was 'a family man'. The two men's statements were added to the growing bundle of documents to be sent to the Crown Court.

Not that it was all plain sailing. Back in 1977 the Hertfordshire detectives had been very meticulous and retained every swab and sample, every peanut shell and piece of chewed gum, just in case the murder was ever solved. By 1988 it had been more than two years since the science of DNA profiling had achieved its first major success with a conviction, and DS Whinnett and his men now looked at the twelve-year-old samples in their original plastic evidence bags and wondered what modern technology could tell them about these exhibits.

Was it just possible that there was enough saliva left within the chewed piece of gum, or on a cigarette end, for it to be identified categorically as having come from Lashley? They dared not hope. In November 1988, the samples were sent off to Cellmark Diagnostics in Abingdon, Oxon, the world's leading DNA testing laboratory, to be microscopically examined by experts.

The chewing gum was carefully separated from the waxed paper it had been placed in, the cigarette ends were tested for traces of saliva and the semen swabs taken from the floor and seats of Janie's Mini were delicately examined. It has been claimed that because DNA is so stable it has been possible to extract it from dinosaur eggs and Egyptian mummies, yet in the case of the swabs taken from Janie Shepherd's car the samples were found to be 'too degraded'. They had deteriorated to such an extent, during their many years in storage, that despite the use of the most sensitive probes available no bands could be detected. The same was true of the cigarette ends. Saliva had been taken from them in 1977 to test for blood grouping and what now remained was of such poor quality that it made identification impossible.

With the semen samples there was an added complication. DNA could only be extracted from the 'live sex cell', the spermatozoa, and there was simply not a good enough sample of spermatozoa for that to happen. Only three were found and they contained insufficient DNA for the profiling technique. Since then, however, the technology has progressed so much that any minute amount of DNA extracted from similar live cells can be grown to make ample DNA for testing. But in 1988, in the run-up to Lashley's arrest, the Hertfordshire team were to be bitterly disappointed with the laboratory's inconclusive results.

On Tuesday 27 February 1990, the trial of David Lashley began at St Albans Crown Court. I was as busy as ever at Acton, but I was determined to get up to the 1970s concrete-rendered courtroom as often as I could to hear the evidence. It was frustrating not being able to sit through the whole trial, and only being allowed into the public gallery, but the glimpses I did get were invaluable.

The defendant was seated in the dock under a heavy guard of prison officers. He had not withdrawn his threat to 'get' a number of people on his hate list, and nobody was taking any chances. I watched him settle into his seat and studied him closely. He looked much the same as he had at Renata's trial, only his muscular frame looked even larger, if that were possible. His twelve years of body-building had made his bulk even more menacing. I was grateful that I was above and behind him and would never have to look into those eyes again.

Janie's mother was sitting in the public gallery a few feet away, watching him too and listening to the evidence. I recognized her from the photographs I had seen of her in the newspapers before Janie was found. I desperately wanted to go and introduce myself, to tell her that in some strange way I shared her tremendous sense of loss. But I knew that I couldn't. Who was I, after all? She didn't know me from Adam.

Michael Kalisher QC, prosecuting, opened the case. He painted a picture of Janie for the jury, describing her as 'an attractive, vivacious healthy young woman of independent means'. He said she had suffered 'appalling abuse', adding: 'Her body was too decomposed to enable rape to be verified, but there can be little doubt that she had been raped.'

Referring to the sworn statement by Daniel Reece, he told the jury: 'The Crown will contend that the confession was so detailed, so accurate and so consistent with the known facts about the murder that it could only have come from the murderer himself. It is overwhelming and, in a sense, too horrifying to be anything other than the truth. Reece had no other possible source of such information. He reported, not to police concerned with the case, who knew some of the details, but to an entirely unconnected prison officer, who had no knowledge of the facts, and who repeated it to the police.'

I felt physically sick as the evidence of Janie's abduction, rape and murder unfolded. Like Angela Darling, I flinched when I saw Janie's Cossack boots presented as exhibits to the jury. They had such an impact on me; they were part of her, or at least they were part of the vision I had of her. I remember thinking, If I feel this upset at seeing them, what on earth must her mother be feeling? I wanted nothing more than to protect her from some of the worst details and gruesome photographs that had been taken of her daughter's mutilated body.

She had looked so nervous and vulnerable when she took the stand as one of the first witnesses to give evidence that the judge asked her if she was all right. Pulling herself together, she insisted that she was there at her own request, before going on to identify the jewellery found on Janie's body.

The trial lasted three weeks and I was able to witness many key moments. There were more than seventy witnesses for the prosecution, and only ten for the defence. Lashley chose to exercise his right to remain silent and not give direct evidence at all. Instead, his aunt and uncle went into the witness box and swore he was at home in bed on the night of the murder.

Prosecution counsel were dreading the cross-examination of Reece because of his previous convictions and dubious super-grass past. Mr Kalisher knew that Helen Grindrod QC, representing Lashley, would do her best to portray Reece as a sneak, a liar and wholly unreliable.

But he needn't have worried. Reece was brilliant. I couldn't take my eyes off him and neither could the jury. He stood tall and proud in the witness box, glaring defiantly at Lashley when the mood took him. He never once tried to hide his past or deny his own despicable crimes and was utterly convincing in his evidence of how Lashley had confessed to him in the prison's wood mill.

'I was just dumbfounded. It was like listening to a Stephen King horror book,' Reece told the jury in his Cockney accent. 'I've had loads of sleepless nights. I've never heard such a sick story in all my life . . . He told me the details because he believed I was the same sort of person as him, that takes pleasure in raping and murdering women.'

Defence counsel asked: 'You did not take pleasure in raping a woman?'

'No, I didn't. I had no pleasure at all.' Reece frowned.

'You were only doing it to punish her husband?'

'No, I done it to punish them all. He was having an affair with my wife.'

'So, in order to get back at him, you raped his wife?' Defence counsel looked meaningfully at the women members of the jury.

'Yes, and it wasn't in a nice calm manner like your client. I didn't crush some innocent girl's throat, and I haven't laughed about my crime like he's been laughing for the past twelve years, and gloating over the details, because he enjoyed doing it.'

Under intensive cross-examination, Reece denied that he would be receiving any special favours from the Home Office or the police for giving evidence. The opposite was true, he said. Lashley had let it be known that Reece had grassed him up and had confronted him about it in Frankland Prison. Since then Reece had been slashed across the back with a razorblade by one of the inmates, and another had tried to stab him in the shower.

He had been moved from modern Frankland Prison, with a toilet in his cell, to Reading Prison and a 'piss pot' in the corner. His visiting rights had been cut in half and he had lost many of his privileges. His son had recently been killed in a road accident and he hadn't even been allowed out to attend the funeral. Furthermore, his recent application for parole had been refused. 'I didn't want to come to this court today, I didn't want all the problems that I have had by coming to this court today,' he moaned from the witness box. 'It's like I've been put on trial again. But by turning away I would be as sick as him; if I turned away and didn't come to this court today.'

Asked again what special treatment he was likely to receive for giving evidence, he repeated: 'I have received nothing. I'm hoping to get nothing. What I'm hoping to get is an end to this, and a good night's sleep.' He added forcefully: 'You can say whatever you want about me, about all this. What I've said in court is the truth. He's an animal, he's a killer, and he enjoyed killing Janie Shepherd.'

Lashley's trial was due to finish on 19 March 1990. Mick Farenden, who had sat through the entire trial with Detective Superintendent Whinnett, told me by telephone that the judge, Mr Justice Alliott, would finish his summing-up of the case to the jury some time in the morning before sending them out to consider their verdict. Mick, like everyone else, fully expected the jury to take at least a day and a night to consider their verdict after such a serious and protracted trial, and, since my work load at Acton had not let up, I was relieved when it was suggested that I shouldn't hurry back to court.

I arrived shortly after three o'clock, parked my car and ambled up the court steps. It was a typical March day, wet and windy and just starting to get dark. I fully expected to see Mick, Mr Whinnett and the others standing in the corridor outside court with Mrs Darling and her family, drinking coffee and smoking cigarettes.

But it was worse. Much worse. There was nobody there. The courtroom where Janie's life and death had been so carefully laid out for the jury was in the process of being locked and there wasn't a soul in sight. My heart was in my mouth as I ran to the court clerk's office and asked what had happened. 'It's all over, dear,' an elderly woman usher in black robes told me. 'They found him guilty.'

My immediate reaction was jubilation. 'Thank God,' I said, but then – almost childishly – I was aware that I felt cheated. Nobody had expected the jury to return so quickly and I had missed it by the skin of my teeth. Having put so much effort into the case, I had now been denied the luxury of seeing Justice finally discharge her great powers.

'What happened?' I asked the usher in disbelief.

'They came back after just two and a quarter hours and returned a unanimous verdict,' she told me. 'Mrs Darling burst into tears, there were cheers from the public gallery and it took the judge several minutes to silence the courtroom.' She went on to explain that, once the verdict had been delivered and the court quietened, Mr Justice Alliott sentenced Lashley to life imprisonment, the mandatory sentence for murder. Knowing full well that life can, in fact, mean parole after a term of seven to nine years, the judge wasn't taking any chances. He told Lashley: 'The decision is such that whoever is responsible must have the utmost careful regard before you are ever allowed your liberty again. In my view, you are such an appallingly dangerous man that the real issue is whether the authorities can ever allow you your liberty in your natural life.'

I learnt later that Angela Darling, who had sat through the trial wearing the same Woodstock charm on a chain that Janie

287

had worn the night she met her death, buried her face in the arms of her niece Camilla and was led away. Confronted by reporters on the steps of the court she told them: 'Justice has been done, we always prayed this would happen. I'd do anything to spare other parents the traumas we've experienced. Anyone with a daughter can feel safer now.'

Following in Angela Darling's footsteps, I now stood outside the court, several hours after the event, trying to absorb all that had happened. Instinctively, I felt drawn to rush into the incident room at St Albans Police Station and congratulate everybody. But I balked with the inner knowledge that this would be an equally special moment for them and I didn't want to do anything that could be considered intrusive. Instead, I got in the car and drove slowly home.

The following day the outcome of the trial was splashed all over the newspapers and I read every word. Janie's boyfriend, Roddy Kinkead-Weekes, now married with children and living in Perth, Australia, expressed his dismay that the prison authorities had released Lashley in 1976 when he had not yet served his full sentence for rape. 'I am angry that those people who were responsible for letting Lashley go free do not appear to be accountable for their mistakes,' he said. 'If Lashley had been kept in prison for the full twelve years, Janie would still be alive. I am not an advocate of capital punishment but I do believe that people who behave like animals should be locked up for ever.'

Jean Lashley was also grateful for her ex-husband's sentence. She said she had wept for joy when he was jailed in 1970 and was appalled by his early release. After the verdict in Janie's case, she said: 'All along people have hinted that because I am a natural blonde it must have been something I did that turned him into a monster. In fact, although I was always proud of my hair and looked after it, he never commented on it. I don't know when blond hair became an obsession with him.'

I devoured every word in the papers and felt elated. It was without doubt the best feeling I have ever had following a conviction. The years of anger, which had first taken root at the sight of Renata's battered features in that hospital bed, were beginning to subside.

The judge was right. Lashley was an appalling, dangerous man. A man who had forfeited all his rights to freedom. He was fifty years old when he was sentenced to life imprisonment. Even if he served twenty years and came out at seventy, he could still exact murderous revenge on those he hated, especially if he continued to keep himself so fit. I sincerely hoped the state would now keep him incarcerated for the rest of his natural life.

One of the worst bad bastards I had ever come across might be off the streets, but sadly there were plenty more lining up to take his place. The rapes and sexual assaults in west London continued and my caseload became more and more burdonsome.

Three months after his trial, on a July morning in 1990, I received a phone call a little after 1 a.m. I was fast asleep and it took me a few minutes to realize that the ringing in my head was for real. It had been nearly four years since I had given up booze and I was sleeping more soundly than ever. It was a deep, untroubled sleep and I usually awoke feeling refreshed and headache-free, something I was already taking for granted.

'Yes?' I finally said into the mouthpiece, switching on the light and reaching for a pen and notepad. I had by then become so accustomed to the late-night phone calls telling me of some new attack, I knew that work would be the only reason for a call at such an hour.

'Report of a rape in Ealing, guv.' It was Christine Douglas, one of my best officers. 'A young mum with a baby in her arms assaulted in her home at Grange Road, a couple of hours ago. Will you attend?'

I rubbed my eyes and scribbled down the address. 'Give me half an hour and I'll meet you there,' I said.

By the time I got to the ground-floor flat off Grange Road the place was swarming with detectives. Sitting in a towelling dressing gown at a neighbour's kitchen table, her hands cupped around a mug of cocoa, her face streaked with tears, was a thirty-five-year-old woman of Middle Eastern appearance.

I picked my way through and, holding out my hand, said: 'Carol Bristow, detective inspector. You must be Mrs Vivash. Can we go into another room and have a quiet word?' The woman looked up at Christine Douglas, who had spent the past two hours holding her hand, and nodded. We wandered through into the lounge and closed the door behind us.

In the next thirty minutes she was able to tell me roughly what had happened. It would be up to Christine to get the full statement from her at the Brentford rape suite later, but for now I needed to know the basic details so that I could plan our line of enquiry.

Estranged from her husband and with a two-year-old daughter, Mrs Vivash told me that the previous evening at ten-thirty she had been in her bedroom, trying to get her daughter off to sleep, when she was disturbed by a noise. 'I thought it was my letterbox or a window latch rattling,' she said. 'I picked up my little girl and went into the hallway to investigate. I went to turn the light on but nothing happened, so I assumed the bulb had blown. That's when he pounced on me in the darkness. A young lad, just a teenager I think, but he was holding two long-bladed knives, one in each hand. He said: "I've come for sex, not to commit burglary. I'm a twenty-one-year-old virgin and my friends laugh at me. Do as you're told or I'll kill you and the child." I was terrified.'

Putting down one of his knives, he pushed her up against the wall, lifted her nightdress and raped her in the darkness, while she held her sobbing child in her arms. Suggesting that they go somewhere more comfortable, he told her to put her daughter down so that they could go to her bedroom and have sex. She did as she was told, terrified of the youth and his knives, but her daughter howled so much when she left her that the young man ordered her to pick her up again and bring her into the bedroom.

In darkness, he raped her next to her small daughter and ejaculated inside her. When he had finished he wiped his penis on the edge of the bed sheet and, although she couldn't see much, she could tell he was smiling all the while.

Desperate to pacify her assailant, the woman offered him a drink and he accepted a glass of orange juice in the kitchen. He then became quite chatty, telling her about himself and his large family and informing her he had been inside for armed robbery.

Asking for her credit cards and car keys, he went into the bedroom, lifted the bottom sheet from the bed and started to slash it violently in an attempt to destroy the seminal staining. Terrified, she picked up her child, ran to the front door, opened it and ran out into the hallway screaming. Fortunately, the people in the other flats heard her and two male neighbours kicked in her front door, looking for the rapist, but he had already legged it through the lounge window by which he had entered.

Mrs Vivash was medically examined and the doctor confirmed the presence of semen. The sheet was taken as an exhibit and the section which had seminal staining on it was cut out and sent to the lab. I then asked the poor woman to recall any details of the conversation she had with her attacker and we made a list of all the things he had told her.

She specifically remembered him saying he had recently been released from prison 'having done a stretch for armed robbery'. In an effort to placate him, Mrs Vivash had encouraged him to talk about himself and during the tiny pockets of calm he had gone on to tell her he had 'five brothers and six sisters', was twenty-one and came from west Ealing. He said he was Irish and that his sister sold Ann Summers erotic underwear and sex aids.

He claimed to have spent the last two years living at Henley-on-Thames, of all places. Mrs Vivash described him as twenty-one to twenty-five years old, white, of slim build, about five feet eight inches in height, with short fair hair, clean-shaven, with blue eyes and a clear complexion. He smoked cigarettes, his breath smelt strongly of beer and he was constantly smiling. She believed him to be drunk and entirely unpredictable.

'If any of what he told Mrs Vivash is true, there should be plenty for us to go on which will identify him,' I told my team the morning after the attack. 'I'm going to check what possible connection he could have with Henley-on-Thames; the rest of you divide the other enquiries up between you.'

I've always regarded Henley-on-Thames as a leafy backwater of suburban Oxfordshire occupied by middle-class toffs, so it came as a total surprise to me when, after making enquiries of colleagues from the Thames Valley police force, I learnt that Huntercombe Young Offenders' Institution was on that patch.

I telephoned the governor's office and asked for his help. I filled him in on what little I knew and he and his staff responded magnificently. 'We can give you a list of every inmate recently released,' he said. 'But, before you get too excited, I'd better warn you that you may have to check hundreds of names.' And hundreds of names is exactly what he gave me. Just over four hundred, to be precise.

I received copies of their profiles and categorized them according to their age, description and the areas they frequented. It took several days to compare descriptions and compile a shortlist of possible suspects, but by the time I had narrowed the list down to around forty names I knew that there was only one way forward and I prayed that I wasn't barking up the wrong tree.

'Gather round and listen,' I told my team as I walked into the office with the bundle of files from Huntercombe. 'I want all these people listed here to be contacted individually and asked to supply a small sample of blood for DNA profiling.' I waited for the impact of what I was saying to sink in. 'The swabs taken from Mrs Vivash have given a reaction to semen and the lab have told me that they should be able to give us the rapist's DNA profile shortly. So please go and find all these sweet little angels, get their blood samples sent to the lab and then let's hope we can get a match.'

The use of genetic fingerprinting in criminal cases was still very new. I had used it before but this was my first case involving such a wide sweep for DNA and, I suspected, the same was true for my team. We knew of its unique possibilities, as it had been hailed as the 'greatest single breakthrough in forensic science this century', and its availability excited me.

292

Originally discovered by Professor Alec Jeffreys FRS in 1984 during basic research, genetic or DNA fingerprinting is the name given to the scientific process which positively identifies individuals using their genetic material. DNA is present in all living cells, with the notable exception of the red blood cell. It provides an identity check based on an individual's hereditary characteristics and in each person (with the exception of genetically identical twins, who are formed by the division of a single fertilized egg) will be unique.

Once DNA has been extracted from the living cell, it is cut into fragments of varying sizes by an enzyme. From this operation, the laboratory technician is able to select the fragments which are of interest to him and transfer them to a nylon membrane which, on being tightly bound, produces a series of straight bands. The end product is a photographic film with the series of bands looking something like a supermarket bar code, where the similarities or differences between individual bands can be readily seen.

A major use of this technology in criminal investigation is the positive identification, or elimination, of suspects. It can be applied to a whole host of substances, for example a bloodstain found at the scene of a murder, a semen sample in a rape case, strands of hair pulled out during an assault, or body tissue found on a car in a hit-and-run accident. Put simply, where any form of biological material containing DNA is found at the scene of a crime the DNA profile made from it may provide a conclusive link to the person or persons who committed the crime.

In 1986 British legal history was made when Robert Melias, a thirty-two-year-old labourer, was convicted of rape at Bristol Crown Court on the basis of his genetic or DNA profile. Two weeks later a second rapist, twenty-five-year-old Nigel Davies, was also convicted through DNA profiling.

The *cause célèbre*, however, and the one which demonstrated the real value of DNA profiling to us all, was that of Regina vs Colin Pitchfork in 1987. In this now famous case, Leicestershire Police used DNA profiling to show that not only was the same man responsible for the murder and rape of two fifteen-year-old schoolgirls within two years, but that a different man who had actually confessed to and been charged with the murder of one of the girls was in fact innocent.

The truth was discovered during the first genetic manhunt in history, when approximately 5,500 men in and around the villages where the two girls were murdered were asked to give a tiny sample of blood for comparison and elimination. Pitchfork, realizing he would be found out by this new science, tried to cheat the system by asking his best friend to give a sample for him, convincing him that he was afraid of hypodermic needles. But when the best friend told others about it in a pub, he was overheard by a barmaid who called the police. Pitchfork was arrested and, when his unique DNA profile was compared with the DNA left in the body fluids on the murdered fifteen-year-olds, they were found to be identical. Forensic science is supposed to take the guesswork out of criminal investigation and in this instance it proved to be incontrovertible proof of Pitchfork's guilt.

The government laboratories at Aldermaston were the first to take on genetic profiling, but suddenly found themselves inundated with enquiries from every police force in Britain, seeking absolute proof from blood and semen samples. In fact they were so overwhelmed that test results were taking up to a year to come through.

Eventually, five police laboratories around the country received the necessary funding from the Home Office for the equipment and training needed. I had always been very interested in the new science and, realizing its potential in cases of sexual assault, I spent time with the scientists, getting them to explain it to me in layman's terms. Armed with that information, I felt able to encourage my team on this inquiry to feel as enthusiastic about it as I did. I desperately hoped to be able to find the same conclusive evidence with which to nail the offending bastard as in the Pitchfork case.

A young DC voiced his concerns. 'But, guv, that will take days, if not weeks, and how do we know the man who attacked Mrs Vivash was even telling the truth?'

'We don't,' I admitted. 'But in the absence of anything else just now, I'm afraid it's all we've got to go on.'

The DC was right. It did take weeks. Many of the addresses we'd been given were out of date, a lot of the former inmates were more than a little reluctant to co-operate and some of them refused outright. We could not force anyone to give a sample. If they wanted to be bloody-minded and say no, then that was their right. Fortunately, 95 per cent seemed quite happy to give their blood up for elimination once they knew we were investigating rape. Three weeks into the inquiry, we had managed to trace and obtain blood samples from about twenty-five on the original shortlist of forty, and these were duly sent off to the forensic laboratory for processing and comparison with the semen samples found at the scene.

Weeks went by and the blood we submitted was examined but one by one the names on our list were being crossed off. After three weeks nearly all of the first batch of volunteered blood had been eliminated. Having exhausted all other en-quiries and with no positive news from the laboratory, we were at our lowest ebb when the telephone rang.

'We suggest you look at number eight on your list of hope-fuls,' the scientist told me. 'His name is Lee Saunders and, although we haven't finalized our procedures yet, we can tell you that he is definitely your man.'

Armed with this information I arrested Saunders, a twenty-one-year-old convicted mugger and burglar who lived less than half a mile from Mrs Vivash's flat, and took him to Acton nick on suspicion of rape. This Pinocchio-faced young lad, who had willingly volunteered his blood, had no understanding of what the new science meant or how it could prove he was there. Despite my spelling out the implications to him time and again, he simply could not understand how his DNA profile could prove that he had had sexual intercourse with Mrs Vivash in her flat.

'You've made a mistake,' he told me, smiling. 'It isn't me you're after. There must be someone else out there who has the same blood as me.' After that, the smiling youth chose to answer 'No comment' to all my questions.

Enquiries established that Saunders had one brother and one sister, not the five and six he told Mrs Vivash about, but his one sister did sell Ann Summers products. His face and build exactly matched the description given to us by Mrs Vivash and he was known to have a problem with alcohol.

Saunders lived on one of the sprawling Brentford council estates. He and his family were extremely anti-police, he had a very poor educational record with severe reading difficulties and was terminally unemployable. He had thirty-nine previous convictions for dishonesty, was thoroughly objectionable and made no attempt to hide his contempt for authority.

After a preliminary court appearance, Saunders was sent to HM Prison Wormwood Scrubs to await his trial, which was listed for June 1991. True to form, he then pleaded not guilty and, refusing to heed the advice of his barrister, promptly sacked him and demanded that someone new represent him under the legal aid system. Much to everyone's annoyance, the whole case had to be relisted for trial four months later, which was a dreadful blow for Mrs Vivash, who had psyched herself up to give evidence in June.

But worse was yet to come. I had failed to anticipate that by the time Saunders eventually stood trial at the Old Bailey he would change his line of defence so completely that he took us all by surprise. The penny had finally dropped about DNA and, knowing that police had irrefutable proof that he had had sex with Mrs Vivash, he now claimed willing compliance on the part of the victim.

He said that on the night in question, having been to a local pub, he felt the need to urinate on the way home. Apparently unwilling to do it in the street, he said he had knocked at the victim's door and asked if he could use her lavatory. He claimed she had invited this complete stranger in for coffee and, within a few minutes, encouraged him to seduce her. According to him, she felt so guilty immediately following the sexual act that she threw a wobbler and ran from the flat, crying rape. He said he left in a hurry to avoid trouble and hadn't mentioned it to anyone because he didn't want to embarrass the lady.

Faced with this wholly unexpected line of defence, Mrs Vivash completely disintegrated in the witness box. She found the whole suggestion so painful and degrading that she burst into tears as the defence barrister cross-examined her about her alleged participation. The case was momentarily stopped to allow her to regain her composure, but all our good work in trying to keep her together failed miserably. Throughout this time, the angelic-looking Saunders, freshly scrubbed with a neatly trimmed haircut and clean, pressed suit, sat smiling at her from the dock. It was absolutely awful.

Fortunately, the jury saw through it all. They took four hours to return a unanimous verdict of guilty and the judge took four minutes to sentence him to ten years. That soon wiped the smile off his face.

I had such high hopes for DNA profiling. When it first started to become available to us for criminal prosecutions, I truly believed – perhaps rather naïvely – that it would put an end to a lot of the misery for rape victims. At that time, rape was just about the only crime where a judge had no option but to warn a jury that to convict in the absence of corroborative evidence was extremely dangerous. How much easier it would be, I thought, for us to nail some bastard to the scene of the crime when he insisted he was elsewhere because DNA would prove it.

But I was wrong. Much as it may have ultimately swayed the jury into believing that the defendant was responsible for the crime, the introduction of DNA evidence often made the giving of a victim's evidence that much harder, because of the cunning employed by the defendants through their articulate barristers. No longer were women to be regarded sympathetically as genuine victims who had, through unfortunate circumstances, been mistaken as to the identity of their attackers. Now they were shameless hussies who had consented to sexual intercourse with the defendants and then – through spite, shame or a change of heart – cried rape to punish the good men they had just slept with. Never mind that many of these women had never set eyes on the defendants before the night of the alleged attack, or that they were covered in bruises. That was now all explained as part of the passionate love-making that had gone on between two consenting adults.

The scheming of some of the defendants sickened me but

when faced with overwhelming scientific evidence of sexual intercourse, they had no compunction about bending the facts whichever way suited them. The dreadful experiences encountered by some of the women was little short of a second rape as first their character and then their honesty were dragged through the mud. 'Was it not the case, Miss Smith, that you were wearing a mini-skirt that night and had told a friend that you were planning on "having a good time" at the discotheque?'

As the victims squirmed under such treatment, so my anger festered. You should have seen the poor girl that first night in hospital when she couldn't even open her mouth for the bruises, I wanted to say. My cynicism suggested that many of these cases were more about winning acquittals at all costs than they were about justice. It no longer mattered whether the victim was a truthful witness or not; it mattered only that the defence barrister, on the instructions of his client, pulled every stroke in the book to ensure a not-guilty verdict.

Once the woman entered the witness box, she was beyond my reach. In much the same way as when a weaker contestant enters a boxing ring, her vulnerable areas were quickly identified and she would be verbally bombarded through the medium of clever oratory. She was isolated and unprotected and, needless to say, many of the blows were well beneath the belt.

It always amazed me how well these women fared under such punishment and, though I wanted to jump in and help them, I had long ago learnt to keep my own counsel. All I could do was walk away, reach for my cigarettes and lighter and gasp for some respite on the courthouse steps, wishing that there could be a better way.

13

'WE SIMPLY CANNOT AFFORD TO GIVE THE INVESTIGATION OF sexual offences a greater priority than other crimes,' my new detective chief inspector was telling me. 'I fail to understand why this division should waste so many of its staff and resources on this one particular area, when your time could be much better used elsewhere.'

'Yes, sir.' I was too tired to argue.

'My predecessor seems to have been willing to spend vast amounts of public money in overtime on these investigations, including those of a relatively minor nature, when burglaries, drug offences and other important matters – all of which rate-payers have expressed concerns about – get less attention because we are so understaffed. The clear-up rate for serious sexual offending on division might well have improved, but you and your team have been allowed too much of a free hand. After some thought, I've made a decision. You will be transferred back to the main office. Do you understand?'

'I do understand. Yes, sir.' In earlier times I might have stood my ground and argued for the continuation of my involvement on the Sexual Offences Unit, but five years on I knew this moment had been a long time coming. Chief Superintendent John Purnell and DCI Searle, who were originally responsible for the team's existence, had long ago transferred and I knew there were rumblings with the new management about cutbacks and so-called better use of resources.

The new DCI was an ambitious university graduate who had joined the Met under the accelerated-promotion scheme, which allowed individuals to enter the force and do the minimum service at each level before being promoted, with a pick of the jobs on the way.

He was wrong to dismiss our success so flippantly, for we had achieved so very much, but in some ways I was relieved to be leaving management's new agenda. It was 1990; I was forty-seven years old with twenty-five years' service under my belt and ripe for a change. I just hoped my next job would be another home posting so that I wouldn't have to commute long distances again. With that in mind, I decided to take matters into my own hands.

I was aware that a vacancy had arisen for a detective inspector in charge of the Child Protection Team at Southall. I had been approached two years earlier and asked if I wanted to set up the new CPT in conjunction with the London Borough of Ealing, but had declined then because I still felt I had much to give the adult victims.

I knew that some might view it as jumping out of the frying pan into the fire, because taking on the job now would mean several more years of investigating sexual offences, but I felt strongly that I had something to offer and it would, after all, remove me from a man who seemed intent on denigrating my work. I was transferred on 14 January 1991.

The CPT comprised ten police officers dealing exclusively with the sexual, physical and emotional abuse of children by parents, carers and members of their extended families. The principle was the same as before, in that all allegations of child abuse would be referred to us, with one big difference. I would now be expected to answer for the entire borough, which gave me double my previous responsibility, when before I had covered just two stations.

Child protection teams were a progeny of the 1989 Children's Act, which, it was hoped, would vastly improve the fragmented and unsatisfactory nature of the existing legislation on children.

The Act came into force on 14 October 1991 and, for me, it meant reading up on 218 pages of new and very complicated legislation. There were no short cuts to learning it and it generally meant taking copies of the relevant sections home for reading in bed. I won't pretend the thought of cocoa, bed and something that had been described as 'the greatest reform of the law relating to children ever attempted by Parliament' excited me, but I did make the effort to get stuck in.

Unfortunately, because of its newness, length and complexity, training programmes were not available when the Act came into force, which meant that many of us worked with the most basic information and kept our fingers crossed that we got it right. The basic theme of the Act was the belief that children are generally best looked after within the family by both parents playing a full part, without the need for any legal proceedings. Its aims were to promote the ideal of the family unit, requiring local authorities to make better provision for children to be cared for in their homes. It was hoped that in this way there would be a greatly reduced need to introduce a child to the frightening and expensive business of welfare proceedings before a court.

The legislation encouraged a close working relationship between the social services and all other agencies that had a genuine interest in the welfare of children. For some of us, this aspect proved to be the most difficult of all, not least because of the stereotypical 'them and us' situation in which many of us were entrenched. I didn't, for instance, know of anyone in social services who had been called 'a right-wing fascist bastard', and I don't pretend it was a label I liked, but the reality was that many of us in the police force were perceived that way, and the totally opposite view was taken of the social worker.

We had to try to put our differences aside as best we could, because there was some very important work to be done. Unfortunately, however, my efforts in this area were temporarily thwarted because several of my Acton investigations still had trials outstanding, which meant that I would be tied up at the Crown Courts for a good time yet.

'Isn't that Daniel Reece?' I whispered into the ear of the black-robed usher who was sitting in the back of the Old Bailey's Number 1 Court, his *Times* crossword neatly folded in front of him. Ever curious to see who was standing in the dock, I had popped my head around the door after a morning of tedious legal argument in Court 4 where my defendant's counsel was suggesting that a particular piece of damaging evidence should be kept from the jury.

'That's right. And the woman sitting next to him in the dock is Linda Calvey,' the usher whispered back. 'The press call her the Black Widow, after the female spider which eats its partner after mating. According to the prosecution, she and Reece make quite a pair.'

I had almost smiled at the sight of the charismatic Reece and wondered if the jury had yet been given the benefit of his beguiling charm. 'What's he charged with?' I asked.

'They're both charged with murder,' answered the usher in hushed tones.

What on earth had Reece been up to? I asked myself. Surely he was still serving his sentence for rape and buggery? I caught sight of an old mate of mine, Billy, sitting in one of the side seats, staring at the dock and lost in thought. Billy had been transferred back to division from the Flying Squad at the same time as me. He caught my eye, looked at his watch, stood up and crept to the back of the court.

'Hello, Billy, fancy a drink?' I greeted him.

'They're just about to rise for lunch. Let's go across the road to the Magpie and Stump before the rush,' Billy whispered.

We grabbed a table as it became vacant and sat down, Billy with his pint and me with my orange juice. 'I'm dying to know, Billy,' I said excitedly. 'What the hell's Reece doing in the dock?'

Billy smiled and said: 'He's really done it this time. He and Linda Calvey are charged with murdering Ronnie Cook, Linda's ex-lover.'

'Not the Ronnie Cook we came to know and love from the Robbery Squad days?' I asked.

Billy nodded as he put his glass to his lips.

'And why does the name Calvey ring a bell?' I asked.

'Linda was married to Micky Calvey,' Billy said. 'He had the dubious distinction of being the first armed robber to be shot dead by police while actively on the job. You remember that supermarket robbery in Eltham in '78? Ron Cook was supposed to have been the getaway driver, although we could never prove it. Anyway, after Micky Calvey's death, Cook chased Linda, showering her with presents, and eventually persuaded her to live with him. Cook was a rich man in those days, on account of all the thieving he was up to, but in 1981 his luck ran out and he was sentenced to sixteen years for his part in the Brinks Matt robbery, leaving Linda almost destitute. Cook then asked his cohort Brian Thorogood to help her out financially but, of course, he forgot about Linda's insatiable appetite for men and within weeks the pair of them were lovers. It all jogged along quite nicely until 1985 when Thorogood got done for robbing post offices and took Linda down with him.'

I interrupted. 'You mean Linda and this Thorogood organized the robberies together?'

Billy nodded. 'They were a real Bonnie and Clyde until they were caught, and then Linda went down for seven years and Thorogood got twenty-one (sentences which were later reduced on appeal to five and eighteen years respectively). When Linda was released in '89, she visited Cook, who was still inside, and led him a right old dance, swearing undying love for him, but in truth she was no longer interested in the poor old sod, although he still believed he was in with a chance. When Cook's time was nearly up and he was due out on parole, he made it clear that he expected their relationship to continue where it left off. That's when Linda's bottle went and she went to see Thorogood for help.'

I was captivated.

'Well, by this time, our Mr Thorogood was in Durham Prison with Daniel Reece, who had got himself locked up for some sexual offences. It seems that the two men got on well together and became firm friends. Cook, in the mean time, was eligible for home leave and began visiting Linda, but she couldn't stand it – the thought of having Cook permanently back in her life was driving her mad.'

'Why didn't she just tell him it was over?' I asked.

'Cook wasn't the sort of bloke to take no for an answer and Linda knew that. So in desperation she went to see Reece, who had been transferred to Verne Prison, and offered him ten thousand pounds to bump Cook off.'

'Bloody hell!' I exclaimed.

'That's roughly what Reece said at first, but Linda can be very persuasive and, after she gave him some sob story, Reece agreed to do it, got the hots for her and allowed her to lead him around by the nose. You could say it was a fatal attraction. So one Saturday last November, when both men were on home leave, Linda supplied Reece with a sawn-off shotgun and sent him to the Bun House pub, in Devons Road, Bow, where she was meeting Ronnie Cook for a drink. Reece was meant to hide outside and do him on the way out, but at the last moment his bottle went and Ronnie lived to fight another day.'

Billy paused for breath and supped his beer. I offered to buy him another, but he shook his head and carried on. 'Linda got really mad with Reece and told him in no uncertain terms that he had to complete the job before he went back to Verne. The scheming woman then invited Cook to her house in Plaistow and instructed Reece to get there first so that he could kill Cook almost as soon as he arrived.

'Reece did as he was told and hid in the garden, and as soon as Cook arrived he burst into the house, levelled the gun and pulled the trigger. But because he had never killed anyone before, his bottle went again and although he fired the gun, at the last minute he shot to the side, hitting Cook in the elbow. He then froze completely, at which point the lovely Linda, realizing that this was a job for a professional, grabbed the sawn-off, ordered Cook to kneel, pointed the gun at his head and fired it, promptly decapitating him.'

I could just imagine Reece's peculiar moral code preventing him at the last minute from killing another robber, but, from what I now knew of the hard-faced forty-three-year-old platinum blonde sitting next to him in the dock, I did not need convincing that Linda Calvey was more than capable of cold-blooded murder.

'What then?' I asked.

'Well, Reece legged it and made his way back to Verne Prison. When the police arrived at Linda's house, she screamed that one of Cook's old adversaries had just broken in and shot him dead. She and Reece might have got away with it, only someone grassed them up and within a couple of weeks we had pulled them both in as number-one suspects.'

'So it's pretty cut and dried?' I said.

'Not exactly,' said Billy. 'Forensics say that the clothing Reece wore that day had debris in the pockets from the firing of the shotgun and that Linda's clothes and shoes were spattered with Cook's blood and brains, but Reece has pulled every nasty trick in the book to try to wriggle out of it from day one.'

'What do you mean?' I asked innocently, sipping my drink.

'Well apparently, last year, he gave evidence against a right evil piece of work called David Lashley who was accused of murdering that Australian girl Janie Shepherd back in '77. It was Reece who had heard Lashley's confession to the crime in prison and that evidence nailed him, apparently.'

I nearly choked on my juice. 'What?'

'Yes, I don't know if you remember Dave Sandlin but he knew Reece from years back and throughout the Lashley investigation in 1989 he dealt with Reece as a witness. So when we started looking at Reece for Ronnie Cook's murder, we called Dave back and asked him to interview Reece on the subject. He confessed there and then to killing him with Linda but then tried to angle for a way out. When Sandlin told Reece there'd be no favours, he went bananas and said that if he wasn't dealt with favourably over Cook's murder, he would retract all the evidence he had given at the Lashley trial. He said he would tell everyone that the details he gave in court were facts which were fed to him by corrupt police who were trying to fit Lashley up.'

I couldn't believe what I was hearing. It was the worst possible news and I didn't know how to respond. Making my excuses suddenly, I got up, brushed a kiss past Billy's cheek and left. I needed to be alone for a minute. I walked into St Paul's Cathedral, sat down in one of the pews and looked up at the mighty dome. If it wasn't so gruesome in its detail, I thought, this case would make a bloody good pantomime.

At four o'clock, when the Old Bailey shut up shop for the day, I rushed back to the office, picked up the telephone and rang the incident room at East Ham Police Station. 'Can anyone please tell me what happened in relation to the case of David Lashley, after Reece got charged with Cook's murder?' I asked, after formally introducing myself to a male voice who identified himself as a DC.

'Reece wrote letters to everyone he could think of, telling them that Lashley was innocent of the Janie Shepherd murder and that he had been fitted up,' said the old-school detective, who sounded about as weary as I felt. 'He wrote about eight letters, including ones to Lashley and several to national newspapers.'

'So does this now give Lashley grounds to appeal against the conviction for the murder of Janie Shepherd?' I asked, almost disbelievingly.

'I suppose it must do,' said the officer. 'He'd be bloody daft not to try anyway, wouldn't he? Because it makes Reece out to be totally unreliable.'

I had to agree with him. Reece had become fickle and the implications of that for the Court of Appeal didn't bear thinking about. I had never felt so impotent in my life. Surely we hadn't come this far only to lose Lashley?

'The Police Complaints Authority', continued the DC, 'have ordered the Kent Constabulary to investigate Reece's allegations.' He paused as he heard me groan. 'I'm sorry to be the bearer of bad news. You sound really upset.'

'Upset' did not adequately describe how I felt. There was a tightening knot in my stomach that made me want to scream. How could Reece do this? He would never understand the enormity of what he had done or the full extent of the frustration he was about to cause every individual who came into contact with Janie Shepherd, in life and death.

I phoned Detective Superintendent Ian Whinnett at St Albans.

'I've only just heard, sir,' I said. 'I can't tell you how sorry I am.'

'There's no one sorrier than me,' he responded gloomily. 'And before you ask, yes, Lashley is going to appeal against the murder conviction, and no, I don't yet know when it will be heard in court.'

I sat back in the only comfortable chair in the office and closed my eyes. I had long ago learnt by heart the Alcoholics Anonymous prayer which I now repeated in my head and which could not have been more appropriate:

> Lord grant me the serenity to accept the things I cannot
>   change
> Courage to change the things I can
> And wisdom to know the difference.

There was bugger-all I could do and I might as well accept it, but wild horses would not keep me away from the Appeal Court when Lashley's case was listed – whenever that was.

Not long afterwards, I heard the news. Reece and Linda Calvey had both been convicted of Cook's murder and given the mandatory life sentence. Reece had shouted at the judge: 'I'll see you in the Appeal Court.' I didn't know whether to laugh or cry.

Two weeks later, on 26 November 1991, two senior officers from the Kent Constabulary went to see Reece in prison. His back was no longer up against the wall and there must have seemed little point for him to continue lying. During an interview which was tape-recorded, he repeatedly withdrew all the allegations about corrupt police fabricating evidence and 'fitting up' Lashley and maintained that the evidence he had given at Lashley's trial for murder had been entirely true.

But the damage had already been done and it wasn't good enough to turn round now and say sorry. Regardless of what Reece was saying, Lashley's lawyers would still be able to proceed with an appeal, not least because the chief prosecution witness's latest change of heart just went to show how unreliable he was as a witness, past or present. As I had hoped and expected, Kent Police cleared all the officers involved in the Janie Shepherd inquiry of any impropriety. But Lashley's lawyers, it seemed, still felt confident that Reece's latest move would have no adverse effect on their client's forthcoming appeal, and that very thought frightened the hell out of me.

My child protection team operated out of a converted nurse's flat in the grounds of Ealing Hospital, so that when children were brought in to talk to us they could quickly feel at ease in the homely surroundings, unlike those of a police station. Akin to the specialized rape suites, the flat had sofas, comfy chairs and toys for the children to play with. None of us wore uniforms, we all called each other by our first names, and the whole atmosphere was much more relaxed than elsewhere. The individual officers, selected for their sensitivity and ability to express genuine care, were as professional as I had found anywhere.

Processing the victims was harrowing. Just as adult victims dissociate themselves from the events of their assault, so do children. I learnt that a child will go to considerable lengths to protect a parental figure who has abused them. They might not have liked what their abuser was doing to them but he was still their father, uncle, neighbour, baby-sitter or family friend, and they loved him unconditionally, as only a child can. In the majority of cases all the child wants is to stop the abuse, not to invoke the force that the law provides. And the biggest deterrent for a child against spilling the beans is the abuser's utterance of words like 'If you tell, I'll go to prison,' or 'If you tell, no one will believe you and they'll take you away and put you in a children's home.'

I had a good team and God knows I needed it. We dealt with an average of four hundred allegations a year and in 99 per cent of cases we knew exactly who the suspect was because he or she was known to the child concerned. Unfortunately, knowing and proving are poles apart and most of our cases were not prosecutable because of the wall of non-co-operation that would suddenly emerge, to prevent the break-up of the family at all costs. The fearful and confused reluctance of children to speak

308

out at times like these was a feature we came to expect and without the child's assistance we were stumped for evidence to prosecute the offender and they knew it. Even faced with a co-operative and truthful victim, it was often a case of adults versus frightened child and we knew there was little chance of winning.

The best we could hope for was to confront the abuser and have him admit the offence – which, on balance, was about as likely as me winning the Booker Prize for literature. By the time we had finished dealing with some of the children, they must have wondered why they had ever complained in the first place, because by the end they would have been branded liars, lost the love and companionship of their siblings and been separated from their families.

Just when I thought my sense of outrage had been exhausted, I suddenly found myself having to deal with a whole new set of injustices, this time against children, and it made my blood boil. The CPT was without doubt the least enjoyable of all my postings. Some of the outside agencies drove me demented and the cases I was dealing with made me sick to the stomach. There was nothing to laugh about with CPT work; I couldn't talk to anyone about what I was doing because it was all so horrible; and I found the whole nature of the work so depressing that it really got to me.

I supervised literally hundreds of investigations and I found that sitting holding a child's tiny hand as they falteringly told me their horror stories was even harder than dealing with the grown-ups. But on my dark days I would remind myself that I only had a few more years to go before being offered retirement and a thirty-year pension.

I often found myself swamped by the work which had piled up. The very urgent stuff was dealt with immediately, while the less crucial material stacked up on my desk accusingly. On one of the days I had set aside to tackle this mountain of paperwork, the telephone rang and Dr Ruth Smith, the consultant paediatrician at Ealing Hospital, asked me to go and see her.

'This is Charmaine Green,' she told me, as she led me into a room off the main ward and pointed to a little angel of a three year old, curled up fast asleep in her cot, sucking her thumb, her blond ringlets framing her pale face. She was attached to an assortment of tubes and drips, and a heart monitor blipped gently in the background. 'She's been very seriously ill, in fact she almost died.'

I went back to Dr Smith's office and took notes as she told me of Charmaine's background. 'She was admitted ten days ago with abdominal pains. Her mother, Susan, told us that her daughter was suffering from appendicitis. She was quite hysterical and demanded that we operate immediately. We told her that we wanted to admit Charmaine for a period of observation before we decided whether or not surgery was required. We invited Susan to stay at the hospital with her daughter, on the children's ward, to give the child support and reassurance.'

Dr Smith said that after a few days appendicitis was ruled out, but her concerns about the toddler did not diminish. 'During the following five days, Charmaine vomited no less than twenty-nine times, sometimes bringing up blood, and we were extremely worried as to what was causing her so much pain and suffering.'

Extensive medical tests were carried out on the sickly child's digestive system – three courses of intravenous fluids, an enema, several X-rays, an abdominal ultrasound and a barium meal – all of which the subdued little girl accepted without complaint. Throughout her illness she was nursed attentively by her mother, who slept at her bedside, washed her, fed her and cleaned her up after she was sick.

Several days later a nurse attending Charmaine caught some of the child's vomit in her hands. Looking down, she noticed that the vomit was streaked with a white powdery substance. Dr Smith was called immediately and samples of Charmaine's vomit, urine and blood were submitted to the National Poisons Unit at Guy's Hospital for testing.

The results were shocking – the samples showed dangerously high concentrations of aspirin, paracetamol and caffeine. The levels of paracetamol were so high that they could have caused liver damage and their continued use would almost certainly have led to her death. All the drugs had been given to the little girl in a finely crushed form.

'Someone was trying to poison her?' I asked, incredulously. 'Who would do such a thing? Was there some maniac coming in from outside and finding his way into the children's ward?'

'Oh, it's not a stranger,' Dr Smith interjected. 'I'm afraid it's far worse than that. In my opinion, these potentially fatal levels of drugs have been administered to Charmaine by her own mother.'

I was staggered.

'It couldn't be anyone else,' Dr Smith said. 'Susan was with the child twenty-four hours a day. She attended to her every need, and always cleared up the vomit before telling the nurses that her daughter had been sick. She must have been feeding the child huge quantities of paracetamol for days before she was admitted and then continued, under our very noses, in the hospital.'

I found what she was telling me almost impossible to believe. Surely one of the most basic human instincts is for a mother to nurture and protect her child, sometimes at risk to her own life. Why then would a mother want to poison such a beautiful little girl?

'It's unusual, but not without precedent,' Dr Smith was telling me. 'The psychological disorder that I believe Susan Green may be suffering from is called Münchausen syndrome by proxy.'

I suddenly remembered Archie, the tramp who swallowed a bottle of blood, and all the material I had read about the syndrome after dealing with his case. It was named after Baron von Münchausen, a German born in the early 1700s who was a gifted raconteur but who was known to fabricate the truth. In 1951, Dr Richard Asher dedicated the newly discovered syndrome to the baron's memory because the wild stories of some of the patients he had seen with self-inflicted injuries reminded him of the eccentric.

'I've heard of that,' I told Dr Smith. 'It's where sufferers crave attention – but I thought they harmed themselves, not others.'

'That's where the "by proxy" comes in,' she said. 'The

311

mothers who harm their children often do it to enhance their own status through contact with doctors and nurses. It can make their otherwise dull and often unhappy lives seem exciting. Everyone sympathizes with them for having a sick child. Everyone rallies round. Nobody thinks for a moment that such an apparently caring mother could be scheming enough to do terrible things to her own child to satisfy her own emotional needs.

'If the deception is not uncovered before the child is of school age, some children start to participate in the game. The mother teaches the child to trick the doctors and to lie, with the result that some children have subsequently grown up to have the syndrome themselves.' Dr Smith went on to tell me that in 99 per cent of cases the mother is the deceiver, leaving the father completely ignorant. In Charmaine Green's case, her father clearly suspected nothing.

I was stunned. 'What should we do next?' I asked.

'I've already asked Susan Green to leave the hospital,' Dr Smith said. 'She knows of our suspicions but, as yet, I haven't gone into any detail with her. I suggest you listen to what she has to say. She'll almost certainly deny it – they always do – but see if you can get any sense out of her.'

She was right. Susan Green appeared to be frightened of her own shadow when I first approached her. I sat opposite her in an interview room at Southall Police Station and said: 'Hello, Susan. Somebody has been doing some dreadful things to Charmaine to make her ill. Do you want to tell me what's been going on?'

Within minutes she threw a tantrum, accusing me of being the devil incarnate. 'I'm a loving and caring mother. Charmaine's my only reason for living. How could you suggest that I would do such a terrible thing to my own little girl?' She ranted and raved, banged her fists on the table and sobbed. It took a long time for her to calm down.

The combination of paracetamol and caffeine turned out to be Anadin Extra, and Susan's handbag was full of them. 'So, maybe I gave her one or two tablets, but she was in pain. What was I supposed to do? That was what they found in her vomit.

But I wasn't trying to kill her, for God's sake. Who do you think you are to make such a suggestion?'

That was the most she would admit to, so I charged her with causing grievous bodily harm and poisoning with intent to endanger life. The social services took such measures as were necessary to prevent Susan from ever interfering with Charmaine again, and the little girl made an amazing and speedy recovery back to full health away from her mother's so-called care. In due course she was successfully fostered and Susan was allowed supervised access.

Prior to her being dealt with at court, Susan Green underwent full psychiatric assessment and was found not to be suffering from any mental illness, although she did have a 'personality disorder'. I agreed with the CPS's view that to take her to Crown Court would be a complete waste of time. It would be like taking a sledgehammer to crack a nut. Charmaine was safe and Susan was, at last, beginning to accept that she might have been culpable.

We offered her the alternative, lesser charge of 'assault occasioning actual bodily harm', which was accepted by her solicitor. A few weeks later she appeared at Ealing Magistrates' Court and, after pleading guilty, was sentenced to three years' probation on condition that she continue to seek psychiatric help. Strange as it may sound, I am utterly convinced that she loved every minute of the attention she was getting, right up to her day of judgement in court, and probably deserved an Oscar for playing the part so well.

The telephone rang. It was WPC Karen Bailey, serving on the Dorset Child Protection Team, asking for me at the Acton CPT unit.

'I'm dealing with two little girls aged five and two,' she told me, 'and I need your help. The kids were referred to us after a teacher noticed that the eldest child, Sarah, was overtly sexual. When we spoke to her, she said that her father regularly forced her and her younger sister Gemma to perform oral sex on him.'

Nothing I heard these days surprised me. 'So how can I help?' I asked.

What followed from that telephone conversation was one of the most complicated and difficult investigations I was ever to undertake, a case which I came to dub 'The Good, the Bad and the Very Ugly' (although the only 'good' thing about any of them was their children). It was quite rare, I felt, that we gave children prepared to speak out against their abusers the justice they deserved, but with this notable exception I think we achieved just that – albeit at a cost.

WPC Bailey carried on. 'Well, it turns out that their father is Danny Porter, who used to live in your area. He moved down here to Dorset with his new wife about two years ago, but we understand he has another ten kids up there, by his first wife. According to Ealing social services, they have a record of him ill-treating those kids and I wondered if you could fill me in.'

It took me no time at all to establish that five of the ten children referred to had been Porter's own children, the others his stepchildren. It appeared that for years there had been innuendo and rumour suggesting that Porter was abusing his children and the social services had acted to remove many of them and place them in care. I relayed all this information to WPC Bailey and promised to look further into the family background and ring her back.

Porter's first wife, June, was living in Northolt in a council flat with an adult son and daughter, while all her younger children were in foster care or residential accommodation. June's sister Sarah had seven children of her own and lived locally with her husband Gary. Their brother Joe Junior, who lived in lodgings around the corner, was a practising homosexual with a penchant for young boys. June's father, a truly revolting individual known as Joe Senior, aged sixty-seven, lived in a nearby tower block with his wife and was the archetypal 'dirty old man' with long, lank white hair, a filthy mac and staining all down his trousers. We learnt later that this appalling man had engaged in the sexual abuse of children for over thirty years, with his own children, now adult parents, involved with him from an early age.

June's ten children and Sarah's seven were known locally as 'wild' kids: filthy, rotten, dirty, running all over the estate at all hours, clad in all sorts of ragamuffin clothes. Often seen to be sporting cuts and bruises which everyone suspected came from their parents or from fighting, none of them could ever be persuaded to say a word about what was going on behind closed doors. According to neighbours, they all looked 'ill-fed, sad and unloved'; some ate food from the dustbins and rubbish chutes, and when denied access to their homes they urinated and defecated in the corridors outside the flats.

Two years earlier, in 1989, while I was still at Acton, I had dealt with Joe Sr for indecently assaulting one of his granddaughters, then aged four, and a grandson aged three. A visitor to the house testified that she had caught him with his hands down the front of the children's clothing. He was sent to prison for twelve months.

In 1973 Danny Porter had been sent to Leavesden Psychiatric Hospital 'without limit of time' after being convicted of serious sexual assault on a fifteen-year-old schoolgirl. Doctors had described him as a psychopath, but still released him after three years. While in hospital he had met Joe Jr, who was undergoing an identity crisis, and ultimately met June, Joe's sister, when she came to visit. When he was released from hospital, Porter moved in with June and her five children and later married her. She went on to give him five children of his own. Years later he divorced her and remarried.

WPC Bailey remained concerned for the safety of the two little girls in Dorset still under Porter's control and, in an effort to help them, she was granted permission to come to London so that all the information on Porter could be pooled and acted on. It was agreed that we should try to track down the elder Porter children, who were in homes or foster care around London and the Home Counties, to try and get them to come clean about the abuse we felt certain had gone on for many years. We hoped that, away from the control of their parents, they might have the courage to speak out.

It was decided that I and certain members of my team and I would each concentrate on specific children. PC Mike Gallagher would try to interview some of the older teenage boys, including one fourteen-year-old called Bobby, who had recently

315

started on a campaign of self-mutilation. DS Charlie Hailstone would try and take on the eldest girls; WPC Di Emms had agreed to deal with some of Sarah's older children; while I volunteered to speak to the younger Porter girls.

Taking on a job of this size, involving a total of nineteen children, is quite rare, but having made the decision to do so I then set about trying to get it exactly right, both from the children's point of view and that of the court, if ever we reached that stage. I knew the judge of the day would not hesitate in having my guts for garters if I got it wrong.

As officer in charge of the case, I also knew I would have to research over twenty years of social history, working backwards from the eldest child. Wading through years of documented evidence and speaking to every officer who had come into contact with the family was not a job for the faint-hearted, and organizing briefings which took us through the mind-bogglingly complicated new legislation pushed most of us to the brink.

We all had to abide by some pretty strict rules governing what we could and couldn't say to the children. 'Did your daddy ever interfere with you?' was not on, although 'Is there anything you want to tell me about your daddy which may, in the past, have upset you?' was. As the video recorder ran, it was like walking on eggshells and difficult beyond belief.

With our noses firmly to the grindstone, we each saw the children we had been delegated and, within a very short time, found that some of them were prepared to speak about their dreadful pasts. Assurances had to be given time and again that they were now safe from Danny Porter, who would not be allowed to contact or intimidate them.

The sexual abuse, they said, was their earliest childhood memory; sometimes between one child and one parent, sometimes with more than one child and several adults, but almost always with Danny Porter, who became very violent if they resisted.

Joe Sr was implicated, and his elderly wife. Joe Jr was said to be an active participant together with his boyfriend. Sarah, her husband Gary and their seven children were involved, and Danny's wife June, who was not the brightest of sparks, was said to be an unwilling partner but too frightened of her husband to complain. In effect, the whole family had been at it for years with no holds barred.

One girl I spoke to said she must have been about three years old when her grandpa held her down so that her father and uncle could rape her. Her grandma, it seems, was downstairs making tea. On a separate occasion, an older brother was forced to sexually abuse her while the men looked on and Bobby, the boy who was mutilating himself, had been forced to have sex with his own mother, June, something which still haunted him. Sarah indecently assaulted one of her daughters, and Gary had done unspeakable things to all the children. During a game of 'doctors and nurses' Joe Jr and his boyfriend had acted outrageously and there were, it seemed, no boundaries to the moral or social behaviour of any of these adults.

Over the years, all the children were repeatedly threatened with a beating if they ever 'told' and when one boy begged Porter not to bugger him again he was dangled over the side of the third-floor balcony by his feet until he apologized. Some of the children ran away from home to escape the abuse, others locked themselves in cupboards and another attempted suicide, but not one of them volunteered a bad word about their adult carers. The ones that stayed were raped, sodomized and beaten. The elder girls did all the household chores while playing mum to the younger ones, and when he ran out of cigarettes Danny Porter sent them into the street to look for discarded butts.

These children suffered a catalogue of physical injuries including punching and kicking, leaving one girl with hearing problems and a boy with missing teeth. But every bruise and scratch had previously been explained away as nothing more than the injuries sustained in the rough and tumble of play. On more than one occasion the social services intervened but, faced with a bunch of kids who wouldn't say a word about what was really going on, there was little they could do. Only later, when it became obvious that things were never going to get better, did they find the evidence to acquire the court orders to have the children removed, but by then irreparable damage had been done.

By the time we arrived to speak to them, we discovered that the children were all so psychologically disturbed by what had happened that most of them were undergoing some kind of psychiatric treatment. On learning the grisly details of their years of abuse, I, for one, felt like joining them.

Once the floodgates opened and they did start to talk, it meant listening to the most vile allegations imaginable. I was told such horror stories that it was difficult not to look shocked and to contain my feelings and, despite the fact that this was a volunteer posting and part of the job, many of us found it impossible to stop the shock waves spilling over into our private lives.

There is nowhere to take the mess of emotions that builds up inside you, except perhaps to talk with colleagues and hopefully dump it in the office, but even that isn't easy. Everyone in the team was struggling in their own way to come to terms with the information they had been given and it affected us all, some worse than others. One confided that it affected his enjoyment of sex with his girlfriend, and another said he had 'gone off sex altogether'. A third said he could no longer bathe his young children without feeling 'dirty and ashamed' and that he had actually asked his wife to supervise him for a time. I offered what help I could, but I knew they were each going to have to sort it out themselves. This type of work was definitely not on most police officers' career chart.

It was the best reason in the world to go down the pub and have a bloody good drink, and who could blame anyone that did? But for this alcoholic, sweet tea would have to suffice.

'Aren't you ever going to drink again?' I was asked countless times.

'I don't know,' was the only truthful answer I could give, 'but for today, I'm going to give it a miss.' It was coming up six years since I'd last taken alcohol and if, at my first AA meeting, someone had said: 'Carol, you can never drink again,' I would have told them to stuff their silly AA and not be so ridiculous. But they never said that. All I was ever asked to do was to try and avoid booze for the next twenty-four hours. 'Take it a day at a time,' I was told – and, for over two thousand days, it had worked for me.

Getting the children to tell us what had happened was one thing, but persuading them to give evidence against their relatives was entirely different. They were absolutely terrified of reprisals and each of us sat with our respective charges for hours, assuring them of our protection. To the older ones I promised: 'When we get to court, you won't have to face them. You can tell your story from behind a screen.' To the younger ones I said: 'You won't even have to be in the same room as them because when you tell your story to the court we'll set up a video link.'

I had no real right to make these promises but I felt that it was the only way forward. The judge of the day might well have refused the prosecution request for such protection for the young witnesses on the basis that it was 'unfair' to the defendant not to see the children give their evidence directly. Had that happened in this case, I'm not sure I could have ever faced those children again without feeling shame.

It took nine months to prepare the case and in the end I chose the seven strongest children to give evidence. Needless to say, I slung the book at the adult offenders, charging Porter, Joe Sr, Sarah, Gary, Joe Jr and his boyfriend with a combination of rape and buggery. The exception was June who, the children said, was as much a victim as they had been.

During the lengthy pre-trial hearings at the Old Bailey, we carried eight four-drawer filing cabinets containing thirty-five thousand documents into the courtroom, listing the histories of all nineteen children. The judge ruled that the defence should have access to many of the documents (which delayed the trial still further) and separated the defendants, so that Joe Jr and his boyfriend would be tried some time after the others. No one was happier than me when he ruled in our favour on screens and video-link facilities and ordered the trial to begin in June 1993.

It was a dreadful case to listen to, even for those of us who had heard it all before. The children gave their evidence with an innocence reserved for angels. They all managed to retain their composure apart from one eleven-year-old girl, who lost it completely and cried when she was called a liar by defence counsel. 'I'm not lying, I'm not!' she screamed and had to be taken from the video-link room in tears.

On 29 June 1993 the jury returned unanimous guilty verdicts on all four defendants. Before sentencing, Judge Capstick QC told them: 'This is about as dreadful a case as I have encountered, involving defenceless and innocent children. All of you behaved appallingly. Porter, you behaved like a monster. You raped, buggered and assaulted very young children. You moved into a family with young children and abused your position as a father, stepfather and uncle.

'There is no mitigation by a plea of guilty and as a result the children had to relive their experiences to this court. It is a pity that you cannot be named, but at least some of the horror for the children can be saved by not being identified.'

Porter got seven terms of life imprisonment, and the others received sentences ranging from twelve years to eighteen months. In terms of justice, it was a fantastic outcome and even though we appreciated the damage done to the children, it was a result they could take away with them and build on because here was irrefutable confirmation that they had been believed. The primary question on the lips of all victims of sexual abuse is 'Will they think I'm lying?', and here was absolute proof that these children were not.

It is a great sadness to have to admit that children who are victims of long-term sexual abuse have the potential to become abusers themselves. Most, of course, do not, but it is my experience that some do. Sexual abuse is as disfiguring as any physical scar and its ugliness creates an emotional rawness that rarely heals. What hope do such children have of leading normal lives with such a dreadful disability? In the case of the Porter children, the eldest have already been involved in dysfunctional partnerships, and at least one child born to such a relationship has been taken into care because of neglect and physical abuse. The cycle will it seems, continue through those particular generations. My only hope is that the younger ones, taken into care at an early age and given psychiatric help, might just stand the chance of leading normal lives.

The case against Joe Jr and his partner was never proceeded with because it was thought that to do so would cause the children too much distress in having to give their evidence all over again.

Needless to say, by the time the case had reached its conclusion every one of us felt as if we had been through the emotional wringer. The judge congratulated us and we each received a Commissioner's commendation, mine for 'professional skill and sensitivity'.

We all had good reason to celebrate and, after a few large tonic waters with my colleagues in the local pub, I attempted to lighten what was fast becoming a grisly post mortem of events. I didn't know a police officer who couldn't tell a story and on this particular evening the responsibility fell to me. I resurrected an old favourite of mine, the story of when I – of all people – fell victim to a series of dirty phone calls.

I was on the Flying Squad and had just got home one evening when the telephone rang. 'Can I speak to Carol, please?' the voice said.

'Carol speaking,' I replied, although I later wished I hadn't. Then began an outpouring of the most filthy, rotten, dirty sexual fantasies you could imagine, as this young man told me all the things he would like to do to me while I was in black lace underwear and silk stockings. I thought of the Marks & Spencer white cotton Aertex knickers I was wearing and I wanted to scream at him that I'd never worn black lace in my life. But instead I said, 'How dare you!' and slammed the phone down.

I was hardly in the front door but now found myself shaking like a leaf. 'For God's sake, Carol, get a grip,' I heard myself saying. If I hadn't been so shocked and upset by what he was telling me I might have seen the funny side of it, for he clearly had no idea I was a copper. Wasn't I the lucky one to have a man who wanted to ravish my less than perfect body? That's what my friends and colleagues would have said, but it wasn't funny and I had hardly recovered from the initial shock when the phone rang again.

'Carol?' It was him again and as he started his monologue of filth I hung up, revolted by what he was saying. I spent the rest of the evening wondering who he could be and how he had got my number. Why me? I asked, but the voice of reason answered, Why not me?

The phone calls soon became a regular feature of my life. For almost five months I put up with the heavy breathing, the smut, the innuendo, the vile language and the plain outrageous suggestions. This was long before the 1990s wizardry of British Telecom which can now trace a call in seconds; in those days it took nearer two weeks and a man working full-time, and he would only be employed in that capacity for 'exceptional' threats. Mine fell into the category of your 'usual dirty phone calls' and were definitely not exceptional.

And so they went on, always on Tuesday and Thursday nights and Sunday mornings. The worse they got, the more obsessive I became about trying to catch the nasty little sod, despite my Flying Squad colleagues thinking it a hoot. Many appeared to find it so funny that they had belly pains trying to suppress their laughter. 'If only he knew,' one of them said. 'A Flying Squad officer, trained to kill, getting dirty phone calls from an unknown admirer.' I quickly learnt that this was the only sympathy I was going to get. It wasn't the crime of the century and I wasn't being threatened, so it was all just a big joke and I learnt to laugh with them.

The next time my caller rang, I decided to try a different tack. Instead of just hanging up, I interrupted and said quietly but firmly: 'If you're going to be rude to me, I'll put the phone down, but if you want to speak to me intelligently, I'll listen to you.'

To my surprise, he said: 'What shall we talk about then?' For the next five minutes I managed to create a conversation about the weather, what was on the television and football. Not that I have a clue about our national sport, but my caller was clearly hooked. I asked him what club he supported and he told me Fulham. I said: 'You have the unfair advantage of knowing my name. What's yours?' There was a pause, and then he answered: 'David.' But before I knew it he lapsed back into his diatribe and I hung up.

I think what unnerved me the most was that during the course of our chat he made it clear that he knew quite a lot about me, not least that I lived alone, which made me feel vulnerable and uneasy. I jumped every time the telephone rang. But he still clearly had no idea that I was a Metropolitan Police officer, and I had no intention of telling him.

The routine of the calls remained roughly the same, but with one minor improvement. He now introduced himself with 'Hello, it's me again.' He would then talk civilly to me for two or three minutes before reverting to his vile fantasies. Over the many weeks that followed, I would encourage him to tell me about himself and, slowly, I began to find out quite a lot about him as he let his guard slip more and more. He told me he lived with his mother after his parents had separated. She now had a new boyfriend and he worked in a greengrocer's on a Saturday.

I now began to get a picture of a spotty-faced, pubescent youth who had recently discovered the wonders of an erect penis. I assumed him to be about fifteen years of age, but in the absence of a father figure and any communication skills with the opposite sex he had opted for anonymity and me to off-load to. I also sensed his despair when he told me about the break-up of his parents' marriage. Knowing this much about him took the sting out of his phone calls and, however bad the language was after that, it never had quite the same impact on me as it did when I knew nothing about him.

Then one day out of the blue, four and a half months after the calls started, he inadvertently announced that he was about to be interviewed for a job with London Transport. I sensed his excitement but hoped he didn't get a whiff of mine. Got you! I thought as I replaced the receiver, grinning from ear to ear and hoping beyond hope that he was telling the truth.

The following morning I could barely contain myself as I rang London Transport in my official capacity and asked a member of personnel for help. Without giving them the exact reason, I told them I required the name of every young man due

323

to be interviewed for employment in the next few weeks. They said they were about to interview prospective apprentice mechanics over a three-day period and gave me a list of sixty names and telephone numbers of school leavers.

Now I was a woman with a cause and I worked like a little navvy to get through that list of names. To my astonishment, there wasn't one David on the whole list – not that I was certain that David was my caller's real name. I started with the telephone numbers from around the Fulham area and, pretending I was looking for an old friend, I rang each and every number, always insisting on speaking to the woman of the house. 'Sorry to trouble you, but I'm looking for David. I don't know his second name but he works in a greengrocer's and supports Fulham Football Club.'

Needless to say, the wives and mums were all very wary of me, but, having established that I was barking up the wrong tree and that they couldn't help me, I thanked them and rang off. Then came that magic phone call. The lady answered: 'It sounds like my son you want, but his name isn't David, it's Stewart. He works in a greengrocer's on Saturday mornings and supports Fulham. Just exactly who are you?'

I formally introduced myself and said I would call at her address within the hour. I couldn't have been any more excited if I had just identified a serial killer. My macho male colleagues didn't take a blind bit of notice and largely ignored me when I told them ecstatically that I had 'got him at last'. Grabbing my coat, I shot out of the office and went directly to Stewart's address.

Stewart's mother answered the door. Before I could open my mouth and introduce myself, she smiled and said: 'Hello, Carol. You're Ernie's daughter, aren't you?' I was dumbstruck.

Eventually I managed a smile and said, rather stiffly: 'Do I know you?'

'Course you do. It's Pearl Bartlett. I knew your dad,' she said. 'We saw you once when we called at the house. He told me all about you.'

I apologized for not recognizing her, before she went on to explain that her husband, from whom she had recently separated, worked with my father in the same bus depot. At social events, when the wives were invited, she got to know my parents, in particular my dad, quite well. She told me that she had a sixteen-year-old son called Stewart who had become very disturbed by the marriage break-up and was 'a bit of a handful'.

Stopping herself suddenly, she said: 'I'm so sorry, Carol, you don't want to know all this. What can I do for you?' I gulped hard, sat her down and told her the true reason for my visit. She was horrified and absolutely refused to believe that 'her Stewart' could have done such a thing. But between us we worked out that the nights he called were always the ones when he was left alone. She also recalled that my father, before he had died, had given her my home telephone number, which she had entered into her telephone book under the name 'Carol'. Dad had apparently proudly suggested that she should call me if ever she needed my kind of assistance. Good old Dad.

My heart went out to Stewart's mum. She cried buckets and was terrified that I was going to arrest her son and take him away from her. She begged me not to take any drastic action until she had had a chance to speak to Stewart herself. I agreed to return in twenty-four hours.

The next day, I called back. She was still very upset but said she had confronted her son and that he had broken down and confessed. 'He admitted it,' she said, horrified. 'Said he didn't know why he did it, he just did. He wants you to know how very sorry he is.'

'I bet he is,' I said. 'Has he any idea what that kind of repeated nasty behaviour does to women? Supposing I'd been fragile or elderly? I could have had a heart attack or a nervous breakdown by now.'

I regretted my outburst when I saw the look on Pearl's face. I wasn't telling her anything she hadn't thought of already. Her eyes filled with tears again as she asked me: 'Are you going to arrest him?'

I took a deep breath and answered, as gently as I could: 'Your son needs help, not locking up. Will you promise to take him to his doctor and explain what's been going on, if I leave him alone?' She didn't need asking twice and promised she would make an appointment straight away. She rang me a week later to tell me that the GP had seen him and referred him for some kind of psychiatric help.

'I can't thank you enough for what you've done,' she told me. Without thinking quite what she was saying, she added: 'I'm just so grateful that of all the people he could have called, he ended up calling you.'

I'll never know if I made the right decision, but it seemed right at the time, and I was never troubled again. Not that the lads in the office didn't make full mileage out of it. When I walked back in after discovering my mystery caller's identity I was confronted with a huge raffia paper banner hung across the ceiling which read: PHANTOM KNICKER LICKER NICKED BY FLYING SQUAD DETECTIVE. For one of the few times in my life, I was speechless.

14

LASHLEY'S APPEAL WAS A LONG TIME COMING AND IT DIDN'T matter how often I rang the list office at the Royal Courts of Justice, nobody could give me a definite date for the hearing, which made me very twitchy. 1992 had been and gone and the best I could hope for was that Lashley's solicitors had either forgotten or abandoned his appeal, but no such luck. His case was in the system somewhere, it was just going to take a considerable length of time to surface, and the waiting was giving me grey hairs.

Not that the emotional stresses and strains of the job were the only things making me feel my age; there were physical aspects that were starting to affect me badly as well. My right knee had never been the same since I had fallen through the ceiling of the burgled house in Notting Hill in 1968. It had certainly not been helped by the kicking I received from the pickpocket a few years later, and the final straw came in October 1993 when I fell arse over apex part-way down a flight of stone steps outside my CPT office.

I had just locked up the first-floor interview room and was feeling my way downstairs in the darkness when I stepped awkwardly, slipped and fell. The pain was so bad that I felt sure that I had dislocated my kneecap, so it came as a surprise to learn at the hospital that it was 'just that old knee playing up again'.

I had had an operation to remove my cartilage in 1988, which had helped for a while, but by the time I fell down the steps five years later my knee was simply reminding me that it had seen better days. I could no longer run because it gave way without warning and it felt about as unstable as a waterbed. In fact, it was now so knackered that I knew any little push or kick would have me on the floor; in other words, I was more likely to be a hindrance than a help in any public disorder situation because of my own vulnerability to injury.

'For God's sake, go and see a doctor about that knee,' one of my colleagues ordered me, having seen me wince as I hobbled into the office one morning not long after my 1993 fall.

'I think I'd better,' I admitted, lifting my aching leg on to a cushion.

My GP showed considerable concern and promised he would write to the Chief Medical Officer of the Metropolitan Police setting out his own reservations about the weakness of my knee. Within days the CMO had responded and I was given an appointment to see him the following week.

As I walked into his surgery at the Medical Branch at Wellington House, I wondered what the hell I was going to say. It wasn't like me to make a fuss; I hated having to see the doctor generally; but I knew I would have to try and prevent further injury to an already troublesome knee. I needn't have worried; I was greeted by the smiling face of Mr Lloyd-Davies, who had the reputation of being one of the kindest surgeons we had. He told me to sit down and tell him what the problem was.

'I'll start at the beginning,' I said, and went through the chronology of my accident-prone leg. 'I was wondering if I could now be granted some form of special authority which would allow me, on medical grounds, to avoid duties which place me in potentially violent situations.' What a mouthful, I thought. Why didn't I speak plain English? So I added, rather shakily: 'I'm scared to death of being kicked or receiving another injury to my knee which may result in me walking on sticks.'

The CMO nodded and, looking at my records, he smiled. 'How many years' service do you have, inspector?' he asked.

'Twenty-eight, sir,' I answered, realizing for the first time just how long that was. Twenty-eight years. Was it possible? Where had the years gone?

The doctor was reading my mind. 'Isn't it time you considered your options?' he asked, an expression of paternal concern on his face. 'I don't know how much more that knee of yours can take and we both know it's not going to get any better. Have you considered that this might be the right time for you to retire from the service on grounds of ill-health? With your service, it would mean that you get the equivalent of a full thirty-year pension.'

'But I don't want to leave,' I spluttered. The police force was my life. What was he suggesting?

'Stop panicking,' he said, gently. 'It's something I want you to go away and think about. In the mean time, I'll put you on a form of light duties which will be discretional but will have the effect of temporarily relieving you from confrontational situations. But I must see you back here after Christmas when I propose to reassess your position within the force with regard to that knee.'

I left Mr Lloyd-Davies's office feeling numb. I was focusing on what had been said in very definite terms. The words 'retire' and 'pension' flashed past my eyes in neon lights time and again and I suddenly felt like some clapped-out geriatric who was fit only for the scrapheap.

'So what exactly did he say?' asked Jackie Malton, an old friend and the first colleague I had rung after my appointment with the CMO.

'He said I should go away and consider my options,' I blurted out, miserably.

'Then think about it, Carol,' Jackie said, trying to calm me down. 'I know you're feeling hurt and angry, but is it right to look a gift horse in the mouth? None of us are getting any younger and it would do you good to slow down, because that way you might just live to see old age.'

'What would I do with myself?' I heard myself asking. 'I'd be fifty years old and bored stiff.'

'You'd soon find something to do; in fact, knowing you, it'd be a million things,' she reassured. 'Why not come over this evening and we'll talk about it?'

'You're on,' I replied.

Thanks largely to Jackie and her soothing words, within forty-eight hours I was starting to think about life after the Metropolitan Police, something I had never previously felt able to do. Suddenly, I felt strangely calm. The thought of further injury to my knee truly frightened me, and maybe they were right, it was time to go after all.

But was it possible to leave a career which had been my salvation without feeling desperately frightened about the future? I had spent the last twenty-eight years totally engrossed in an utterly brilliant job which had become my life, and I had seen more violence, hatred and evil than anyone should ever have to witness in a lifetime. But the investigations had fulfilled me – there had never been a dull moment.

By the time I returned to see the CMO on 25 January 1994, I was already preparing myself for the possibility of premature retirement. In fact, I had thought of little else for the past three months. My AA programme had taught me to accept those things that cannot be changed, so what was the point of getting angry about a leg which was always going to be weak? The same programme had also taught me that when one door closes another will open, just so long as I decided to push on it.

I was now in my eighth year without alcohol and my quality of life had changed so much that sometimes I could not believe my luck. I had actually accepted who I was, 'warts and all'. I no longer saw myself as bad, just different. My new optimism was beginning to convince me that I could go on to live a full life doing all those things that I had always said I would do 'if only I had the time'. Well, here is your chance, I told myself, so stop moaning and if retirement is still on offer you should accept it gratefully and get on with it.

'According to my calendar, your last day will be the fourteenth of June 1994,' mused the CMO, as he studied me over the top of his spectacles. The niceties had already been gone through and he and I were now facing the nuts and bolts of the situation. 'But in the run-up to your retirement you will get ninety days' sick leave, which should cushion the blow.' He smiled. 'So your last working day will be somewhere around the middle of March. I hope that suits.'

'Thank you, sir,' I said as I got to my feet and held out my hand. He shook it warmly and I left. Now it was official. In a little under five months, I would be a pensioner.

I returned to the office to find a message on my desk. It read: *David Lashley's appeal is due to be heard on 30 June 1994.* One way or another, I thought, June is going to be a memorable month.

As March loomed I volunteered for less and less work. My office was already littered with case files which needed updating for my successor and as I started to clear away my papers, books and photographs I began to feel the kind of uselessness that others must have felt when told that they were being made redundant. On a good day I could accept that retirement was the right thing, but on others I felt rooted to a state of the unreal.

Trying to prepare myself for the freedom I knew to be just around the corner, I began to make mental lists of all the things I had said I would do in retirement if only I had the time. I could now write that book; I could even sign up for an adult education class in criminology which had always interested me; and what about travelling around the world, learning bridge and how to play golf?

As I tidied up my papers, my eyes fell on a tattered brown folder which I had marked in big red letters: ANABOLIC STEROIDS. I shan't be sorry to see that one go, I thought, as I picked it up, ready to file away. And then, as if renewing memories from a photograph album, I opened the cover and started reading.

Like most of my theories in life, I based my opinions on the case histories of my investigations and the people I met who became inextricably linked with them. A particular case in point where I felt I had important and valuable information to impart was as a result of meeting and arresting a young Adonis called Jack who introduced me to anabolic steroids.

Jack and I met at Acton when I was investigating a series of apparently motiveless attacks on women where the attacker had always managed to stop short of committing a more serious sexual act. Jack opened my eyes to something I had never previously come across.

The youngest of four children, a formerly placid young man from an excellent family background with no previous contact with the law, Jack was a fanatical body builder and ruggedly handsome. By the age of twenty-one, he had been using anabolic steroids for four years. In that same period, he had carried out the sexual assaults that I was investigating on eight women aged between twenty-one and seventy, each time losing control of his libido and acting like a wild animal.

No one had warned Jack (not that he would have listened) that massively exceeding the safe dose of anabolic steroids by fifty times and more (as many body builders do in the quest for the perfect body) could have an adverse effect on his personality. He had not bothered to read the small print that accompanied his daily injection of testosterone cypionate, which spelt out the warnings: 'Anabolic steroids can cause excessive frequency and duration of penile erections [the kind that are not satisfied despite multiple ejaculation]. They can cause depression, anxiety, increased irritability and aggression [often referred to as 'roid rage']. Anabolic steroids can cause cancer and heart disease, nausea, cholestatic jaundice and internal bleeding.'

Jack started body-building at the age of seventeen because he believed he looked weak and puny. Yet when I arrested him his frame was so huge that he had to manoeuvre his shoulders sideways to get through the door of my office. At seventeen and a half, he was introduced to anabolic steroids as the short cut to achieving muscle and bulk and began to take high doses of the drugs. At eighteen, he attacked a middle-aged woman in the street in broad daylight for no apparent reason by putting his hand under her skirt. At nineteen, he punched and kicked out the windows of a bus when the driver was unable to find change for the ten-pound note that Jack tendered for his fare.

Jack never denied the attacks, but blamed anabolic steroids

entirely for his uncontrollable mood swings. He appeared in court and was placed on probation for two years when he agreed to be supervised for his addiction. He would say that his addiction was psychological, not physical. 'It makes me feel great to look this good, I couldn't imagine a day without taking them, and anyway my body needs them,' he told me. Meeting him caused me to think that there might be others in the criminal justice system who had been charged with violent or sexual crime who had been taking anabolic steroids as well.

With this in mind, I randomly drew the files of the first fifteen men I could think of who had made the headlines because of their heinous crimes, including John Steed, the M4 rapist, who raped three women and murdered a prostitute. To my astonishment, nine of those fifteen were body builders and in court three of them, including Steed, had cited their addiction to anabolic steroids as being the cause of their terrible behaviour. The second had suddenly lost his temper and set fire to his own house, burning to death his two young daughters, while the third, in a fit of 'roid rage', had crushed the life out of his two-year-old stepdaughter.

None of the three had previously been reported for violent crime and the six who did not introduce anabolic steroids into their defence were never even asked if they were users. I couldn't help but think that if David Lashley knew about anabolic steroids then he would certainly have been a candidate for their use.

Excited by my findings, I went on to examine the medical literature on the subject and found that extensive research had been done in America. More limited analysis had been done in the UK, although a recent study in Wales found that anabolic steroids were a major factor in 'motiveless acts of aggression, including murder and rape'. It also estimated that one in twenty weight lifters and body builders used the drugs, which meant, in reality, that several thousand men were abusing them.

The doctors in the American studies described men who had no previous history of antisocial behaviour who impulsively committed violent crimes – including murder – while taking anabolic steroids. Psychiatric interviews revealed that steroids played a necessary, if not primary, role in the causes of the violent behaviour and, while it was recognized that the men may have exaggerated the effects that steroids played in their crimes in the hope of improving their legal position, their individual accounts were consistently corroborated by other factors.

My next port of call was to Professor V. H. T. James, from the University of London, who had worked in the field of steroid endocrinology for the past thirty-five years. According to him, anabolic steroids can 'cause the development of manic psychotic behaviour which may culminate in violent crime. Androgens have well-recognized effects on the central nervous system and there are convincing clinical reports which support the view that anabolic steroids, taken in large doses, in some individuals, can cause serious changes in mood and result in aggressive, violent or irrational behaviour.' Adolf Hitler is said to have administered anabolic steroids to his stormtroopers to make them more fearless and aggressive.

I went on to examine the law and took legal advice but discovered that the only control police could exercise to halt the supply of steroids was under the Medicines Act, which placed restrictions on the supply of 'prescription-only' drugs. As this was rarely enforced and was a relatively minor offence, it meant that certain individuals felt free to peddle steroids, knowing that there was nothing of substance to stop them.

I did not need further convincing that the continued unrestricted use of anabolic steroids would contribute to the rise in violent sexual crime and decided to send a report to the Commissioner, setting out my findings. Knowing it was never going to be easy, I got on my soapbox and said my piece. Quoting the experts, I told everyone who would listen about the appalling side effects of steroids only to be criticized repeatedly by academics and other individuals outside the force for over-reacting and 'scare-mongering'.

I was very chuffed to discover, however, that, with the aid of others who helped me beat the same drum, something of what we said must have eventually made its mark because within a few years we had legislation which adequately fitted the bill.

*   *   *

'I suppose, with you not drinking, there'll be no boozy farewell for you to remember us by?' said a colleague of mine who I knew liked a good drink.

'You could be right, but just in case you're wrong, I suggest you carry on with the collection for my leaving present so nobody gets embarrassed in the event that I do have an official retirement party,' I said, with a straight face.

I knew exactly what I wanted, a sit-down dinner, not just some wild piss-up where everyone but me got legless. No, it was going to be done properly. There'd be a free bar to start with, and then forty or so close friends and colleagues and I would sit down to dinner. I organized a seating plan and put myself at the top table with Mo Dennison, who had taught me beats all those years ago, and Commander John Purnell, with whom I had joined training school and who was awarded the George Medal for his bravery during the famous Balcombe Street siege. Then there were Detective Chief Superintendents Ken John and Graham Searle, who set up the Acton Rape Squad, Chief Superintendent Stewart Higgins and a whole host of lovely people, whose ranks and positions were not important, who had touched my life at some stage of my service.

The function was held on 27 May 1994 at Sudbury Golf Club, Greenford. I arrived early and on my own so that I could put the name cards on the tables and greet everyone as they arrived. I was as nervous as a kitten. What if nobody turned up? How would I feel if half the tables were empty?

I had bought a white silk blouse especially for the evening, and wore it with a smart black skirt, black tights and black shoes. The tables were all laid out on my arrival, and as I began to put down the neatly written cards a woman's voice behind me made me jump. 'You're early, love,' she said. I turned and saw a matronly woman with a tea towel in her hand and an apron round her middle.

'Yes, I wanted to make sure everything was all right,' I told her.

'That's fine,' she replied. 'Well, now you're here, you'd better make yourself useful and come and help me polish these glasses.' I was half-way across the room to help her before I remembered I was paying for this lot, so she could polish her own flipping glasses.

'Isn't there anyone else who can help you?' I asked, stopping myself in the middle of the floor.

'What's wrong with you?' she asked, quizzically. 'I mean, that's why you're here, isn't it? I asked the agency for extra waitresses and they sent you, right?'

'Wrong,' I said, looking down at my outfit and realizing that, dressed as I was, it was easy to mistake me for a waitress. Laughing, I put the poor woman straight and she offered me a thousand apologies before walking off red-faced.

Despite an unpromising start to the evening, it was a wonderful night; without doubt one of the best of my life. I felt like a bride at her wedding reception – all eyes were upon me, everyone was dressed up to the nines. The only difference was that my honeymoon was going to be the rest of my life away from police work, not just a couple of weeks in the Seychelles. Probably for the first time in my life, no one had a bad word to say about me, in fact they were sweet and generous in their praise.

Commander Purnell gave the first of two speeches, and after being presented with gifts and flowers I was asked to respond. Following my expression of genuine thanks I racked my brains for inspiration and something funny to say.

'There are lots of stories I could tell you about my life in the Met,' I began. 'And having been mistaken for a waitress when I arrived here tonight, I remembered a story about the time when I was a young detective in training at Notting Hill over twenty-five years ago.'

I explained how a number of us had been invited to Marylebone Lane nick's Christmas party, held, as ever, in the Chamber of Horrors at Madame Tussaud's. Young TDCs (temporary detective constables) like me were welcome at these functions, not least because we could be used to do the running about for the senior officers, and most of us were only too pleased to volunteer because, of course, it brought us to the attention of the particular governor we were helping. Suffice to say that at this particular do one of the DIs got very drunk and I was asked to drive him home before he fell over.

'Yes,' I said, only too willing to help out but equally mindful of the fact that I too had had a good drink and probably too much to pass any breathalyser test. However, I agreed to drive the drunken sot home and felt good when he told me that he lived in Wandsworth, south-west London, because it was an area I knew fairly well. I sat the DI in my car and drove off in the general direction of Hammersmith before he tugged at my sleeve and said: 'Where are we going, or is this the scenic route?'

'I'm driving you home to Wandsworth, sir,' I answered.

'No you're bloody not,' he growled, 'because I live in Wanstead.'

I stopped. 'Wanstead? In east London?' I asked in disbelief. 'I was sure you said Wandsworth.'

'That's because you're going deaf,' he said, and roared with laughter, finding it all a huge joke. Realizing that I was then driving in completely the wrong direction, I changed tack and drove off on his instructions to east London. I eventually dropped him off at his home address and watched him topple through the front door.

The area around Wanstead is a total mystery to me. It is so far away from the areas of London I know that even today I'm not sure I could drive there without first consulting a map. I knew I was lost, but I did manage to find my way back to Wanstead underground station and I knew that Bow must be somewhere nearby. I hoped that from there I could find some signs so that I could make my way home.

Well, there were absolutely none that I could see and I decided that my only hope was to drive slowly around the area, looking for someone who could give me directions. It was now about 1 a.m., the roads were all but deserted and I hadn't got a map of London with me, so I drove round and round.

Then, as if by some miracle, I saw a young man standing at a zebra crossing, waiting to cross, holding his hand to his jaw as if in agony. I wound the window down and shouted across to him: 'Excuse me, I'm afraid I'm lost, could you point me in the general direction of Bow?'

'Yes,' he mumbled, 'it's that way,' pointing somewhere out

to my left. 'I'm trying to get to the London Hospital in Whitechapel because I've got chronic toothache. If you wouldn't mind giving me a lift, I'll direct you from there.'

I was so relieved. 'Great,' I said, 'hop in.' Once he was safely in the passenger seat it was easy to see how much pain this young man was in and it was only when I knew he was comfortable that I drove off. I reckon I had driven all of fifty yards when a police car appeared. It seemed to be right up my tail, having materialized from nowhere.

The police siren sounded briefly and I saw the police driver waving his arms, directing me to pull in to the kerb to stop. Bloody hell, I thought, the bugger's going to breathalyse me and I'm sure I'm over the top. Remembering something I'd heard a long time before, I decided I might stand a chance if I was terribly polite and spoke straight at the windscreen, in the vain hope that he wouldn't smell the alcohol on my breath. I stopped, the police car pulled up in front of me and the driver got out.

'Good morning, officer,' I said brightly.

'What's your game then, gal?' he asked, sounding more like a Cockney barrow boy than a Metropolitan Police officer.

'Sorry,' I said, 'I don't understand.'

'It's a bit late for you girls to be working, innit? Is he going to be your last customer then?'

I've never been one to accept an insult gracefully and in different circumstances I would have been out of the car and smacked him straight in the mouth – but here I was, doing my very best to avoid being breathalysed, with no option but to act like a lady.

'I'm sorry, officer, but you're mistaken,' I said indignantly. 'I am taking this young man, who has toothache, to the London Hospital for treatment.'

'And I'm the tooth fairy,' he replied. 'I've just seen you drive round and round these streets doing all of ten miles an hour, looking up and down, waiting for someone to turn up, and then he came along and I saw you proposition him not two minutes ago.'

Before I could answer back, I saw it: the pink form which I

knew so well from my days in Soho. The prostitute's caution, the official warning given to someone caught soliciting for prostitution. I was so outraged I wanted to grab him by the throat and tell him who I was, but thought better of it when I remembered how some uniformed officers regarded detectives. I realized that, had I said what I wanted to, it probably would have inspired him to throw the book at me, starting with the breathalyser.

Thereafter I deserved a bloody medal for self-control. I sat there smiling sweetly as he finished writing out the form, tore it off and gave it to me. 'Count your lucky stars I didn't nick you,' he told me. 'Now be on your way and get rid of the john.' With that he got back in his car and drove off. I turned to my passenger to see him trying to stifle a giggle behind the hand that was still holding his jaw. I was livid, but I bit my tongue and dropped him off at the hospital.

The following morning, I made the mistake of telling my colleagues at Notting Hill. When they had picked themselves up off the floor from laughing, one of them suggested that I ring the man in charge at Wanstead and demand an apology. Yes, why not? I thought, riled by their laughter. 'Only he'll want to know why you didn't challenge the PC at the scene,' my friend added as I picked up the telephone receiver. 'And we'd love to hear you give him a reason why.' On second thoughts, I put down the phone and contented myself with being the only woman detective in the Met who has been cautioned for soliciting.

My story went down extremely well; in fact everything did. The dinner was smashing, the evening a dream, and when it was all over I wanted to go back and do it all again. A friend took photographs and they are among my most treasured possessions. I didn't shed a tear, but it was close. It was a wonderful send-off and I fell into bed that night happier than I had been in years.

June 14, D-Day, came and went without incident. I had expected to feel more as I woke up on the official date of my retirement, but I felt nothing. Perhaps because I had packed up my last few belongings and walked out of my office several weeks earlier, or because it had been over two weeks since my party – which seemed to finalize everything – the day itself was no more significant than any other. It was merely the day that my pension started, the day when I was no longer a serving officer with the Metropolitan Police.

The true realization of that fact was only brought home to me a few days later when, as a retired detective inspector, I made my way to Lambeth by train to deliver a talk on anabolic steroids to a group of forensic medical examiners in training at the laboratory. Armed with nothing more than my briefcase and my travel pass, I found a seat on a Metropolitan Line train from Uxbridge Station and sat down to read through my notes one last time.

At Harrow-on-the-Hill Station most of the passengers disembarked and I was left with a man opposite, one to my right across the aisle, and an old woman a few seats down. At the next stop the man opposite me got off and two minutes later something made me glance across at the man to my right, who couldn't have been more than thirty. To my absolute horror, I realized that he was sitting staring at me, a grin across his face, with his left hand gripping his exposed penis.

'I don't believe it!' I nearly exclaimed, although I stopped myself. Why me? I thought. Turning away quickly I stared hard at my own reflection in the window, trying to make out his shape behind me, so that I could be prepared if he made any sudden moves. I suppose I will have to take him in to the British Transport Police at Baker Street, I thought. What a bloody nuisance – it's always the hot weather that brings them out. What was I on about? Had I forgotten? I was retired. I didn't even have my warrant card any more. I was just a member of the public, an ordinary woman travelling into London on a summer's morning. I stared at the glass, contemplating my next move.

Do nothing, I told myself. You'll be late for your meeting if you do, and anyway, it's not your problem. Keep calm, look away and wait for your stop. Only a few to go now. Don't let it bother you.

But the more I told myself not to worry, the more I did. In the reflection, I could see the man's face still turned towards me and then I saw his hand start to move slowly up and down. I sighed with exasperation, thinking, This pathetic pain in the arse is really enjoying himself. Just then we pulled in to Finchley Road Station and the doors opened. A group of teenage girls got on and sat down at the far end of the carriage. Thank God for that, I thought. Three men in suits stepped in and sat in the middle; a young couple and a woman with a child stood in the centre aisle. Just as the doors were about to close, a grey-haired woman pulling a shopping trolley darted smartly in and, oh no, sat opposite my flasher.

I gulped and watched her face. I didn't want to look at him, but I knew if I watched her I could tell whether he had put it away or not. After a few seconds of looking up at the Tube map, she looked down, and the colour draining from her face told me all I needed to know.

'Right, sunshine! That's it!' I yelled as I leapt to my feet. 'I'm a police officer and you're nicked!' I reached into my pocket and pulled out my travelcard, an official-looking red pass with my photograph stuck in the middle. Thrusting it into his face as if it were a warrant card, I grabbed him by the sleeve of his jumper and hoisted him to his feet. He was so busy fumbling with his hands, trying to stuff his rapidly deflating pecker back into his underpants, that he didn't put up any resistance. It was only when I yanked him up to his full height that I realized he must have been at least a foot taller than me.

Trying not to look daunted by his size, I dragged him into the centre of the carriage – much to the astonishment of everyone around me – and cleared my throat.

'Ladies and gentlemen,' I began, as the flasher's expression changed from one of shock to one of confusion. 'May I have your attention, please. I don't know this man from Adam, but from Northwick Park to here he has sat with his flies open playing with himself. He undoubtedly travels on this train on a regular basis, so I want you to have a good look at his face so that you can recognize him in the future and warn others about him. All right?'

As I finished my speech and noted with pride that my flasher's face had turned as red as my travelcard, the train slowed down at Baker Street Station. I knew that if I got off and handed him over to the British Transport Police I would be stuck there for hours, filling in forms and making a statement. I would miss my meeting and, having taken so much care preparing myself for it, I didn't want that to happen.

The train stopped and the doors opened. I looked up at the embarrassed young man in front of me and let my hand slip from his sleeve. Quick as a flash, he darted off into the crowd and up the stairs to the barrier. I stood in the carriage doorway, watching him go. I reckoned I'd taught him a lesson. I doubted if he would flash again that day, well, not on this train, anyway.

Two weeks later, on 30 June 1994, I made my way to the Royal Courts of Justice in the Strand to hear Lashley's appeal against conviction in front of the Lord Chief Justice, Lord Taylor of Gosforth, sitting with Mr Justice Kay and Mr Justice Dyson. I had been so busy that I hadn't been able to catch up on all the news, so I was grateful to a colleague who rang me to tell me that Daniel Reece and Linda Calvey had married in Parkhurst Prison on Valentine's Day. Well, bully for them, I thought.

Once again I was to find myself sitting in a courtroom a few feet from David Ronald Lashley. There was no reason on earth why I needed to be there for the appeal, but I felt that Lashley had taken up such a big part of my life that I couldn't bear to miss the final chapter – even if the ending looked to be far from a happy one.

I caught the train bound for Farringdon that morning with a heavy heart. Even though the sun was shining and everyone seemed to be enjoying the summer, the weight of the world seemed to be resting upon my shoulders and the day felt doomladen.

As the world sped past outside my window and commuters came and went from my carriage, I was lost in a wave of sadness. Sadness for Janie, for her family, and for all the women who had fallen foul of men like Lashley. It seemed so ironic that the man who had come to represent the composite rapist in my mind, the sum of all the evil parts, could now be released back into the community just as I was no longer there to do anything about him. Not that I supposed there was much I could have done to stop him, but without a warrant card I had no powers whatsoever and I felt totally impotent.

I had recently read a book by American sociologists William and Joan McCord, and when I came to their definition of a psychopath I thought it summed up all that I knew about Lashley.

> The psychopath is asocial . . . driven by primitive desires and an exaggerated craving for excitement. In his self-centred search for pleasure, he ignores restrictions on his culture . . . He is an impulsive man for whom the moment is a segment of time detached from all others. He feels little, if any, guilt. He can commit the most appalling acts, yet view them without remorse. He has a warped capacity for love. His emotional relationships, when they exist, are meagre, fleeting and designed to satisfy his own desires. These last two traits, guiltlessness and lovelessness, conspicuously mark the psychopath as different from other men.

I am in favour of capital punishment; but only where society, having judged the crime to be so abhorrent, has said enough is enough. I firmly believe that life is the most precious gift and anybody who destroys another person's right to breathe air and exist should know that he may end up paying the ultimate price himself. Selfish premeditated acts of wickedness and bloody-minded violence are no longer a distant threat. They lurk in the shadows of our own space, putting constraints on our lives that our forefathers would have found intolerable.

Murderers have a fast-growing lethal destructiveness which permeates all our lives. Their numbers increase daily because they know they are safe from extinction, and not a day will pass without us being touched by them one way or another, but particularly through the media. They are real. They are here to stay. They are alive and living in your neighbourhood.

The professional criminal now considers the possibility of murdering someone in the same way that he would plan to rob or rape. It was Lashley, after all, who made the point that it was easier to kill the main prosecution witness to the crime than it was to allow her to live on to give evidence against him in court. And in the absence of some substantial deterrent, what is there to stop these warped individuals continuing in this way? As to the question of who would play executioner, look no further. I would have no trouble pushing the button.

I was shaken from my solitary thoughts by the train doors shutting as we pulled out of Preston Road. I looked up and studied the people around me. Smart individuals dressed in business suits, others in more casual clothes. How had their lives been affected? I wondered, and given the chance I would have asked the question out loud and openly debated the issues with them. But for now they were absorbed in thought or reading matter and they didn't need me to depress them. Not for the first time, I realized how jaundiced and cynical my view of life sometimes was and I envied those who could lose themselves through the medium of fiction. When all's said and done, there was enough of the real stuff for everyone, I thought.

The first person I saw as I entered the oak-panelled chamber of the High Court was Michael Kalisher, the brilliant QC who had successfully prosecuted Lashley for Janie's murder. 'Hello, sir. What do you think?' I asked him, not sure that I wanted to hear the answer. But he smiled at me and patted my hand reassuringly.

'I feel pretty confident, inspector,' he told me and winked. I allowed my heart to lift a little until I looked up and saw the huge Lashley standing heavily guarded in the witness box, his brilliant white shirt a stark contrast against his black skin. His overnight bag was packed and ready at his feet and he stood looking menacingly around the courtroom at the rest of us as if to say, 'I'll be out there among you in no time at all.' I shivered and reflected yet again on what on earth would happen if such a man were ever allowed to walk free.

I had survived confrontation where I felt terrified, standing in the front line of fire. I had coped with injuries sustained on duty, I had worked all hours God sent me for as long as I could remember. I had taken flak from every quarter of society at large and I had frequently been so saddened by what I had seen that I had been reduced to tears. But I had never felt so desperately useless and uncomfortable as I did when I walked into that packed courtroom.

Camilla, Janie's cousin, was there as the family's representative. Mrs Darling had asked her to telephone her in Australia with the judge's decision the minute the appeal hearing was over.

There were suddenly two loud knocks on a wooden door behind the judges' bench and a court clerk announced: 'Silence; be upstanding for the Queen's Chief Justices.'

The Lord Chief Justice emerged from his chambers, severe-looking in his robes and wig, and the court fell silent as he walked in and took his seat with the two other judges at his side. We all stood until they were seated and then settled back on to the uncomfortable wooden benches at the back of the court. As the rustling died down and the silence crept across the courtroom from the judges' bench, I held my breath. I had never been to an appeal hearing before and I didn't have a clue what to expect.

Helen Grindrod, QC for Lashley, rose to her feet and, adjusting her barrister's wig, started to make her representations on her client's behalf. She spoke for what seemed like hours but in reality it was considerably less. She made some excellent points which gave credence to her argument and became so persuasive in her speech that my spirits plummeted further.

Her four grounds for appeal were that the trial judge had failed to direct the jury adequately in relation to the evidence of Reece and the other witnesses; that the verdict was unsafe and unsatisfactory because of 'lurking doubt' as to the credibility of the witnesses; that Lashley's aunt and uncle should not have been cross-examined about the fact that they had given him an identical alibi in his previous trial; and that Reece's later retraction of the evidence he gave at Lashley's trial rendered the verdict unsafe. Labouring Reece's unreliability as a witness, she said there should never have been a conviction. The judges clearly knew the details of the case and interrupted her several times to highlight particular features. I was hugely impressed.

Then it was Mr Kalisher's turn. As he rose to his feet to speak, I leant forward in my seat. In a speech which probably lasted no more than thirty minutes, I was amazed at the speed with which he seemed to kick defence counsel's argument straight into touch. He argued that the judge's direction to the jury about the evidence of Reece and the other witnesses was both adequate and fair. The judge had warned the jury of the need for 'great caution' and had cited all the reasons for Reece's possible lack of credibility – including his previous convictions, supergrass status and his role as a 'self-appointed angel of justice'.

The judge had also directed the jury not to convict Lashley just because he had been previously convicted of another crime, a matter which was obvious to all because the chief prosecution evidence came from fellow-inmates. Mr Kalisher argued in support of the trial judge's decision to allow the jury to know that Lashley's aunt and uncle, who told the court that he was at home in bed on the night of the murder, had provided a virtually identical alibi in the Renata case – an alibi which had been 'manifestly rejected as untruthful or unreliable' by the Renata jury in 1977. Mr Kalisher said it was important that this fact be known to the jury when assessing the credibility of Lashley's relatives.

Mr Kalisher said that Reece's reliability should be considered only at the time he gave evidence. 'Subsequent events have no or limited relevance,' he told the court, referring to Reece's later statements. He said the retraction was designed only to discredit DI Sandlin for 'betraying his friendship' and not helping Reece out in the Cook murder case. He cited the case of R. vs Flower and Others, a legal test case which bore similarities to the Lashley retrial and in which it was ruled that just because a witness was later accused of being unreliable it was 'a fallacy' to assume that the verdict was therefore unsafe.

Mr Kalisher told the judges: 'The witness's state of mind at the time of the trial and what he had to gain from giving evidence was what had to be taken into consideration. Reece knew he would forgo many privileges. He had already been stabbed by a fellow-prisoner once and would spend the rest of his term of imprisonment locked in his cell for twenty-three hours a day and in fear of his life for turning Queen's evidence.'

The judges listened and then told Mr Kalisher that they were acquainted with the case law and had already referred to it in preparation for this hearing. My heart started to beat a little faster. When Mr Kalisher sat down, the judges announced that they would retire to consider their judgement. The clerk called for silence once more and we all stood up as the eminent lords swept from the courtroom and into their private chambers.

I felt as nervous as a kitten. I couldn't bear to leave the courtroom in case I missed anything and my fingers twitched for a cigarette.

They were gone for just over twenty minutes. Then, before we knew it, the knocks came and they all swept back into court. You could have heard a pin drop as the Lord Chief Justice cleared his throat and started to speak.

A lot of what he first said seemed to me to be incomprehensible legal jargon, but then he began to say something which made my heart pound in my chest. 'If the witness's new version of the case is disbelieved, this may well show he is now unreliable, but it is a fallacy to assume from this that he was also unreliable at the trial . . . the crux of the case is whether the content of what Reece said at the trial was credible, cogent evidence which, supported as it was in some respects by other evidence, rendered the jury's verdict safe and satisfactory.' There was some more legal talk and then he said: 'After anxious consideration of the points argued by the defence as well as the additional grounds prepared by the appellant himself, each member of this court is of the view that the verdict of the jury is safe and satisfactory. Therefore we dismiss the appeal. Full judgement shall be given in writing in twenty-one days.'

Had I heard him right? I looked around the room, seeking some sort of reassurance, some evidence that I wasn't imagining things, that, despite my brain convincing me that we were going to lose, it was Lashley who had just lost his appeal.

Standing as if on auto-pilot as the judges left the courtroom for the last time, I watched in amazement as the four burly prison guards suddenly closed in on Lashley and bundled him unceremoniously, with his overnight bag, through a small door behind the witness box that led down to the cells. He wasn't even given time to look round at the rest of us standing open-mouthed in court. Mr Whinnett and I sat blinking at Mr Kalisher's grinning face, wondering if we were dreaming.

The full judgement was later to indicate just how carefully the learned judges had considered the appeal. Twenty-two pages long, it went into every detail and cited whole passages of the trial judge's directions, including his comments to the jury: 'You may think this case stands or falls by Reece.'

The judge had reminded the jury: 'Truth is not a commodity only available to the honest, law-abiding and respectable. Bear in mind that the wickedest villain can on occasion tell the truth.' The judges pointed out that the scientific and other evidence lent 'considerable support' to Reece's evidence and, as Lashley did not give evidence at the trial, there was no sworn testimony from him to 'undermine, controvert or explain the evidence from the Crown'. Their lordships said the criticism of the judge's summing up and his decision on the alibi question was, in their view, unfounded. They too were saying, if not in so many words, that they believed Lashley to be guilty of the murder of Janie Shepherd.

I couldn't have wished for a better end to my career. I felt a little breathless as I sat in the courtroom trying to take it all in. It had taken seventeen years and four months for the different investigating teams to travel this road, but they had finally arrived and now they could relax.

I felt good as I reflected on what had been the last act of a great tragedy. Despite having taken no active part in the investigation, I had been the fly on the wall for as long as I could remember, and the memories would stay with me for ever. I am sure I must have skipped across the mosaic floor of the building's grand central hall and out into the bright June sunshine. Standing on the court steps in the Strand, I spoke two words to anyone who might have been listening. 'Thank you,' I said.

No longer a police officer, no longer a drunk, in better shape both psychologically and physically than I had been for years, I inhaled the summer air deeply. It had never smelt so good. If I could start all over again, would I have done it any differently? I thought. But I didn't have to ask myself the question twice because the answer was obvious to me: no. How could I feel this good if I hadn't first learnt the lessons of what it had been like to feel that bad? Hadn't I read some lines in a book which said it all for me? 'No man can live in his heaven until he's first lived in his own hell.' I had arrived at a kind of heaven on earth and I knew I was one of the lucky ones.

I closed my eyes and thought of Janie. I saw the photograph that the newspapers had carried of her seventeen years earlier, which I always found easy to conjure up in my mind.

'God bless you, dear Janie,' I whispered. 'Now rest in peace.'